TRIUMPH
B O O K S

ON THE CLOCK: VANCOUVER CANUCKS

ON THE CLOCK: VANCOUVER CANUCKS

Behind the Scenes with the Vancouver Canucks at the NHL Draft

DANIEL WAGNER

TRIUMPH
BOOKS

No part of this publication may be reproduced, stored in a retrieval system, or transmitted in any form by any means, electronic, mechanical, photocopying, or otherwise, without the prior written permission of the publisher, Triumph Books LLC, 814 North Franklin Street, Chicago, Illinois 60610.

Library of Congress Cataloging-in-Publication Data available upon request.

This book is available in quantity at special discounts for your group or organization. For further information, contact:

Triumph Books LLC
814 North Franklin Street
Chicago, Illinois 60610
(312) 337-0747
www.triumphbooks.com

Printed in U.S.A.

ISBN: 978-1-62368-052-7

Design by Preston Pisellini

Page production by Nord Compo

Photos courtesy of Getty Images unless otherwise indicated

CONTENTS

FOREWORD

SO, YOU'RE A CANUCKS FAN, you say?

For how long now? Two years? Ten? Don't tell me you've been around since day one! Regardless of the amount of time you've dedicated to cheering for this team, it's clear (as long as you haven't taken a timeout from this mostly fruitless endeavour) that you're loyal, stubborn, and likely a bit of a sucker for punishment.

Listen, I understand that cheering for any sports team is always going to be more pain than pleasure. However, I have covered the Vancouver Canucks very closely for nearly 25 years now, and this organization seems to have perfected the art of torturing its fans over the years. It's not that the Vancouver Canucks as an organization have wanted to do this to the fan base but many of the best intentions have morphed into self-inflicted wounds. And let's not even begin to talk about how the league has it out for the Canucks (wink).

Sure, there have been moments of brilliance and extended periods of excellence, but the valleys FAR outnumber the peaks. And the same can be said for this franchise's history when it comes to the NHL entry draft. The mere fact that the Canucks lost their first-ever draft lottery on the spin of a carnival wheel couldn't have been a better predictor of the circus that would follow.

Now this book is not going to be a could have/should have historical look at the Canucks draft history. Everyone has done that over the years. And frankly, it's too depressing.

MATTHEW TKACHUK WAS RIGHT THERE!

THEY PASSED ON DAVID PASTRNAK TWICE IN THE FIRST ROUND?

THEY COULD HAVE HAD JAROMIR JAGR AND KEITH TKACHUK IN THE SAME DRAFT!

Sorry, I said this book was not going to be like that.

Instead, *On the Clock* will dig into the stories behind the drafts, explore the reasons why the Canucks picked who they did when they did, and get the dirt directly from the people that were at the draft tables. It picks the brains of the scouts who were sent to those rinks in the middle of nowhere.

As a Canucks fan you probably know the team took a bit of a gamble selecting Pavel Bure in the sixth round in 1989. It was a gamble that would pay off handsomely, of course. But did you know that the NHL voided the pick with a month to go before the next year's draft? And if it wasn't for the Professor and a Russian statistician, Bure would have been back in the queue to be picked by someone else in 1990?

You likely understand that the Canucks had to make some wild trades to get both Daniel and Henrik Sedin in 1999. But did you know about the $115 million deal that threatened to scuttle the whole thing and potentially leave the Canucks with neither Sedin?

And surely you've heard how the Canucks scouted Alex Edler playing in a glorified beer league (a bit of a stretch, but we'll allow it for the purpose of creative licence) in the middle of nowhere in northern Sweden. But how exactly did they discover him? And which NHL team did they beat at their own game in order to call his name first on the draft floor? These are the types of stories in the pages of *On the Clock*. And who better to bring them to life than Daniel Wagner?

It feels like Daniel has been writing about the Canucks nearly as long as I have covered them. One of the co-founders of the hugely popular Canucks blog *Pass It to Bulis,* Daniel began his career as a fan who wanted to muse about the team that he fell in love with. Furthermore, he wanted to share those thoughts with others who might view the sport of hockey and the team they love/hate through a slightly different lens than how traditional writers might. Like many other successful sports bloggers that have helped shape this industry, Daniel understood that entertaining was just as, if not more important than, informing the audience.

His writing talents have only grown since then. Sure, Daniel continues to have fun with his craft. He can still build a creative lede with the best of them. However, as he has delved into more serious reporting, Wagner has proven to know what questions to ask and how to follow those up. Storytelling is an art, and when it comes to really digging up the tales of the ghosts of Canucks drafts' past, I couldn't think of a better artist or writer to inform and entertain.

Is *On the Clock: Behind the Scenes with the Vancouver Canucks at the NHL Draft* a comedy or a tragedy? I'm not totally sure. But it's a must-read if you're a fan of the Canucks or just a fan of good stories in general.

Dan Murphy has been hosting the Vancouver Canucks' television broadcasts since 2001 and covering the Canucks even longer, getting his start in broadcasting as a reporter for Sports Page *in 1995.*

INTRODUCTION

WHEN IT COMES TO THE NHL ENTRY DRAFT, it feels like the Vancouver Canucks have been cursed by the hockey gods.

The Canucks have never won a draft lottery and have never picked first overall. They have seen numerous top picks become busts and have traded away some of their best draft picks right before they became stars. All too often, when they manage to pick a good player, it comes just before or after another team picks a Hall of Famer.

It sometimes seems like the only way the Canucks have found success at the draft is through trickery, like Prometheus stealing fire from the gods. They drafted a rocket when no one else believed he was eligible, executed a series of absurd trades to snatch a pair of twins, and stole a hidden gem when they weren't even supposed to know it existed.

Maybe that's why the Canucks have been subsequently tortured—brought to the edge of winning the Stanley Cup only to have it cruelly torn away, like Prometheus condemned to have his liver repeatedly eaten by an eagle.

In the Greek myth, it took a hero like Heracles to save Prometheus from being tortured worse than this metaphor. Perhaps that's all the Canucks need to break the curse: a legendary hero who can kill monsters, divert rivers, and hold up the heavens—that shouldn't be hard to find, right?

The Canucks' history at the NHL draft is a reflection of their history as a franchise—decades of futility punctuated by a few glorious moments fueled by a combination of hard work, talent, and luck. Yes, the Canucks have had plenty of bad luck at the draft, but they've also had some preposterously good luck along the way.

Perhaps at least one of the hockey gods is secretly a Canucks fan, sneaking them some good fortune every now and then to make up for all the liver-eating.

I promise, there are a lot fewer livers in what you're about to read. Instead, I dug up the best and most interesting stories from the Canucks' history at the draft and did my darnedest to cut through the myths and legends surrounding them and get to the true story underneath.

You'll read about how the Canucks defined their identity when they drafted Stan Smyl and Harold Snepsts; how they built the foundation of a Cup run by picking Trevor Linden and Pavel Bure; how they nabbed two Hall of Famers out of one of the worst drafts ever in Henrik Sedin and his lesser-known brother, Daniel Sedin.

You'll get the story behind the Cory Schneider trade that gave the Canucks Bo Horvat, the debate that delivered Elias

Pettersson, and how everything went right for Quinn Hughes to fall into their laps.

We'll have a few laughs, cry a few tears, and eat a few livers. It'll be fun.

1

THE CARNIVAL
WHEEL OF FATE

THE VANCOUVER CANUCKS' bad luck at the NHL draft started right from day one, when a carnival wheel cost them a Hall of Fame forward in their very first draft.

It was Tuesday, June 9, 1970, and representatives from all 14 NHL teams were gathered at the Queen Elizabeth Hotel in Montreal, Quebec. That included two entirely new expansion franchises joining the NHL for the 1970–71 season: the Vancouver Canucks and Buffalo Sabres.

At the front of the room, the president of the NHL, Clarence Campbell, had a carnival prize wheel set up on a table—a red-rimmed crown and anchor wheel with numbers written around the outside. Only, the prize wasn't a plush bear or a chalkware figurine, but a 19-year-old hockey phenom.

The wheel would be spun twice—once to determine whether the Canucks or Sabres would pick first in the expansion draft the next day and then a second time to decide the first pick in the amateur draft. That second spin is the one that really mattered. The winner of the second spin would earn the right to draft the consensus first-overall pick: Gilbert Perreault, a centre out of Quebec that was expected to be the next Jean Beliveau. Perreault was billed as a future superstar with his fluid skating, exceptional stickhandling, and knack for finding the back of the net. His dazzling end-to-end rushes thrilled fans, excited NHL scouts, and won hockey games. Perreault racked up 51 goals and 121 points in 54 games for the Montréal Jr. Canadiens, then dominated the playoffs with 17 goals and 38 points in 16 games en route to winning the Memorial Cup.

His NHL career lived up to the lofty expectations created by his play in junior. In 17 NHL seasons, Perreault surpassed his idol Beliveau in career points, tallying 1,326 points in 1,191 games. He was inducted into the Hockey Hall of Fame in 1990.

Jim Kearney, sports columnist for the *Vancouver Sun,* called Perreault "the best prospect since [Bobby] Orr," and he quoted Bernie "Boom Boom" Geoffrion, then a scout with the New York Rangers, as saying, "You could build a franchise around him." That was the idea. The wheel would decide which franchise would get to use Perreault as its foundation.

At the Buffalo table, awaiting that fateful spin, sat Sabres general manager and head coach George "Punch" Imlach in an ill-fitting green suit that he bought after winning the Stanley Cup with the Toronto Maple Leafs in 1967. He called it his lucky suit but later admitted, "I put on some weight since '67 and could hardly close the front buttons."

From a *Sportsnet* video, a shot of the infamous crown-and-anchor wheel that decided the fate of the Canucks' first draft, with no sign of the number one. (Courtesy of *Sportsnet*)

With Punch at the Sabres table was director of scouting John Andersen and his hastily assembled scouting staff, which included Al Millar, a former goaltender for the pre-NHL Canucks in the Western Hockey League. Millar was new to scouting but had plenty of experience watching hockey as a backup goaltender. Before he retired, he was frequently on the bench furiously tallying statistics during Canucks games for his head coach, Joe Crozier.

Punch was a controversial character in the NHL—a cocky and quick-witted hockey man who clashed frequently with players who didn't always appreciate his coaching and motivational tactics and made some questionable decisions in management. But he won four Stanley Cups with the Maple Leafs, so the Sabres were happy to have his experience in the front office and behind the bench to kick off their fledgling franchise.

In the year leading up to this moment, many thought that Punch would be sitting at the Vancouver table instead. Punch had been fired as head coach and general manager of the Leafs on April 6, 1969—two minutes after the Leafs were eliminated from the Stanley Cup playoffs by the Boston Bruins in four games. Speculation ran rampant that he would join his friend, Joe Crozier, the head coach and general manager of the WHL Canucks, to help head up the team in Vancouver as they transitioned to the NHL.

In fact, prior to taking the job in Buffalo, Punch owned shares in the Canucks, as well as their sister team, the Rochester Americans in the AHL, who would become the Canucks' first farm team. More than that, Punch was secretly on the Canucks' payroll. Crozier, himself a significant shareholder in the Canucks, had hired Punch as a scout and personnel consultant without notifying the Canucks' other directors, Coley Hall and Cyrus McLean. Crozier was a popular figure in Vancouver, so he was confident he would continue in his role as coach and general manager as the Canucks joined the NHL and it was believed Punch would join him.

It was not to be.

Given the $650 million expansion fee paid by the Seattle Kraken to join the NHL in 2021, the Canucks and Sabres' expansion fee of $6 million each may not seem like much. But it was a significant increase from the $2 million paid just three years earlier by the California Seals, Los Angeles Kings, Minnesota North Stars, Philadelphia Flyers, Pittsburgh Penguins, and St. Louis Blues.

"If the National Hockey League gets that $6 million asking price for each of the two new franchises, the deal will constitute the biggest heist since The Great Train Robbery," said Eric Whitehead of *The Province*.

As Crozier put it, "Twelve governors sat around a table and simply decided that they wanted a million bucks apiece." The price was too rich for oil magnate Frank McMahon, a member of the Canucks' ownership group headed up by McLean, who purchased the WHL Canucks from their previous owner, former Vancouver major Fred "Friendly" Hume. McMahon and McLean originally had rival bids to join the 1967 expansion but merged their groups together in hopes of joining the NHL in 1970.

McMahon believed, perhaps justifiably, that one of the other expansion teams would struggle to the point that they could purchase them and move them to Vancouver for much cheaper than the $6 million expansion fee. He was out and, with him, the Canucks' biggest source of cash.

Crozier wasn't worried: "With or without McMahon, we'll have no trouble at all raising the $6 million," he said.

He wasn't entirely wrong. While the various investors in the WHL Canucks balked at the hefty expansion fee, they eventually did find someone willing to pay it. The Minneapolis-based Medical Investment Corp., otherwise known as Medicor, provided the financing and bought a controlling interest in the Canucks. But, by the time the deal was done, Crozier was out and so was Punch.

The new owners, headed up by president Tom Scallen and vice president Lyman Walters, were at first open to keeping Crozier on board and bringing in Punch.

"Obviously, Joe Crozier is a candidate," said Scallen in December 1969, after the deal was made official. "We will talk to Punch Imlach and several other qualified men."

In fact, Crozier and Punch had already sold all of their Canucks shares to the new owners. It's estimated Punch and Crozier made around $250,000 each from the sale of the Canucks to Medicor. Less than a week after Medicor purchased the Canucks, the Buffalo Sabres announced the hiring of their new coach and general manager: Punch Imlach. Subsequently, Campbell gave Lyman Walters a call to ask if the new owners of the Canucks were aware that the new GM of the Sabres was also registered with the NHL as authorized to make player deals and transfers for the Canucks.

Punch wasn't just on the Canucks payroll as a scout. Crozier gave Punch the authority to make deals and transfers for the Canucks without telling anyone else in the Canucks organization, perhaps anticipating that the two of them would soon be working together in Vancouver. They did end up working together—two years later, when Crozier stepped in as head coach of the Sabres after Punch suffered a heart attack and was ordered by doctors to take it easy.

The new owners of the Canucks were less than thrilled that they hadn't been informed of Punch's secret role. While they wanted to retain Crozier as general manager and head coach—after all, he was a proven winner en route to taking the WHL Canucks to back-to-back Lester Patrick Cups—Scallen and Walters planned to install an experienced hockey man in Bud Poile as a special assistant over Crozier, giving them more control over the team's direction. It would also keep Crozier from hiring more old buddies on the sly.

Scallen and Walters were going to inform Crozier of this new hierarchy in a meeting but someone tipped him off. Crozier refused to even show up and, as a result, Medicor fired him for "rank insubordination."

"[We] were not happy with Joe Crozier's business practices—he's a good hockey man but not, in my judgment, a good businessman," said Scallen. "We have a considerable investment in the club. We did not know where some of the money was going even when we asked."

To replace Crozier, Scallen had just the man for the job. Instead of a special advisor, Poile would be the first general manager of the Vancouver Canucks in the NHL and would make the team's first-ever draft pick.

At the Canucks' table on June 9, Poile was anxiously waiting to find out if that pick would be Perreault. Among those with him were head coach Hal Laycoe—who took over the WHL Canucks when Crozier was fired and ably coached them to the Lester Patrick Cup—chief scout Johnny "Peanuts" O'Flaherty, and president Coleman "Coley" Hall.

The original owner of the WHL Canucks before "Friendly" Hume, Hall was the man who gave the team the name "Canucks" in the first place, on the suggestion of a bootlegger friend, Art Nevison.

Also with Poile at the table was a special guest—his son, David Poile, who would go on to become the winningest general manager in NHL history in four decades as GM of the Washington Capitals and Nashville Predators.

The younger Poile had just turned 20 years old and had finished his final year at Northeastern University, where he was captain of the hockey team. He led Northeastern in scoring by a wide margin with 37 goals and 45 points in 23 games and went to the Canucks' first-ever training camp to vie for a spot on the roster. His dad cut him and sent him to the Rochester Americans in the AHL instead.

David may have been done at Northeastern but in Montreal, he was schooled in the art of hockey management. "We had a big suite at the Queen Elizabeth," recalled Poile. "We just hung out there and hockey people, managers, would come up and talk. It was eye-opening to me. It was normal business, but for me, it was an education.

"It was a smaller league at that time—my dad was a player before he was a coach before he was a manager. His relationships are with the people, they grew up with each other, they played with each other—there were just so many connections."

"I was a fly on the wall. Kept my mouth shut," he added with a laugh.

Bud was a tremendous athlete right from a young age growing up in Fort William, Ontario, competing not just in hockey but hitting cleanup for the local baseball team, the Fort William Rangers. Hockey captured him the most, however, and he earned the attention of the Toronto Maple Leafs, likely because he was considered to have "one of the hardest shots in amateur hockey," according to 1942 newspaper clippings.

Bud made his debut for the Leafs at just 18 years old and shone in his rookie year, putting up 35 points in 48 games, second in rookie scoring behind his Leafs teammate Gaye Stewart, who was a year older. His hockey career was interrupted by World War II—Bud joined the Royal Canadian Air Force, briefly playing for their hockey team before they were barred from competition. By the end of the war, he was stationed in Germany.

Upon returning from the war, Poile found success with the Leafs on a line called "the Flying Forts," with fellow Fort Williamites Stewart and Gus Bodnar. Together they won the Stanley Cup in 1947, but that was his last full season in Toronto. He was part of a six-player trade to the Chicago Black Hawks the following season, where he finished fifth in NHL scoring in 1948.

Poile wound up playing for five of the Original Six teams, missing only the Montreal Canadiens in his tour of the NHL. He then became a player-coach for minor league teams like the USHL's Tulsa Oilers and the WHL's Edmonton Flyers, eventually transitioning off the ice as just a coach, first for the Flyers, then for the San Francisco Seals of the WHL. Along the way, he developed a passion for growing the game.

"He was very gregarious, very outgoing. My mom and dad were very social," recalled David. "Even at that time, it wasn't unusual for media to come over to our house for dinner back when I was growing up in Edmonton or in San Francisco. He loved people and he loved the game of hockey."

After his stints in NHL management, Bud became a commissioner, first for the Central Hockey League, then the International Hockey League, developing it into one of the top minor leagues in North America in competition with the American Hockey League, with most of its teams serving as farm teams for the NHL.

"He wanted the game to grow and develop," David said. "A lot of his roots were in American cities like in San Francisco, where I went to high school. He even worked for

USA Hockey—there's the untold story of helping the U.S. Olympic team in 1980. They had nobody really to play, so they scheduled games against teams in the IHL, which Craig Patrick and Herb Brooks would tell you went a long way toward getting them more ready for the bigger games that came at the Olympics."

His long career in the game eventually led to Bud getting inducted into the Hockey Hall of Fame in the builder category in 1990, in the same class as none other than Gilbert Perreault.

"The one thing that really stood out to me is that he was always looking for fairness in terms of what was right for the game against winning at all costs," said David. "He loved the game itself more than winning—not that he didn't like winning, but at all costs? No."

BUD POILE HAD a strong résumé to head up the expansion Canucks. He was one of the few hockey executives that actually had experience building an expansion franchise as the first-ever general manager of the Philadelphia Flyers. Under Poile, the Flyers won the newly formed West Division in their inaugural season and put together the foundations of the team that would go on to win back-to-back Stanley Cups a few years later.

Like Punch, Poile had recently been let go from his NHL job after getting fired by the Flyers because of "fundamental differences of opinion" with ownership, but he was on the same page as Tom Scallen and Lyman Walters. As an added bonus, Poile was familiar with Vancouver and the Canucks thanks to years of coaching against them in the WHL. His new coach, Laycoe, was a rival from those WHL years as the former coach of the Portland Buckaroos, who were consistently one of the best teams in the league.

While Poile had experience building an expansion franchise, no one had much experience with the amateur draft. The draft was introduced to the NHL just seven years prior, in 1963. Before the draft, NHL teams sponsored amateur teams and players, restricting the NHL future for those players to just one team. When the draft was introduced, initially only players who didn't have a sponsorship deal could be selected, leaving a limited number of players available.

Just 21 players were selected in the first amateur draft in 1963, but that was far from the fewest players ever picked in a single draft. A change in the minimum age of prospects in the 1965 draft resulted in just 11 players getting picked and the Maple Leafs chose not to participate at all.

Under the sponsorship system, Perreault would have belonged to the Montréal Canadiens, who sponsored Perreault's team, the Montréal Junior Canadiens. Up until 1969, the Canadiens could have had Perreault even without the sponsorship system—the French Canadian rule gave them the privilege of picking two French Canadian players before other teams could even draft. When the sponsorship system finally ended in 1969, however, so too did the French Canadian rule, leaving Perreault available to either the Canucks or the Sabres, depending on who won the spin of the wheel.

In the first of the post-sponsorship drafts in 1969, Poile picked a prospect who would go on to define the future of the Flyers, nabbing Bobby Clarke of the Flin Flon Bombers in the second round when other teams were scared off by his type 1 diabetes. Undoubtedly the greatest Flyer of all time, Clarke still holds the franchise record for most points by a wide margin, and his feisty, gritty, hardworking style gave the Flyers their identity.

That's what Poile wanted for the Canucks in 1970—a franchise-defining player. He wanted Gilbert Perreault.

On Tuesday morning, before the wheel was spun, Hal Sigurdson of the *Vancouver Sun* reported that Imlach tried to make a deal with Poile to spin the wheel just once. The winner of the spin would get first choice in the expansion draft but second pick in the amateur draft. That way, both expansion teams would get to pick first in one of the drafts.

That meant if the Sabres won the spin, the Canucks would get first pick in the amateur draft and get Gilbert Perreault.

According to Sigurdson, Poile turned Punch down—"This way he could have first choice in both drafts...or second in both," said Sigurdson.

BEFORE THE FIRST spin, there was a coin toss to determine which team got first dibs on players on waivers. Punch and the Sabres won the toss and the waiver wire served up Joe Daley, who served as the Sabres' backup goaltender in their first season. Then the wheel was spun for the first time, establishing the first pick in the expansion draft.

There were six big red sevens on the wheel and an assortment of other numbers spread around the wheel up to 12. There were 36 numbers in total—one team would get the numbers below seven, the other team got the numbers above seven. If the wheel landed on one of the big red sevens, they would spin again.

Imlach got to pick whether the Sabres wanted the high numbers or the low—"You know me, I always go for the top, so I say higher," he recounted later.

Campbell gave the wheel a spin and the clapper clicked and clacked as it collided with the pegs along the outside of the wheel before coming to a stop on the number eight and granting the Sabres the first pick in the expansion draft.

So far, the Canucks were 0-for-2, losing the initial coin toss and the expansion spin, but the most important spin still remained. If the wheel stopped on a number below seven, Poile and the Canucks got Gilbert Perreault; above seven, he belonged to Imlach and the Sabres.

Whoever lost the spin of the wheel would have to go with the second choice on their draft list. Some argued that this should be Reg Leach, a dominant goal scorer who played for the Flin Flon Bombers of the WCHL like Clarke. But the odds-on favourite for the second pick was Dale Tallon, a powerful and versatile two-way player for the Toronto Marlboros in the OHA, who could play either forward or defence.

Poile wasn't thinking of second-best as Campbell stepped to the wheel, however. He was hoping for Perreault.

"Remember, it's Buffalo high, Vancouver low," announced Campbell as he stepped up and spun the wheel. The loud clacking sound of the clapper on the pegs resounded through the room. Poile and Punch held their breath as the wheel came to a stop.

"The number is one!" announced Campbell authoritatively.

The Canucks' table leaped to their feet to celebrate, applauding and shaking hands. With the wheel stopping at a number under seven, the first-overall pick was theirs and, with it, the great Gilbert Perreault. Poile was delighted that his new team had just been handed the franchise cornerstone they could build around for the future.

But before the celebrations could go on too long, a yell could be heard from the Sabres table.

"Miscall!" yelled the voice, as reported by Sigurdson. "That's not number one, it's number 11!"

It was Millar, who honed his eyesight on the bench as the backup goaltender for the Canucks, tallying statistics for Crozier. Sure enough, Millars' eagle eyes were right— Campbell had called the wrong number. The wheel hadn't stopped on number one; it had stopped on number 11. The Sabres had won the spin and, with it, Perreault.

The partitions on the wheel for each number were slim. In order to fit the two-digit numbers on the wheel, the digits were not side-by-side but instead stacked on top of each other. That meant the number 11 was a one on top of another one. Campbell looked at the wheel and saw only the one on top and called it out, lifting the Canucks' hopes high into the air only to dash them to the ground.

On either side of the number 11 were the numbers two and three. One number to the left or right would have given the Canucks the first-overall pick.

"I miscalled it," acknowledged Campbell. "The correct number is eleven!"

Now it was the Sabres' turn to celebrate, jumping up out of their seats as the Canucks sadly returned to theirs. The

Sabres cheered and clapped each other on the shoulders, while Punch pulled his glasses off and pantomimed wiping the sweat off his forehead with the back of his hand as he laughed. "I told you I was going to win them both," said Punch later. "I knew it all the way."

Here's the kicker: there were no ones on the wheel at all. There were 36 numbers on the wheel. That's enough room for the numbers 1–12 to each appear three times, but with six giant sevens on the wheel, one number had to be removed: they took away the number one. The Canucks had numbers 2–6—with three of each, that was 15 chances to get the first-overall pick, same as the Sabres who had three each of numbers 8–12.

When Campbell said, "The number is one," it should have been met with confusion rather than excitement—it was an impossibility. Ironically, the removal of the number one from the wheel was to avoid confusing it for any of the two-digit numbers 10–12. Instead, it had the opposite effect.

"It was shocking," recalls David Poile about the mood around the Canucks' table. "It went from elation to shock."

The mistake would surely have been spotted either way—there were television cameras recording the proceedings, after all—but it was an added gut punch that the one who spotted the error was a former Canuck. There appeared to still be some residual bitterness even months later.

"Punch and Al Millar say they outdrafted us," Bud Poile would say later when the Sabres came to town. "They say they know us inside and out. Well, they should, they had two people on our payroll for quite a while."

Poile had a zinger available for the media right after the fateful spin, as he tried to keep his spirits up about losing out on Perreault.

"It's just as well Imlach gets used to picking first," quipped Poile. "He may be doing it for a long time."

Behind the verbal jabs, however, Poile was feeling pessimistic after losing a coin toss and two spins of a wheel.

"I'll tell you this," he said. "I'm not going to call home tonight. The way things are going, my wife is likely to tell me the house has burned down."

Punch didn't have to say anything at all. He let his actions give the Canucks one last jab. He knew exactly the number to give to his newly acquired superstar, one which Perreault would wear as he carried the Sabres to the Stanley Cup Final in just their fifth season and for the rest of his Hall of Fame career.

That number was 11.

THE EXPANSION DRAFT: "$6 MILLION WORTH OF TALENT"

"$6 million buys 37 goals," read the headline from the *Vancouver Sun* after the Canucks made their picks in the expansion draft on June 10, 1970, the day before the amateur draft.

The hefty $6 million expansion fee for the Canucks and Sabres gave them the right to select players from the 12 existing NHL teams in an expansion draft. It didn't, however, buy them a lot of talent. The 18 skaters and two goaltenders selected by the Canucks had scored a grand total of 37 goals between them in the previous season.

"There you go, Hal," cracked Poile to head coach Hal Laycoe. "There's $6 million worth of talent. Don't foul it up."

Compared to recent expansion drafts for the Vegas Golden Knights and Seattle Kraken, the Canucks got swindled. For the Golden Knights and Kraken, teams were only allowed to protect a maximum of seven forwards, three defencemen, and one goaltender, although first- and second-year professionals and unsigned draft picks were exempt. In addition, teams were required to leave players exposed at each position with a minimum amount of NHL experience.

This left enough good players exposed that the Golden Knights, with the help of some savvy side deals, were able to put together a legitimate contender, making it all the way to the Stanley Cup Final in their first year.

The Canucks and Sabres weren't so fortunate.

Similar to the modern expansion draft, amateur players and first-year professionals were exempt from the draft. Unlike the modern version, teams could protect two goaltenders and 15 skaters each. To make it even more absurd, the first two times a player was selected from a team, that team could add another player to their protected list. That meant teams could protect a total of 19 players compared to the maximum of 11 protected in the Vegas and Seattle expansion drafts.

That left a paucity of players to pick from, particularly when you consider that two separate teams were picking from these scraps. Still, Poile did the best he could and managed to mine a few decent players.

Notable Canucks picks from the expansion draft include defenceman Gary Doak with their first pick, defenceman Barry Wilkins, centre Rosaire Paiement, and wingers Mike Corrigan and Wayne Maki. In net, Poile picked veteran Charlie Hodge and prospect Dunc Wilson, who Poile called the best goaltender not in the NHL. The two split starts in the 1970–71 season, then Hodge retired, and Wilson took over for a couple of seasons until Gary "Suitcase" Smith stepped into the Canucks' net.

Poile's best pick wasn't technically in the draft. After all the picks were in, Poile signed an undersized winger from the St. Louis Blues for the sum of $30,000—a bargain compared to the $300,000 per player they were paying via the $6 million expansion fee. That player was Andre Boudrias, who became the team's first star. He led the Canucks in scoring in four of their first five seasons and earned the nickname "Superpest" for his constantly aggravating presence on the forecheck.

By the end of the expansion draft, the Canucks didn't have a lot of talent but they had toughness to spare, with a roster that wouldn't back down from anybody in the league.

"We may not win many games," said Poile, "but we should win a few fights."

The two most significant players taken by Poile in the expansion draft were two legendary Canucks leaders, neither of whom lost many fights: Orland Kurtenbach and Pat Quinn.

The Canucks were looking for a veteran captain with their second pick in the expansion draft and they got one in Kurtenbach, who previously played for the Canucks when they were in the WHL.

"An expansion team just has to have a leader," said Poile. "A coach has to have a tough, strong right arm to take charge on the ice, to lead the way. That's why Kurtenbach is here. I think he's the man."

The 34-year-old centre helped give the Canucks their gritty, lunch-pail identity in their early years in the NHL. Kurtenbach was one of the most feared fighters of his day, with a long reach and heavy fists, though he was seen as a gentle giant off the ice and was never a goon.

"He never started many fights," recalled Quinn about Kurtenbach in a 2010 interview on *Hockey Night in Canada*, "but he could finish them."

The aging centre had a bad back—he had spinal surgery in 1968—and was known more for his defence and fighting than any offensive prowess, with a career high of 37 points recorded seven years earlier with the Boston Bruins.

In Vancouver, however, Kurtenbach found his scoring touch, playing on a line with Wayne Maki and Murray Hall, as well as getting prime power play time. The rough-and-tumble captain hit career highs in goals and points and was the lone Canuck to finish with more than a point per game in the team's inaugural season, scoring 21 goals and 53 points in 52 games. If not for a knee injury that knocked him out of the lineup for more than two months, he surely would have led the Canucks in scoring.

He did exactly that in the Canucks' second year, tying Boudrias with 61 points in 78 games. In his four seasons with the Canucks at the end of his career, Kurtenbach tallied 62 goals—more than his previous nine NHL seasons combined.

"It was such a wonderful feeling for all of us, coming to Vancouver, having an opportunity to play lots of hockey and a chance to prove ourselves as NHLers," said Kurtenbach in 2010. Later that year, Kurtenbach was the first player inducted into the Canucks' Ring of Honour.

While the Canucks found their first captain in Kurtenbach, Poile also selected a player who would lead the franchise decades later in Quinn.

At the time, however, Poile said that Quinn "needs coaching." The 28-year-old defenceman Quinn was tough as nails but a little rough around the edges.

To Quinn's credit, Poile also called him the fourth-best defenceman available in the expansion draft. Perhaps that was damning with faint praise but Quinn became a solid defenceman in the Canucks' first two seasons and his gregarious personality turned him into a leader off the ice as well.

"I remember what a great example Pat Quinn's work ethic was to the other players," said goaltender Charlie Hodge to onetime Canucks director of public relations Norm Jewison. "He may have been just an adequate player but he was a great person. His character made him a superstar on that team."

"He was the guy you wanted to be with after practice," recalled David Poile, who first met Quinn at the Canucks' first training camp, then got to know him better when he was in the front office of the Atlanta Flames, where Quinn was their first captain. "When Pat spoke, everybody listened. He had a great sense of humour, a fun-loving guy—everybody wanted to be like Pat."

Quinn's impact on the Canucks became far greater two decades later, when he served as the Canucks' president and general manager from 1987 to 1997 and was head coach from 1990 to 1994. He was credited with taking the Canucks from irrelevancy to Stanley Cup contention. Quinn and the Canucks will forever be intertwined.

In 2014, Quinn was inducted into the Canucks Ring of Honour, seven months before he passed away after a long illness. Two years later, Quinn was elected into the Hockey Hall of Fame as a builder. The year after that, the Canucks unveiled a life-sized bronze statue of Quinn outside Rogers Arena, next to a bench with a lineup card in hand, so he can continue to coach the game he loved for the rest of time.

2

DALE TALLON, THE DEFENCEMAN- CENTRE

DALE TALLON'S BIGGEST flaw is that he wasn't Gilbert Perreault.

After the fateful spin of the wheel and before the amateur draft took place, the Canucks front office tried to talk themselves into being as excited for Tallon as they had been for Perreault.

"Maybe it's just as well," said Johnny "Peanuts" O'Flaherty, according to Hal Sigurdson of the *Vancouver Sun*. "Tallon is tougher than Perreault. Stronger defensively too."

"Who knows, maybe Perreault will break a leg," said Coley Hall optimistically.

General manager Bud Poile, meanwhile, suggested he still wasn't sure who he would pick: Tallon or right winger Reg

Leach. Leach was known as the Riverton Rifle for his hometown in Manitoba and his deadly shot. He had just put up
65 goals and 111 points in 57 games for the Flin Flon Bombers
in the Western Canada Hockey League, but the WCHL was
considered a lesser league than the OHA, where Tallon and
Perreault plied their trade.

As much as Poile tried to suggest there was still a debate
to be had, there was no doubt—Tallon was their man.

That came as a surprise to Tallon himself.

"We all knew that Buffalo or Vancouver was going to take
Gilbert Perreault. If Vancouver lost [the spin of the wheel]
they were probably going to take Reggie Leach, because he was
a western kid and I was probably going to go to the Bruins,
who had the third pick," said Tallon in a 2010 interview on
Hockey Night in Canada. "It was kind of startling that I ended
up in Vancouver."

TALLON WAS BORN and raised in Noranda, which got its name
from "North Canada" and it was about as cold and rugged
as that implies. Along with its sister city, Rouyn, with which
it merged into the singular city of Rouyn-Noranda in 1986,
it was a major mining centre in Québec. Noranda was particularly known for its copper smelter, which led to the name
of one of Tallon's early teams.

The Noranda Copper Kings had been around since the
1930s but, by the time Tallon started playing for the local
team, it was owned and coached by his father, Stan Tallon.
At just 15 years old, Tallon was a star for the Copper Kings,
scoring 20 goals and adding 33 assists in 24 games. He was

utterly dominant the following season, racking up 70 goals and 134 points in just 30 games.

While with the Copper Kings in 1966, Tallon even earned comparisons to Bobby Orr from overzealous sportswriters. To be fair, Orr was just a prospect himself at that time, as a dominant defenceman for the Oshawa Generals who had yet to make his NHL debut. Tallon certainly loved to rush the puck up ice like Orr, slaloming through opponents to go end-to-end, bringing fans out of their seats.

However, Tallon was bigger than the sister cities of Rouyn-Noranda and high-end junior hockey came calling. After Orr's spectacular rookie season with the Bruins, Tallon replaced him on the Generals in the Ontario Hockey Association.

"He was supposed to be the new Bobby Orr in Oshawa and the kid had to take a lot of guff from the fans when the pressure started building up," said his father.

"They expected me to be some kind of redeemer," recalled Tallon a few years later. "We finished ninth again and at the time I was sorry. But I'm not now because it taught me to cope with that sort of situation."

The Orr comparison was always going to be an unfair one, but Tallon had a solid season as a 17-year-old rookie with the Generals, tallying 43 points in 50 games. He was subsequently traded to the Toronto Marlboros for five players. It wasn't just a hockey deal—according to Matt Leyden, the Generals' general manager, Tallon's parents wanted Dale in Toronto so he could be mentored by Al Balding, one of Canada's top professional golfers.

Tallon wasn't just a top-end hockey talent; he was also one of the best young golfers in Canada. At 14, he was the juvenile champion in the Northern Ontario Golf Association. At 17, he was winning tournaments against pros, such as the Noranda Invitational.

"It takes a while to get used to golf after playing hockey," said Tallon at the 1970 Ontario Open, one month after he was drafted. "In hockey, you can belt somebody if you get mad, but in golf, there's nobody to take it out on but yourself."

The year before he was drafted by the Canucks, Tallon was already in B.C., winning the Canadian junior golf championship in Kelowna by one stroke and helping Ontario take home the interprovincial championship. After the win, Tallon credited his lessons with Balding and fellow pro Ken Duggan at Toronto's Markland Wood Golf Club.

"Balding got rid of my loop and shortened my backswing," explained Tallon. Evidently, it was a good thing he got traded to the Marlboros.

Tallon also played good hockey in Toronto. He put up 49 points in 48 games in his first season, then at 19 broke out with 39 goals and 79 points in 54 games, then another 12 goals and 29 points in 18 playoff games.

The young phenom played every position except goaltender for the Marlboros—in the postseason awards, his votes were split between so many positions that he didn't even make the All-Star Team despite being among the league's leading scorers. His position in junior hockey was sometimes listed as "centre-defenceman" because he played both positions in about equal measure.

After that final season in Toronto, Tallon was eligible for the NHL draft but was still uncertain about his future.

"I'm a free agent, so if I don't get picked up in the draft in June for the right money, I'll probably try for a golf scholarship in the States," said Tallon after winning the Canadian junior championship. "I don't know what I'm going to do. I love hockey and golf equally well."

Tallon was offered golf scholarships at both Ohio State University and the University of New Mexico, so going to the U.S. to play golf was a legitimate option. But the scholarships also provided something else for Tallon: leverage in contract negotiations.

TALLON'S FATHER RECOGNIZED his son's talent early on and got in touch with Alan Eagleson, who grew to prominence after negotiating Orr's first contract with the Bruins. Stan Tallon had a simple desire: he didn't want his son to do the same type of backbreaking work that he had done to support his family.

"The kid isn't going to work with his back," said Stan in an interview with Red Fisher at the *Montreal Star*. "I was lucky. I had the back and I had the muscles and I worked like hell…but the kid isn't going to work with his back."

Stan had been a talented hockey player in his own right but never had a chance in the professional game. Instead, he became a bricklayer and a contractor, working long hours to provide for his family and adding to those hours with coaching junior hockey and being a bird dog for the Montreal Canadiens. He was known for being gruff and tough at times, but with a soft heart for the kids that skated at the local rink.

According to Stan, Dale made a promise when he went off to play professional hockey. "Even if the kid makes it, he has to keep up with his schooling. Nothing else really counts," said Stan. "Even if he takes only one college subject a year...even if it takes 10 years to get his degree, he'll stay with it. He promised us that." While Tallon never fulfilled that promise, he never had to work with his back—apart from the hard work of playing in the NHL, of course. After 10 years in the NHL as a player, Tallon became a hockey broadcaster, working as an analyst on radio and television broadcasts for the Chicago Blackhawks. In 1998, Tallon stepped into the Blackhawks' front office as director of player personnel, then became their general manager in 2005.

Long before he was negotiating contracts in an NHL front office, he and Eagleson were negotiating his first contract with the Canucks.

"Money talks," said Tallon after the draft when he was asked about playing for the expansion Canucks. "If the money isn't right, I'll take a golf scholarship."

With that leverage in hand, Eagleson negotiated a larger signing bonus for Tallon than what he had gotten Orr, making Tallon the highest-paid rookie in the league.

AT THE CANUCKS' training camp in the fall, the pressure was on immediately. Vancouver had been waiting a long time for the NHL and the media attention was overwhelming, particularly for the team's hotshot first draft pick, who came roaring into town in a white Pontiac Firebird Trans Am Special.

"He's someone the girls will talk about," read one headline in *The Province*, extolling Tallon's handsome features. "Everybody was excited. The fans were excited that the NHL was coming, the city was alive," said David Poile. "You have a big media in Vancouver and they were hungry for it."

Poile was at that first Canucks camp, but not just as a guest of his father. Instead, he was there to try out for the team. His father sent him an invite, reasoning that he didn't want to overlook his potential just because David was his son. For a player just coming out of college hockey, the experience was a lot to take in, but even in the midst of the chaos, he could see the weight on Tallon.

"The younger players, especially Dale Tallon, felt the pressure—Dale was smothered by it," recalled goaltender Charlie Hodge to Norm Jewison. "I came here as a veteran; I was used to it."

Beyond the external attention from fans and the media, there was the internal pressure from the Canucks' brass. After missing out on Gilbert Perreault, the Canucks were hoping that Tallon could be the team's franchise centre instead. At the start of training camp, head coach Hal Laycoe lined Tallon up at centre instead of on defence.

"The history of expansion teams is that their weakness has been in the middle," reasoned Bud Poile. "We are definitely inferior to established clubs at centre ice and we must fill that spot well."

Tallon had been talked up ahead of the draft as a potential centre like Perreault—less skilled, but perhaps better equipped for the more physical game of the NHL. Oddly enough, the

Canucks' own head scout, "Peanuts" O'Flaherty, disagreed; he didn't think Tallon was a centre or a defenceman. "Tallon is bigger and stronger and a good two-way player," said O'Flaherty in comparing Tallon to Perreault. "[He's] a good skater, his big forte is bursting out of his own end. And he has a fine shot. His weakness is that he's not a good playmaker. He doesn't distribute the puck well. As a matter of fact, he's not really a centre. I think his position is left wing. He'll stand a better chance of making the Canucks there than at centre."

Tallon struggled at centre at camp and in the preseason and aired his frustrations.

"I just don't feel right there. I feel uncomfortable. It just doesn't seem like my position," said Tallon early in training camp according to Eric Whitehead of *The Province*. "However, I'll play where I'm told to play."

Where Tallon wanted to play was on defence. As Orr was revolutionizing the position in Boston, dazzling opponents and fans in equal measure with his end-to-end rushes, Tallon wanted to do the same on the west coast.

As Tallon continued to struggle in the preseason, the Canucks reluctantly admitted that Tallon wasn't going to be the franchise centre they were looking for. They briefly tried him on left wing but when Pat Quinn was ejected from a preseason game early in the first period, Tallon took over on the blue line, playing almost the entire game on defence in his place. It became eminently obvious that was where Tallon belonged.

"I'm not the skater to be a centre," admitted Tallon near the end of his rookie season. "They need the lateral movement and the quick starts and stops. Me, I like to crank it up and unwind."

By the time the season started on October 9, 1970, against the Los Angeles Kings, Tallon was officially listed as a defenceman. He lined up at right defence, playing his offside as a left-handed shot. That allowed him to step into one-timers in the offensive zone, drilling them like a tee shot down the middle of a fairway.

"I guess we have to face facts," said Poile ahead of the game. "As a junior, he had so much talent you could play him anywhere you wanted to. In the NHL, his best spot is defence and that's where he'll have to play."

After Tallon scored his first NHL goal later that month, it seemed clear that defence would be his permanent position.

"Defence is where he'll be a superstar," said Poile after the goal. "That's where he'll stay."

The pressure was on. If Tallon wasn't going to be a franchise centre like Perreault, he needed to be a superstar defenceman.

"OBVIOUSLY, THERE WAS some disappointment that they didn't get Gilbert," said Tallon years later. "I would have been too because he was the best player in that draft by a mile."

The thing is, Tallon was still a talented hockey player. Perhaps without the constant comparisons to Perreault and the pressure to be a franchise player for an expansion team, things would have gone differently for Tallon.

It wasn't just the comparison to Perreault but the perception that Tallon was overpaid that kept the pressure on.

With a bigger signing bonus than Orr, Tallon faced unflattering comparisons to the greatest defenceman of all time. People claimed that Tallon couldn't be as good a centre as Perreault, and that he couldn't be as good a defenceman as Orr. How could he possibly live up to those types of expectations?

Canucks fans, accustomed to winning after back-to-back Lester Patrick Cups in the WHL, were perhaps not as patient as they could have been. *Vancouver Sun* sportswriter Jim Taylor recorded that Tallon was getting booed and catcalled as early as mid-December—just two months into his rookie season.

On one occasion when the Montreal Canadiens were in town, a Montreal writer, surprised at the reception Tallon got from the hometown crowd when he made a mistake, asked Laycoe if the fans were too hard on "the kid."

"The kid?" replied Laycoe. "You mean Tallon? No, I don't think so. They pay their six dollars, so I supposed they're entitled to voice an opinion. Besides, I think it's a challenge, and a player like Dale will respond to it."

Tallon did respond. As much as he struggled at times defensively—not a unique problem in the early years of the Canucks—he was still a star and was the team's first representative at the All-Star Game in 1971, then again in 1972. He finished his first season with 56 points in 78 games, placing him at fifth in rookie scoring and first among rookie defenceman. That still stands over 50 years later as the Canucks' franchise record for most points by a rookie defenceman.

And yet, the Canucks couldn't stop trying to play Tallon at forward. Early in the 1971–72 season, Laycoe kept trying

Tallon at centre or left wing, believing he could be a true superstar at forward. "It all hinges on Dennis Kearns," said Laycoe in November 1971. "If Dennis can't hack it as an NHL defenceman, I'll have to use Dale back there."

Kearns could hack it—he would play all 10 seasons of his NHL career for the Canucks. He retired with 321 points, which stood as a franchise record for Canucks defenceman for nearly 30 years until Mattias Öhlund broke the record in 2009. As a result, Tallon continued to be shuttled between defence and forward.

The position shuffling continued under a new head coach, Vic Stasiuk, in the 1972–73 season. In one game against the Buffalo Sabres early in the season, Stasiuk sent Tallon out at centre for a power play, but he wasn't the only defenceman out of position. His wingers were Gregg Boddy and Jim Hargreaves, who were also defencemen. With Kearns and Jocelyn Guevrement at the points, the Canucks had five defencemen on the ice for the power play.

Facing those five defencemen were four other defencemen—Vancouver's old WHL coach Joe Crozier, now coaching the Sabres, sent out four defencemen to kill the penalty, meaning nine defencemen were on the ice all at once.

The Sabres won the game 6–0. Gilbert Perreault had a four-point night.

WHEN SPORTSWRITER CLANCY Loranger handed out his end-of-season awards in his March 28, 1973, column in *The Province*, he named Tallon the "Best Defenceman Playing Centre."

"The only reason I play centre is because I'm told to play there," said Tallon after a January game. "I scored 56 points that first season when I went the whole way on defence," he said later. "It was a good year. They let me play defence." Stasiuk also stripped Tallon of the alternate captain's "A" in January just before a game against the Atlanta Flames. Tallon was told he could have it back "when and if he earns it."

The pressure kept piling on. As Perreault was thriving in Buffalo, Tallon was getting upbraided by Vancouver fans and branded a "sulker" and "malcontent" in the media. Continuously shuffled from forward to defence, Tallon was understandably frustrated.

"I've been shifted around so many places, it's tough to learn. I'm just starting to get my confidence back," said Tallon in March of 1973. "I'd like to come to training camp with one position in mind....If I had three years of continuous defence, I'd be better today."

Eventually, the frustrations came to a head and Tallon wanted out. Eagleson, his agent, gave the Canucks an ultimatum: they "had until May 1 to trade him to Boston, New York, or Chicago, or else he'd go to the World Hockey Association."

The May 1 deadline passed with no trade but two weeks later, the Canucks' first-ever draft pick was heading to the Chicago Black Hawks after just three seasons in Vancouver. Tallon played enough at centre that season that his position was once again referred to as "defenceman-centre" when the trade was announced.

"Maybe I should have taken a different attitude, but it's tough enough to play one position all season without playing a different one every game," said Tallon in the 1973 off-season, adding that Laycoe and Stasiuk "didn't treat the players right."

If Tallon was hoping that he could finally stick to playing defence once he was out of Vancouver, his hopes were quickly dashed.

"Tallon is the big centre we have been looking for," said Black Hawks GM Tommy Ivan. "Tallon will play centre full-time for us."

DENNIS VERVEGAERT AND THE TRAVELING PANTS

The signing of the Canucks' first-round pick from the 1973 Amateur Draft was overshadowed by a pair of falling pants.

Many expected the Canucks to take Lanny McDonald, a western Canadian sniper with the Medicine Hat Tigers, with the third-overall pick in 1973. So, it was something of a surprise when they drafted Dennis Ververgaert instead.

McDonald was apparently asking for a hefty contract—his first contract with the Toronto Maple Leafs was for $1 million over five years, $200,000 per year. Just a few years earlier, Tallon caused a stir when he signed for a then-rookie-record $60,000, so it's understandable that the asking price for McDonald might have scared the Canucks off.

Or maybe it wasn't the money at all.

"The brain trust simply decided they liked Ververgaert… better than McDonald, who was picked right behind him by Toronto," reported Clancy Lorager after the draft.

Ververgaert was coming off an outstanding season in the OHA, where he finished second in scoring behind Blake

Dunlop with 58 goals and 147 points in 63 games. A pre-draft scouting report said he was "strong and truculent, rugged in the corners, rated high on shooting and aggressiveness, tough, and an outstanding passer."

The decision to pass by McDonald was a regrettable one for the Canucks—the burly winger with the bushy moustache scored more than 1,000 points for the Toronto Maple Leafs, Colorado Rockies, and Calgary Flames and was inducted into the Hockey Hall of Fame in 1992. Ververgaert did manage some solid seasons for the Canucks, leading the team in scoring with a career-high 37 goals and 71 points in the 1975–76 season, but he couldn't hold a candle to McDonald.

Before all that, Ververgaert had to get signed. That wasn't always a guarantee thanks to the rise of the World Hockey Association, a league that hoped to rival the NHL and was offering players a lot more money to lure them away. Fortunately, Ververgaert was eager to play in the NHL and there were no issues.

The Canucks held a press conference with the newly signed Ververgaert on May 28, 1973, presided over by general manager Hal Laycoe and director of hockey operations Coley Hall. The 66-year-old Hall, a former high-level baseball player, was still in fantastic shape and was boasting a glowing tan from a recent trip to Hawaii. An enterprising photographer at the press conference jokingly suggested that Hall should compare his muscular build to that of Ververgaert.

Surprisingly, Hall agreed, shrugging off his suspenders and taking off his shirt. Laughing, Ververgaert doffed his shirt as well and the two struck bodybuilding poses next to one another.

Then Hall decided he needed to puff himself up a little bit more and sucked in his belly for one last pose. That's when his pants, no longer held up by his suspenders, plunged to his knees, exposing his underwear.

The next morning, Hall's muscles—and briefs—were on full display on the front page of the *Vancouver Sun*. Sigurdson called it "the first time in living memory the canny Hall has ever been caught with his pants down."

3

THE STEAMER

DALE TALLON wasn't a franchise-defining player for the Vancouver Canucks like Bobby Clarke had been for the Philadelphia Flyers, but he wasn't alone in that regard. It wasn't until 1978 that the Canucks finally drafted the player that would give them their personality as a hardworking, blue-collar team.

That's not to say the Canucks didn't draft some good players before 1978.

Don Lever was one of the better players picked in the 1972 draft. He played more than 1,000 games in his NHL career and served three seasons as captain of the Canucks, but he was never quite a star. It doesn't help that a Hall of Famer, Steve Schutt, was taken right after the Canucks took Lever third overall, and another, Bill Barber, was taken a few picks later.

It's something that would happen frequently to the Canucks in the '70s—both picking third overall and just missing out on a Hall of Fame player.

It was particularly painful in their inaugural 1970–71 season, when the Canucks were three points behind the Detroit Red Wings for second to last in the NHL with five games remaining, putting them in line for the second-overall pick. The Canucks went 3–1–1 over their final five games, passing the Red Wings by one point to give themselves the third-overall pick in the 1971 Amateur Draft. After Guy Lafleur went first overall, the Red Wings took Hall of Famer Marcel Dionne second overall.

The Canucks took Jocelyn Guevrement, a decently productive offensive defenceman who finished third in points on the Canucks in his rookie season, but he couldn't hold a candle to Dionne, who the Canucks missed by just one point in the standings.

Dennis Ververgaert was a good player for the Canucks after they took him third overall in 1973, but Hall of Famer Lanny McDonald was the very next pick. The Canucks also missed Hall of Famer Bob Gainey by one pick that year when he was taken just before the Canucks selected his fellow Bob, Bob Dailey, ninth overall.

The Canucks traded their first-round picks in the 1974 and 1976 drafts. It's just as well—two Hall of Famers, Clark Gillies and Bernie Federko, were taken with the picks before where the Canucks would have selected, so they simply passed on their draft luck to other teams.

The Canucks kept picking third overall because they were bad enough to miss the playoffs but not quite bad enough to finish at the very bottom of the standings and earn one of the top two picks. They managed to make the playoffs in 1975 and 1976 but were knocked out in the first round both times and were back out of the playoffs again in 1977 and 1978.

That gave the Canucks the fourth-overall pick in the 1978 draft, but that's not where they found their franchise-defining player. He didn't get selected until 40ᵗʰ overall in the third round.

STAN SMYL WAS already a legend in Vancouver after winning back-to-back Memorial Cups with the New Westminster Bruins. The first of those Memorial Cup wins, in 1977, even came in Vancouver at the home of the Canucks, the Pacific Coliseum. It was at the 1978 Memorial Cup, however, that the 20-year-old Smyl came into his own.

The 1977–78 season didn't start particularly well for Smyl, who collided with a goalpost and was knocked unconscious during an exhibition game against the Seattle Breakers. He suffered a fractured skull and rib injuries that caused him to miss both the preseason and the first five games of the regular season, which also slowed him down when he did get in the lineup.

"I was knocked cold, so I don't remember anything about what happened," said Smyl a couple of months into the season. "I've had no aftereffects, but it's taken me a while to get into proper shape."

It wasn't all bad news. While he was sitting out, Smyl was named captain of the Bruins.

As much as it took him time to get rolling, Smyl still set a new career high with 76 points in just 53 games and earned a spot on Team Canada at the 1978 World Junior Championship. There, he won bronze alongside a few

future Canucks teammates in Curt Fraser, Rick Vaive, Steve
Tambellini, and William Huber, as well as a scrawny 16-year-
old kid who led the tournament in scoring: Wayne Gretzky.
Smyl was on the smaller side at 5'8", but he packed a ton
of power in that compact frame, throwing hits with reckless
abandon.

"A lot of opposing players make the mistake of overlook-
ing Stanley when he's coming at them," said Harold Phillipoff,
a Bruins teammate who had seven inches on Smyl. "They soon
get smartened up fast."

Smyl already had a nickname when he came to Vancouver.
He first played a couple of seasons with the Bellingham
Blazers in the BCJHL, where they started calling him "Stanley
Steamer," after the steam-powered cars produced by the
Stanley Motor Carriage Company in the early decades of the
20th century. The Stanley Steamer was kept alive in popular
culture thanks to appearances in movies, not to mention the
American carpet-cleaning company founded in 1947 called
"Stanley Steemer."

Smyl's style was much more akin to a steam engine than
a carpet cleaner. He was like a locomotive on the ice, or
perhaps the Little Engine That Could because of his size. His
nickname was eventually simplified to just "the Steamer" and
when he built up a head of steam, Smyl seemingly couldn't
be stopped.

Even injuries could barely slow Smyl down. A severely
sprained ankle threatened to derail the end of Smyl's 1977–
78 season with the Bruins but, with the playoffs on the line, Smyl
got his ankle taped by former BC Lions trainer Roy Cavallin
to take the ice at the end of the season. Smyl came through in

the clutch, scoring the game-winning goal in one of their final games to secure a playoff spot by one point over the Breakers. Despite the heavily taped ankle, Smyl elevated his game in the postseason. He was dominant in the WCHL playoffs, racking up 14 goals in 20 games to lead the Bruins to the WCHL championship. He was even better at the Memorial Cup, leading the competition in scoring by a wide margin with four goals and 10 assists in five games.

In the championship game against the Petersborough Petes, Smyl steamrolled the competition with a five-point effort en route to a 7–4 win. When it was all over, there was no doubt that Smyl was the tournament MVP.

Smyl already had the attention of NHL scouts but his MVP performance at the Memorial Cup evidently wasn't enough to get him drafted in the first two rounds. Perhaps there were questions about his size—not just that he was small, but that the style he played, crashing into an opponent every shift, wouldn't work out well in the NHL for a 5′8″ winger.

Or maybe it was his skating, which even Smyl admitted wasn't strong enough. Being small and slow has been the downfall of a lot of junior stars when they tried to make the NHL. Perhaps that's why Smyl didn't seem to care what team drafted him.

"Where? Heck no. Anywhere will do just as long as I play," he said, with his typical folksy charm.

SMYL DID HAVE the support of one NHL scout: Ernie "Punch" McLean, his head coach with the Bruins and bird dog for the Detroit Red Wings.

Stan Smyl (centre) paces Tiger Williams (left) and Harold Snepsts (right) in a practice drill.

McLean was a character who had experienced some serious trials and tribulations in his life. He was literally born in a coal mine because his parents' house was too cold and the mine was the warmest place in town. He nearly died in a plane crash in northern Saskatchewan in the early '70s—he wrapped a T-shirt around his mangled face and walked miles in the snow to get help, losing sight in his left eye from the accident.

Perhaps that's why McLean had little patience with players who whined and complained but plenty of time for a tough kid like Smyl. Although he was supposed to be scouting for the Red Wings, he couldn't keep himself from crowing about his captain and calling for the local NHL team to take him in the draft.

"I think Stan would make a hell of a second-round draft for the Canucks," said McLean to Lyndon Little at the

Vancouver Sun. "He's a great leader and his all-out style of play would really help."

"Stan's one of the smartest players I've ever coached," said McLean to Little on another occasion. "He's got a good shot and sense of anticipation. And, of course, he's always working hard."

For Smyl, hard work was a given.

"My work ethic probably helped me get to where I did," Smyl said to Mike Beamish of the *Sun* after his playing career was over. "I didn't get there on my scoring ability or my talents or my stats. I never gave up. It's something I'm pretty proud of. I guess, basically, I played with a lot of heart. I never took the easy way out. It took me a long ways."

Smyl credited McLean for teaching him how to play a strong two-way game—he was known more for his goalscoring before his arrival in New Westminster—and he nearly ended up in Detroit because of him. On the day of the 1978 draft, McLean pushed hard for the Red Wings to pick Smyl in the second round.

"I was arguing back and forth with [Red Wings scout] Rudy Pilous about whether to take Stan or a kid from Flin Flon named Glen Hicks," McLean said to Beamish. "[Red Wings GM] Ted Lindsay decided there was only one way to settle it. 'Who's the better skater?'"

McLean admitted that Hicks was a better skater than Smyl and the matter was settled: the Red Wings took Hicks 28th overall in the second round. They had another chance to take Smyl a few picks later and McLean continued to plead Smyl's case.

"Ted, I can't tell you what the guy's got in his heart, what he brings to a hockey club," recalled McLean. "It's a lot more than skating ability."

Instead, Lindsay decided the Red Wings needed to pick a goaltender, so he took Al Jensen 31st overall, hoping Smyl would still be available later in the third round. But he was already gone—at 40th overall, the Canucks drafted Smyl.

McLean was choked that the Red Wings missed out on Smyl even as he was happy to see him drafted. "Smyl is the most underrated player in the draft," he said. "He's a tough right-sider—he's just what the Canucks need."

Jake Milford, the Canucks' general manager, was certainly pleased.

"We were delighted to get Stan," he said. "We felt it was a bit of a steal because we didn't think he'd be around for our third pick."

Milford had taken over from Phil Maloney as Canucks general manager in 1977. Under his leadership, the Canucks drafted well, finding several stars and few, if any, busts. Milford had been around the game for over four decades by that point and earned a reputation for being a shrewd talent evaluator.

"Jake was a great guy, very astute, and [he was] a good hockey guy," said Mike Penny, who Milford hired as a scout in 1980. It was a savvy hire—Penny would work for the Canucks for the next 20 years and played an instrumental role in the Canucks drafting Pavel Bure.

Milford also expanded the scope of the Canucks' operations. The round after he selected Smyl in 1978, Milford selected Harald Lückner, the first Swedish player drafted by the Canucks. He acquired a bevy of Swedish players led by Thomas Gradin and also lured Ivan Hlinka and Jiri Bubla out of Czechoslovakia. At the draft in later years, he found a couple more European stars in late rounds in Patrik Sundström and Petri Skriko.

As much as Milford led the Canucks to look internationally, his best draft pick came right out of the Canucks' backyard in Smyl. First, however, Smyl had to make the team. He was well aware of what scouts saw as his shortcomings.

"I always thought I could make it to the NHL, but the scouts kept saying I was too small and too slow," recalled Smyl in 1991. "[McLean] kept telling me, 'Size has nothing to do with this game. You play hard for me and you're going to go a long way.'"

Smyl wasn't worried about his size—thanks to McLean, he knew he was tough enough—but the skating was a problem. So, after he was drafted, Smyl took power skating lessons in the off-season and dramatically improved.

"Three solid weeks of power skating this summer has improved my mobility," said Smyl when he came to training camp. "Maybe no one else has noticed, but I have. I'm turning better and my stride and takeoff are stronger."

The improved skating combined with his ever-present hustle quickly erased any concerns that Smyl might be too slow. As for being too small, one of his own Canucks teammates learned the hard way that Smyl's size wasn't going to keep him from playing a hard, physical game. During a scrimmage at his first NHL training camp, Smyl hit 6'3" defenceman Harold Snepsts so hard that Canucks head coach Harry

Neale said, "If the glass hadn't been there, Harold would still be flying."

Snepsts didn't seem to take it personally. The next day, the defenceman cheerfully said, "That Stan Smyl is just the type of guy we need."

Smyl was turning heads with every aspect of his play in training camp and if there were any concerns about him being able to play the same way for 80 games, Smyl didn't share them.

"Sure, I can keep it up for a whole season," said Smyl. "I ran into people for three years with New Westminster and you meet quite a few big boys in the corners in the Western Canada League."

It became clear that Smyl was going to make the team out of camp. Smyl and second-round pick Curt Fraser were matched with another Canucks rookie, trade acquisition Thomas Gradin, and the line quickly found chemistry. The rough-and-tumble Smyl and Fraser proved to be a great fit with the skilled Gradin—they stuck together as a trio until Fraser was traded away in 1982.

"I should be down having a beer with the guy who decided to draft him," said Neale of Smyl to Tony Gallagher of *The Providence*. "He never seems to play a bad game."

WHILE TALLON HEARD boos when he didn't live up to expectations, fans rallied around Smyl, who became a fan favourite due to his work ethic and willingness to take on anyone on the ice, no matter how many inches or pounds they had on him.

"If you play a hard game consistently, people appreciate it," Smyl said simply.

The Steamer played all 13 seasons of his NHL career with the Canucks and he personified the team's underdog identity. Despite Smyl's best efforts, the team never once had a winning record during his career, finishing below .500 every single season. But through it all, Smyl was the model of consistency.

"He's either great or good every game and never bad," said Neale during the 1979–80 season. "I don't think there's another winger in the league who has more hits than Stan does."

Regrettably, there's no way of knowing if that's true. The NHL didn't start tracking hits as a statistic until after the 2005 lockout. He certainly led the Canucks in every single other statistic. In the 1979–80 season, Smyl became the first player in NHL history to lead his team in goals, assists, points, and penalty minutes.

It was one of just two seasons Smyl led the Canucks in scoring, but he led the team in so many other ways. On the eve of the 1982 playoffs, Canucks captain Kevin McCarthy suffered a broken ankle when Fraser accidentally fell on him during an optional practice. In his place, Smyl was named the team's temporary captain.

The first thing Smyl did as captain of the Canucks was lead the team on a Cinderella run to the 1982 Stanley Cup Final. Smyl tallied nine goals and 18 points in that playoff run, one point behind Gradin for the team lead.

After the Canucks were swept by the Islanders in the 1982 Stanley Cup Final, fans swarmed outside the Canucks dressing room chanting, "Stan-ley! Stan-ley!" not for the Cup, but for

Smyl. The newly crowned captain had given everything he had and, as he predicted, the fans appreciated it.

Smyl was named the team's permanent captain the following season and served as captain for eight seasons. By the end of his career, Smyl proved to be the steal Milford believed him to be. Among players taken in the 1978 draft, Smyl tied for third in points behind first-overall pick Bobby Smith and seventh-overall pick Ken Linseman. The Steamer scored 673 points in 896 games across 13 seasons, all of them with the Canucks. He retired as the franchise leader in games played, goals, assists, points, and penalty minutes.

When Smyl retired, he simply took one step back, from sitting on the bench to standing behind it as one of the Canucks' assistant coaches. It was a natural progression for a natural leader.

On November 3, 1991, Smyl's No. 12 was retired to the rafters, the first ever retired by the Canucks. Cliff Ronning, another undersized Canuck, was there to see it. He grew up in Burnaby watching Smyl play and knew exactly what Smyl meant to the Canucks.

"He was the heart and soul of the Vancouver Canucks for all the years he played—it's as simple as that," said Ronning as he headed into his first full season with his childhood team. "Seeing Stan's number retired means something to us. You want to work that much harder because, maybe 10 years down the road, if you put in hard work that's what happens.

"People respect you."

HAROLD SNEPSTS

The man that Stan Smyl nearly put through the glass at his first Canucks training camp defined the first two decades of the Canucks nearly as much as Smyl did. Harold Snepsts was never the most talented player on the ice, just like the Canucks weren't the most talented team in the NHL, but no one worked harder.

And no one had a better moustache.

Long before the facial hair, however, Snepsts was just another kid in Edmonton, Alberta, who loved to play hockey. While the other kids dreamed about playing in the NHL someday, Snepsts dreamed a little bit smaller—he just wanted to play indoors.

"I was playing for Beverly Heights and that was the elite—to make it to the Maple Leafs and the indoor rink," said Snepsts to Mark Spector at the *Edmonton Journal* about his lofty goal of playing for the local Maple Leafs Athletic Club when he was 11.

Even back then, Snepsts was short on talent but had plenty of determination. Jim Stewart, one of his coaches with the Maple Leafs, said, "Harold Snepsts was the worst skater on the team but he could run like crazy on the ice." But even though his dreams started small, they grew with every step he took.

"Initially, you were just happy to play Bantam AA," said Snepsts. "Then as you started playing there, you realized that a good portion of the guys that made the Oil Kings were from the Maple Leafs."

Playing major junior with the Edmonton Oil Kings in the WCHL became Snepsts' next goal but it took him some time—he couldn't make the cut at 17, then broke through as an 18-year-old in the 1972–73 season. One of his Oil Kings teammates that season was Darcy Rota, who would be a teammate with him on the Canucks years later.

"When he played junior, he was a guy who couldn't skate very well, couldn't handle the puck very well—but he was the guy where we would just say, 'Harold, sic 'em,'" recalled Rota years later during a "Greatest Canucks" segment on Global News. "He was a great battler and a good fighter back then."

Even after fulfilling his goal of playing for the Oil Kings, Snepsts still didn't dream of playing in the NHL. In his mind, that was for players with more skill and better skating. Instead, he thought he might go to school and become a teacher. But then he saw Rota, and others like him, make the jump directly from the Oil Kings to the NHL.

"I figured, 'Hey, I'm playing on the same team with those guys,'" said Snepsts to Jim Taylor of the *Vancouver Sun* in 1976. "'Why couldn't I make it too?' So, I sat down with my parents and we decided that rather than go to school right away, I'd give it one more shot."

Snepsts worked tirelessly on every aspect of his game and improved by leaps and bounds in his second season with the Oil Kings. With his size at 6'3", a reputation for making opponents' lives miserable along the boards, and the type of work ethic and off-ice character that coaches dream about, Snepsts went from someone with no future in hockey to someone with a chance of being drafted.

"Harold Snepsts is certainly one of the finest competitors I've ever met. I think he's the most improved 19-year-old in the league," said Oil Kings coach Ken Hodge to Terry Jones of the *Edmonton Journal*. "I know that Harold is the toughest player in the league.... He certainly has a great deal of pro potential. He's just a little late developing."

Despite his improvements, Snepsts was still an awkward skater and was limited offensively. There were serious doubts he could play at any level of professional hockey, let alone the NHL. And yet, Snepsts wasn't just drafted once—he was drafted twice.

The upstart World Hockey Association had caused chaos with the NHL by conducting a secret two-round amateur draft three months earlier than the NHL draft, giving them a head start on luring top prospects with lucrative contracts. In response, the NHL decided to hold the 1974 draft just before the WHA held their public amateur draft on May 31.

In an arduous three-day process, the NHL secretly held a 25-round draft—the draft continued until every team stopped making picks, so teams could take as many players as they wanted. The draft list was not publicized, in hopes of preventing the WHA from stealing players from NHL teams.

Snepsts was selected in both drafts—in the fourth round by the Canucks in the NHL draft and in the sixth round by the Indianapolis Racers in the WHA draft. New Canucks general manager Phil Maloney went with size over skill at the 1974 draft, believing that the bigger players would perform better in the physical NHL.

"This year, we decided to concentrate on big, aggressive kids, who want to play even if there were smaller, more talented kids still available," said Maloney to Hal Sigurdson of the *Vancouver Sun.* "I figure two or three years down the road, the bigger kid will be the better player."

The 6′3″ Snepsts, with his 239 penalty minutes with the Oil Kings, fit the bill. The WHA proved to not be a threat— like Rota, Snepsts wanted to play in the NHL and the Canucks had been bold enough to use a fourth-round pick on him.

As a fourth-round pick, the 20-year-old Snepsts wasn't expected to make the Canucks out of training camp, but Snepsts impressed Maloney, who was also the Canucks' head coach, with his willingness to drop the gloves with—and clobber—Los Angeles Kings tough guy Dave Hutchison in a preseason game.

It wasn't just his fists that impressed Maloney. Snepsts proved he could play at the NHL level and Maloney praised his simple, no-frills defensive game. After one preseason game against the Kings, Maloney rattled off the three things that Sneptsts did well to Tom Watt of *The Province:* he moved the puck to his forwards "without making a production of it," pinned players to the boards, and punished opponents in front of the net.

"I just hope he continues to do these things," said Maloney. "I hope some of the veterans on this club were watching him last night. They could have learned something from him."

Snepsts made the Canucks out of camp and kept doing those three things for the rest of his career, which proved longer than anyone expected. Just one player from the 1974 draft played more NHL games than Snepsts: Hall of Famer Bryan Trottier. By the time Snepsts retired in 1991, he had played 1,033 NHL games, 781 of them with the Canucks.

"The only thing that keeps me here is my determination," said Snepsts to Taylor a couple of years into his career. "But I'm here and I'll do anything I have to [in order] to stay." He didn't just stay—Canucks fans fell in love with him. Vancouver was a working-class city and he was a working-class hero and someone the fans could latch onto even as the Canucks struggled. Snepsts was the ultimate underdog on a team full of them, who matched up against the best players in the NHL purely through hard work.

"People always love to see the goal scorers and the fancy players. I don't think they can relate to these types of players as they can to myself," said Snepsts. "I just go out there, I give it 110 percent. I don't have the world's talent in this body, so what I do give, I think everybody can relate to."

Snepsts gave everything he had every single night and, after games, even when he was exhausted, always took the time to talk to fans and sign autographs. The fans responded with adoration, chanting his name—"Har-old! Har-old! Har-old!"—when he would throw a big hit or score one of his rare goals.

"The fans loved him," said Canucks colour commentator Tom Larscheid. "He didn't have a lot of talent, but boy, he had a lot of heart."

Snepsts and Smyl were the heart and soul of the Canucks. When they won the Campbell Conference championship in 1982, team captain Smyl snagged Snepsts as he skated to centre ice to lift the Clarence S. Campbell Bowl.

"I grabbed Harry and said, 'Come on, you're coming with me,' and he said, 'You're damned right I'm coming,'" said Smyl. "Nobody deserved to be out there more than Harry.

He's played so well all through the playoffs and he's waited eight years for this to happen."

When Rota met up with Snepsts again in Vancouver, he marveled at the progression he had made from the kid who couldn't skate with the Oil Kings.

"He worked on his game to become a quality, All-Star player in the National Hockey League and make it when many said he couldn't do it," said Rota.

That's right—an All-Star. The kid from Edmonton who had never even dreamed of playing in the NHL played in two All-Star Games for the Canucks.

4

DRAFTING THE 1982 CANUCKS

THE BUFFALO SABRES, thanks in part to their luck at the wheel, quickly saw more success than their expansion cousins in Vancouver. Gilbert Perreault was joined by Rene Robert and Rick Martin—drafted fifth overall in 1971 after the Canucks took defenceman Jocelyn Guevremont third—to form the French Connection line, which dominated the '70s and took the Sabres to the Stanley Cup Final in just their fifth season.

It took the Canucks a bit longer to reach their first Stanley Cup Final; they did it in 1982. It was the first time they had even made it past the first round of the playoffs.

It was an extremely unlikely playoff run for multiple reasons. Just before the playoffs started, the Canucks lost their captain—and top-scoring defenceman—Kevin McCarthy to a freak broken ankle suffered during an optional practice.

Two other key defencemen, Rick Lanz and Jiri Bubla, were also injured, leaving the Canucks with a depleted blue line heading into the postseason.

Even before the injuries, the Canucks were not the most talented team. The Canucks finished the regular season with a 30–33–17 record, three games below .500. In the dreadful Smythe Division, however, 77 points was good for second place behind the juggernaut Edmonton Oilers and their 111 points.

But even juggernauts can fall. The Oilers were stunned in the first round of the playoffs by the Los Angeles Kings, who won the best-of-five series three games to two. That included the "Miracle on Manchester" Game 3, where the Kings came back from a 5–0 deficit in the third period to win 6–5 in overtime.

That miracle meant the Canucks didn't have to overcome the Oilers after sweeping their first-round series against the Calgary Flames. Instead, they faced an exhausted Kings team and dispatched them 4–1 in their best-of-seven series in the second round.

That sent the Canucks to the Clarence Campbell Conference Final against the Chicago Black Hawks, who had a Cinderella postseason of their own. The Black Hawks finished even lower in the standings than the Canucks with 72 points, but had upset the division-leading Minnesota North Stars in the first round, then slipped past the St. Louis Blues in the second round.

It was an ideal matchup for the Canucks, who cruised to a 4–1 series win and the conference championship, sending them to the Stanley Cup Final against the powerhouse New

York Islanders. Their only loss of the series was its own sort of victory. When interim head coach Roger Neilson raised the white flag—a towel on the end of a hockey stick—in mock surrender to the referees in Game 2 for what he viewed as unfair officiating, it galvanized the fan base. Fans greeted the Canucks at the airport while waving white towels over their heads, then twirled more towels in Games 3 and 4 at the Pacific Coliseum.

Towel Power was born.

THE TEAM THAT went to the Stanley Cup Final to face the New York Islanders dynasty wasn't exactly built through the draft. The few drafted players on the team were not even first-round picks. They were led by third-round pick Stan Smyl, who was the heart and soul of the Canucks, and fourth-round pick Harold Snepsts, who encapsulated their scrappy, hardscrabble identity.

But beyond Smyl and Snepsts, only five players drafted by the Canucks made an appearance in the 1982 playoffs and most of them barely played.

Instead, the 1981–82 Canucks were largely built through trades and some savvy free-agent signings, like Czech players Ivan Hlinka and Jiri Bubla—the first crest of a wave of players to come to the NHL from Czechoslovakia. When Hlinka stepped on the ice for Game 3 against the Islanders after missing the first two games with a shoulder injury, he became the first Czech player ever to play in the Stanley Cup Final.

Several of the top players on the Canucks came from trades with their opponents in the 1982 playoffs. Their first-round opponent, the Calgary Flames, was the former home of Ivan Boldirev and Darcy Rota when the franchise was still in Atlanta, coming over in a trade for the Canucks' 1972 first-round pick Don Lever. The Canucks' leading scorer, Thomas Gradin, came to the Canucks in a trade with their third-round opponent, the Black Hawks. The Canucks' starting goaltender, Richard Brodeur, was part of a minor trade that saw the Canucks swap fifth-round picks in 1981 with their Cup Final opponent, the Islanders, where Brodeur had been their third-string goalie.

Of the draft picks who actually played for the Canucks in the 1981–82 season, most of them played a minor role.

Glen Hanlon, who was drafted in the third round in 1977, was the team's backup goaltender but was traded to the St. Louis Blues mid-season. Hanlon had been a top goaltending prospect after a great WHL career with the Brandon Wheat Kings but his ascension to number one goaltender with the Canucks was blocked when they acquired Brodeur. That allowed the Canucks to trade Hanlon to the St. Louis Blues for a pack of three players and a fourth-round pick. One of those players, Jim Nill, put up seven points in 16 playoff games during the 1982 playoff run for the Canucks and was one of their most frequent fighters.

Hanlon played parts of 14 seasons in the NHL but his biggest claim to fame from his playing career was, regrettably, that he gave up Wayne Gretzky's first career NHL goal when he was in net for the Canucks in 1979.

"I created a monster," Hanlon would later quip.

Hanlon returned to Vancouver in the early '90s, serving as a goaltending coach and scout for the Canucks, then saw a promotion to assistant coach from 1995 to 1999. After a decade of coaching in the AHL, NHL, and Europe, including a stint as an NHL head coach with the Washington Capitals, Hanlon came back to Vancouver as an assistant coach with the Vancouver Giants for two seasons, then came back again as the Giant's general manager for two more seasons.

Garth Butcher was the Canucks' first-round pick in 1981, but he was just a 19-year-old rookie during the 1982 playoffs and appeared in just one game. Butcher went on to be a key defenceman for the Canucks during the '80s, even if he didn't quite live up to expectations as a 10th-overall pick.

At the time, the Canucks were over the moon that Butcher was even available. His combination of skill and toughness in junior had him ranked third overall by *The Hockey News*, but his toughness outweighed his skill once he got to the NHL. He was a punishing defender and loved to get under the skin of his opponents, making him difficult to play against, but he wasn't known for his offensive contributions, unlike Hall of Fame defenceman Al MacInnis, who went five picks later.

Butcher is widely considered one of the toughest players in Canucks history. When the *Vancouver Province* compiled a list of the 101 greatest Canucks of all time in 2014, Butcher landed at number 44.

Marc Crawford was a fourth-round pick from the 1980 draft and he played a depth role during the 1982 playoff run, appearing in 14 games and tallying just one point, a goal. Scoring wasn't his job—Crawford was more of a feisty pest on the ice, aggravating opponents rather than scoring on them.

Crawford would go on to a lot more success in the NHL as a coach, winning the Stanley Cup with the Colorado

Avalanche in 1996. He came back to Vancouver as head coach of the Canucks for seven seasons, from 1998 to 2006.

Rick Lanz, selected seventh overall in 1980, was one of the few first-round picks by the Canucks still with the team in the 1981–82 season, but he missed the entire playoffs with torn knee ligaments. Like Hlinka and Bubla, Lanz was born in Czechoslovakia but grew up in Canada after his family defected in 1968, when he was eight years old.

"We left Czechoslovakia suddenly and with hardly any of our possessions when there was a rumour the Russians were coming into the country," recalled Lanz to Arv Olson of the *Vancouver Sun* after he was drafted. "We were on vacation in Bulgaria at the time and we had to go through Vienna to get to Canada. I think we arrived here with $25."

After the 1982 playoffs, Lanz became the team's top offensive defenceman in the early '80s, with two 50-plus point seasons. Injuries ultimately derailed his career after the Canucks traded him to the Toronto Maple Leafs for Dan Hodgson and future Canucks general manager Jim Benning.

Andy Schliebener was a third-round pick in the 1980 draft and a depth defenceman for the 1981–82 Canucks, forced into action thanks to the team's injuries on the blue line. He played just three playoff games in 1982 and bounced between the Canucks and the minors for a few more seasons before retiring at 24.

Gerry Minor made an appropriately minor impact in the 1982 playoffs. The sixth-round pick from the 1978 draft played just nine games during the 1982 run to the Stanley Cup Final, but he came through in some big moments. His four points—a goal and three assists—all came in the Final against the Islanders.

Minor was an adept scorer at the AHL level but struggled to produce in the NHL, except in one somewhat surprising situation: he set a franchise record for the most shorthanded goals by a Canuck in the 1980–81 season with six. That record would stand for over a decade until Pavel Bure scored seven shorthanded goals in the 1992–93 season.

Those picks may not have been the most important players for the Canucks' run to the Cup Final, but one other draft pick definitely was: Curt Fraser.

FRASER WAS BORN in Cincinnati, Ohio, where his dad, Barry Beatty, played minor pro hockey with the IHL's Cincinnati Mohawks. His family moved back to Winnipeg when he was little and then to Vancouver when he was nine, landing him right in the Canucks' backyard. His two older brothers dragged him to the rink on a nightly basis—"They were probably the main reason I developed as a hockey player," Fraser recalled years later when he was head coach of the AHL's Grand Rapids Griffins.

His older brothers also toughened him up, as they regularly got into scraps with each other. That proved important as he took steps into higher levels of hockey, first with the Kelowna Buckaroos in the BCJHL, then with the Victoria Cougars of the WCHL.

"Back then it was tough, tough hockey. You had to step up and be counted or you'd get run over," Fraser said. "I was probably one of the smaller guys on the team but I still liked sticking my nose where I probably shouldn't have."

Hockey became a year-round obsession for Fraser and he began working out in the gym to get stronger. He took boxing and Tae Kwon Do lessons to improve both his fitness and his fighting skills and it paid off.

Fraser had the combination of toughness and skill that NHL scouts love—he tallied 48 goals and 92 points in 66 games in his draft year but also 256 penalty minutes. He was a hardworking two-way player, who did his best work in the corners, coming away from board battles with the puck more often than not. He used his hands in two ways: putting the puck into the net and laying an opponent out on the ice.

It wasn't just NHL scouts that had their eyes on Fraser. The Winnipeg Jets tried to lure Fraser to the World Hockey Association, but Fraser had one goal.

"I listened to the WHA offers, but basically I had my mind set on the NHL," said Fraser to Lyndon Little of the *Sun* after he was drafted.

After taking the skilled Bill Derlago with their first-round pick in 1978, the Canucks were eager to take a couple of tougher players, starting with Fraser in the second round, then Smyl in the third round.

"With good, tough boys like these two joining us, I wouldn't feel too complacent if I were a veteran right winger or left winger on the Canucks," said Jake Milford about Smyl and Fraser.

Fraser could go toe-to-toe with the heavyweights of the NHL with the gloves off but he was more valuable to the

Canucks when he kept them on. Unlike most of those other heavyweights, Fraser played on the first line.

"There is not a guy in the league who can really handle Fraser," said Dave "Tiger" Williams, the NHL's all-time leader in penalty minutes, to Archie McDonald of the *Sun*. "I've never played with a guy who could put someone to his knees with one shot. Another thing that makes Fraser so valuable is that he's consistently a 25–30 goal scorer. He's a good hockey player."

At his first training camp in 1978, Fraser was put on a line with Smyl and the Canucks' new acquisition out of Sweden, Thomas Gradin. The rookie trio, dubbed the "Kid Line" as rookie lines so often are, was immediately a success, thriving in training camp and the preseason. While first-round pick Derlago was sent down to the minors, Fraser and Smyl easily made the Canucks out of camp, and their line with Gradin stuck together for the next four seasons.

"When Fras and I got put together as a line with Thomas at training camp, we hit it off from day one," recalled Smyl to Ben Kuzma of *The Province* years later. "In skating drills, we tried to keep up to Thomas and figured if we could do that, then we'd be better."

Fraser brought a physical edge to his game that complemented the sublime skill of Gradin and Smyl's fearless grit, but his own skill shouldn't be discounted. Fraser scored 28 goals and 67 points in the 1981–82 season and led the Canucks with 11 power play goals, using his great hands around the net to corral rebounds and finish off passing plays.

FRASER MADE AN immediate impact in the 1982 playoffs. Off the opening faceoff in Game 1, Fraser sent the puck ahead to Gradin, who set up Smyl in front for the game's opening goal, just eight seconds into the game. Moments later, Fraser added a fight to his assist. He dropped the gloves with Flames tough guy Willi Plett, then dropped Plett with a single punch. Just 14 seconds into the first game of the Canucks' post-season, Fraser had a point and a fight. It set the tone for how the rest of the playoffs would go for the Canucks, as they fought all the way to the Stanley Cup Final.

Three players from the 1982 Canucks landed in the NHL's top 20 all-time in playoff penalty minutes: Tiger Williams (116), Curt Fraser (98), and Colin Campbell (89). Fraser fought in every game of the Canucks' three-game sweep of the Flames in the first round—four times in total. He fought less as the playoffs progressed but still piled up penalty minutes for other physical fouls and several misconducts, as he stuck his nose into every post-whistle scrum. He contributed offensively too, scoring 10 points in 17 games along the way.

As a team, the Canucks fought a whopping 34 times in 17 games in the 1982 playoffs, averaging two fights per game. The Canucks weren't the highest-scoring team—their leading scorer, Thomas Gradin, had 8 fewer goals and 10 fewer points than the Islanders' leading scorers, Mike Bossy and Bryan Trottier—but they scrapped their way to the Stanley Cup Final.

Even though the Canucks fell short against the Islanders, there was no shame in it. It was the third of four-straight Stanley Cups for the Islanders—they beat everyone.

Roger Neilson and the 1981–82 Canucks raise the white flag in mock surrender to the officials during the 1982 Stanley Cup Playoffs, starting Towel Power in Vancouver.

The Islanders, unlike the Canucks, did build through the draft. The vast majority of the 1981–82 Islanders were Islanders draft picks. Trottier and Bossy were both Islanders' draft picks, as were Denis Potvin, Clark Gillies, Lorne Henning, Bob Nystrom, John Tonelli, Duane Sutter, Brent Sutter, Stefan Persson, and many more. Even goaltender Billy Smith was an Islanders draft pick of sorts, taken in the 1972 expansion draft.

The Canucks got a few key players from the draft and that was enough to go on one miraculous run to the Stanley Cup Final, where they were tremendously fortunate to face three teams who finished below them in the standings along the way. But they were no match for a team that was actually built through the draft.

CURT FRASER AND THE CHICAGO 6

While his Canucks teammates loved what Curt Fraser did on the ice, he was also well-liked off the ice, with a kind and gentle demeanour that belied his tough reputation. "He's a pussycat," said his head coach, Roger Neilson, during the 1982 playoffs. "If you were to bump into him in the street, he would be all over himself apologizing. He doesn't often go looking for fights. He's not the kind of guy who scares other players but he scares other fighters."

Fraser's off-the-ice pursuits took a more creative turn. He played guitar while growing up—he played in a band called Bull Rug Sludge when he was just 12 years old—and he took those talents to a bigger stage after he was traded to the Chicago Blackhawks for Tony Tanti in 1983.

Along with two of his Blackhawks teammates and three members of the 1986 Super Bowl–winning Chicago Bears, Fraser played guitar and sang in a band called the Chicago 6, playing gigs around Chicago for charity and even playing shows in Puerto Rico and New York.

The band was put together by an enterprising editor for *Chicago Sports Profile* magazine during the 1987 NFL strike. The three Blackhawks were Fraser and Surrey's own Gary Nylund on guitar and centre Troy Murray on saxophone, while the Bears contributed defensive tackle Dan Hampton on bass, safety Dave Duerson on trumpet and trombone, and legendary running back Walter Payton on drums.

The main appeal of the band, which primarily played covers of Motown and classic rock hits, was that they were all professional athletes, but they could legitimately play, and all members of the group took a turn behind the microphone singing lead vocals. Despite throwing plenty of punches on the ice, Fraser's fingers were still dexterous enough to play a mean blues lick, trading guitar solos with Nylund.

"Those Canucks from up north," said Hampton in a behind-the-scenes video put together about the band. "When we got together, it was apparent right off that they were very serious about it."

The group stayed together for four years, even when Nylund and Fraser were traded away from the Blackhawks, though Murray was replaced by Bears linebacker Otis Wilson, a multi-percussionist.

Music wasn't to be Fraser's post-playing career, however. Like his fellow Canucks draft picks Hanlon and Crawford, Fraser became an NHL head coach—he was the first-ever head coach of the Atlanta Thrashers. It seemed like the Canucks were better at drafting future head coaches than future stars in their early years.

5

THE ONES WHO GOT AWAY: DERLAGO, VAIVE, AND NEELY

THE NHL DRAFT hasn't always been kind to the Canucks, particularly in their first couple of decades. Prospects that seemed like certain stars never lived up to their potential, while others suffered injuries that derailed their careers. At best, the prospects the Canucks drafted in the first round were good players while their opponents were drafting future Hall of Famers.

But the Canucks also suffered a few self-inflicted wounds along the way. The few star players that the Canucks did draft early in their history were traded away before they could break out.

When the Canucks went to the 1982 Stanley Cup Final, for instance, it might have been nice to have two of their recent first-round picks on the roster—Bill Derlago and Rick Vaive—but they were both long gone, traded in 1980 to the Toronto Maple Leafs.

BEFORE HE WAS drafted, Bill Derlago was one of the all-time greatest goal scorers in junior hockey, leading the Western Canada Hockey League with 89 goals in just 52 games in his draft year. It was the 1977–78 season and he reached the 50-goal mark in just 27 games, a junior record. He was the consummate sniper, beating goaltenders cleanly with his quick release.

The Canucks desperately needed goalscoring. In an era when the top goal scorers were regularly putting up 50 to 70 goals per season, the Canucks didn't have a single 30-goal scorer in the two seasons leading up to the 1978 draft. Mercurial veteran Mike "Shaky" Walton was their leading goal scorer in the 1977–78 season with just 29 goals.

Derlago seemed like the perfect fit for the Canucks, and they wanted him badly. They felt there was a good chance they would get him too. The Canucks held the fourth-overall pick and Derlago wasn't likely to go first or second to the Minnesota North Stars or Washington Capitals. Bobby Smith and Ryan Walter were considered safer bets, partly because Derlago was coming off knee surgery and partly because he was considered a one-dimensional player.

"Known around the Western Canada League as 'Billy D,' one scout skeptical of Derlago's defensive play suggested a more appropriate nickname might be 'Billy No D,'" said Lyndon Little in the *Vancouver Sun*. It was a flaw in his game that Derlago was aware of and was prepared to handle with a pithy quote.

"Defence is my biggest weakness," said Derlago. "It's tough to backcheck when you've always got the puck."

Even if Derlago was questionable defensively, his ability to put the puck in the net had scouts salivating. One anonymous NHL scout quoted in the *Philadelphia Inquirer* even said Derlago "could be another Gilbert Perreault."

Imagine—eight years after a spin of the wheel cost them Perreault, the Canucks had the chance to draft the next Perreault.

There was even speculation that the Canucks made a deal with the St. Louis Blues, who held the third-overall pick, to take someone other than Derlago. Just before the draft, the Canucks traded their leading scorer, Mike Walton, to the Blues for only a fourth-round pick and undisclosed future considerations. Some thought those "future considerations" were a promise not to pick Derlago.

The draft went exactly as expected. The North Stars selected Bobby Smith first overall, the Capitals drafted Ryan Walter, and the Blues took winger Wayne Babych, the older brother of defenceman Dave Babych, a Canucks fan favourite in the '90s. That left the Canucks with exactly who they wanted.

"We got our man in Derlago," said Canucks general manager Jake Milford.

DERLAGO MAY HAVE been Milford's man, but Canucks head coach Harry Neale wasn't a fan when he arrived in Vancouver for training camp. The junior star was reportedly overweight and out of shape and was swiftly sent down to the minors to start the season with the Dallas Black Hawks, while second- and third-round picks Curt Fraser and Stan Smyl stayed in the NHL. It was the first time a first-round pick of the Canucks started the season in the minors—a dubious distinction for Derlago.

After just 11 games in the minors, Derlago got the call back up to Vancouver after a rash of team injuries. While in Dallas, Derlago cut weight and found his rhythm, putting up 13 points in 11 games. He kept on rolling in the NHL, scoring four goals and four assists in his first nine games with the Canucks. Six of those points came in just two games, heating up heading into his ninth game against the New York Islanders.

That's when the Islanders' Denis Potvin blew out Derlago's knee—the same knee that was injured in his draft year with the Brandon Wheat Kings. Newspaper reports at the time called it a "clean, hard hip-check" but that's not the way Derlago remembers it.

"It was an offside play with a late whistle," recalled Derlago years later in an interview with the Wheat Kings. "The whistle blew and then he hit me two seconds later."

The injury ended Derlago's rookie season and may have played a part in his slow start the next season. Derlago struggled to score, with long slumps that frustrated both his head coach and Canucks management. He had just 11 goals and 15 assists in 54 games for the Canucks in the 1979–80 season when Milford decided it was time to trade him away.

Perhaps Derlago could have been a star in Vancouver if Potvin hadn't thrown that dirty hit. We'll never know.

WHEN MILFORD TRADED Derlago to the Toronto Maple Leafs in 1980, he didn't go alone. The Canucks' first-round pick in 1979, Rick Vaive, went with him.

Vaive already had a year of professional hockey under his belt when the Canucks selected him fifth overall. In the summer of 1978, the Birmingham Bulls of the World Hockey Association made the unprecedented move of signing seven 18-year-old junior hockey players to professional contracts. The players were too young to be drafted into the NHL but felt they were ready to make the jump to pro hockey.

Six of the seven made the team in Birmingham and came to be known as the "Baby Bulls." They included some of the most promising prospects in junior hockey, such as Vaive, future Hall of Famer Michel Goulet, and future All-Stars like goaltender Pat Riggin and defencemen Craig Hartsburg and Rob Ramage.

Hailing from Charlottetown, Prince Edward Island, Vaive moved to Quebec at age 17 to dominate for the Sherbrooke Castors in the QMJHL, where he was named rookie of the year. At 18, he was one of the league's top scorers with 76 goals and 155 points in 69 games in the 1977–78 season. That put him at fifth in the league in scoring, with the four players ahead of him all a year older. He was a prime target for the WHA.

After merging with the WHA a couple of years later, the NHL lowered the draft age to allow 18-year-olds to be selected, but that wasn't the case in 1978. Vaive, with little left to prove in junior hockey, was perfectly justified in turning pro and demonstrated as much in the WHA—he led the Bulls in scoring with 59 points in 75 games and proved his grit by also leading the entire league in penalty minutes. "I don't think I'll ever get this many minutes again," said Vaive to E.M. Swift at *Sports Illustrated*. "It's my style of play. I hit a lot of guys, and since I'm a rookie they want to try me."

That was the end of Vaive's WHA career. The league ceased operations after the 1978–79 season, with four WHA teams—the Edmonton Oilers, New England Whalers, Quebec Nordiques, and Winnipeg Jets—joining the NHL.

Veteran WHA players on teams that didn't merge were free to sign anywhere they wanted but the 19-year-old Baby Bulls were put back into the NHL amateur draft, where they were considered some of the top players available. Ramage went first overall to the Colorado Rockies, and all six were selected in the first two rounds. The seventh junior player who signed with the Bulls but didn't make the cut for their roster, Kevin Lowe, was also a first-round pick.

The second Baby Bull to get drafted after Ramage was Vaive at fifth overall to the Canucks.

THE CANUCKS NEEDED a right winger and Vaive was one of the best in the 1979 draft. They even passed over Vaive's teammate, defenceman Craig Hartsburg, who was higher on their list. Milford later admitted they made the pick based on position rather than picking the best player available. Head coach Harry Neale wanted a gritty scoring winger.

"Neale, and not the scouts, pushed the hardest for the selection of Vaive," reported Arv Olson in the *Sun*. "He was highly recommended by Neale's former coaching cohorts in the World Hockey Association."

Neale had coached in the WHA for seven seasons with the Minnesota Fighting Saints and New England Whalers. Beyond just the recommendation of the coaching fraternity, Neale liked a specific element of Vaive's WHA statistics.

"I like guys who lead their club in scoring and in penalties," said Neale to Clancy Loranger at *The Province* during Vaive's first training camp. "We picked him because we thought we needed a guy capable of stirring things up."

Perhaps Neale took it personally when Vaive had an underwhelming training camp, with little of the aggressiveness that Neale was hoping to see. He bluntly said, "Vaive is not in shape," and played him repeatedly in the preseason while other players rested. Vaive threw few hits and when he took hits or was slashed, Vaive didn't retaliate—the opposite of what Neale wanted.

Once the season started, Vaive was in Neale's doghouse, as was Derlago. Both first-round picks were having a disappointing season given their draft pedigree and weren't clicking with their head coach. Meanwhile, Milford was shaking up the Canucks, making multiple moves to try to transform the team into a contender, including trading away team captain Don Lever.

When Lever was traded in February, he had plenty of praise for Neale's coaching, but added, "His biggest fault is that he hasn't given the younger players the time to prove themselves. He's been too hard on Vaive, Derlago, and Fraser."

Vaive and Derlago didn't get the time Lever thought they needed—10 days after Lever was traded to the Atlanta Flames for Ivan Boldirev and Darcy Rota, Vaive and Derlago were on their way to the Toronto Maple Leafs.

"I know we're going to get a lot of flak over this trade," said Milford to Olson. "But I don't care what people say. The way they were playing, we had to trade them or send them to the minors if we weren't going to use them."

Derlago was 21 years old and Vaive was just 20; a stint in the minors might have been just what they needed. Instead, they were moved for older, proven veterans: 26-year-old David "Tiger" Williams and 28-year-old Jerry Butler.

Milford said that Derlago and Vaive didn't have the high-end potential the Canucks needed.

"I've watched Derlago and Vaive closely and I know they can play in the league, but I don't think they'll be superstars," said Milford to Loranger. "What Vaive was supposed to give us was aggressiveness and we didn't get that from him. I really don't think he has enough ability. He's got that big slapshot and that's about all.

"And Derlago, sure he's got the ability, but the only time he showed it was in those nine games last year. I don't think he's willing to sacrifice enough to make it big. He's a good kid but he's not dedicated. He doesn't work that hard even in practice."

Milford and the Canucks felt good about the trade early on. Tiger Williams was a unicorn—an enforcer who could also score goals—and he became a fan favourite in Vancouver. He scored 35 goals in his first full season with the Canucks and delighted fans with his exuberant goal celebrations, such as riding his hockey stick like a hobby horse down the ice on December 10, 1980.

The magic of that first season couldn't continue, unfortunately, and Tiger slowed down in his remaining three seasons with the Canucks, scoring 17, 8, and 15 goals.

Butler, who was more of a defensive specialist, played just one full season with the Canucks, tallying 27 points in 80 games. The next year, in the 1981–82 season, he suited up in just 25 games with the Canucks—he lost his spot in the lineup and was sent down to the minors to play for the Dallas Black Hawks, missing the 1982 playoff run entirely.

"We gave up two promising players and five years down the line it may turn out to be a better deal for the Leafs but in all honesty, neither of them has lived up to our expectations," said Neale. "A lot of people will say we didn't have enough patience, but I think we gave them enough time to show us what they could do."

It didn't take five years for the trade to be a better deal for the Leafs. It didn't even take two.

Vaive scored 33 goals in his first season with the Leafs, then, in the 1981–82 season, he erupted for 54 goals. It was the first 50-goal season in Maple Leafs history, and it stood as a franchise record for 40 years until Auston Matthews scored 60 goals in the 2021–22 season.

Named the captain of the Maple Leafs, Vaive went on to score 50-plus goals in two more seasons and scored at least 30 goals in nine seasons. Vaive's 441 career goals is still the most ever by a Canucks draft pick—four more goals than Pavel Bure.

Derlago became Vaive's centre in Toronto. He hit a career-high 84 points in 75 games in the 1981–82 season and had a 40-goal season in 1983–84. He finished his career with 416 points in 555 games, 19th all-time among Canucks draft picks.

It's hard not to wonder what might have been in 1982 if the Canucks hadn't traded Derlago and Vaive. They would have been first and third on the Canucks in regular-season scoring, with Vaive leading in goals by a country mile.

That said, Tiger was a fierce competitor, who helped galvanize the underdog Canucks to embrace their hardworking, blue-collar identity. In the 1982 playoff run, Tiger was tied for fifth on the team in scoring with 10 points in 17 games and scored the game-winning goal in both games two and three of the Canucks' three-game sweep of the Calgary Flames in the first round.

Maybe the Canucks still would have lost in the Stanley Cup Final to the dynastic New York Islanders if they'd had Derlago and Vaive on the team. Maybe they wouldn't have even made that Cinderella run without Tiger's influence.

Still, it's hard to avoid wondering what if—what if the Canucks had two of their best draft picks of the previous decade in their lineup in the 1982 playoffs? What if the Canucks had a 54-goal scorer like Vaive and an 84-point centre like Derlago to support the likes of Stan Smyl, Thomas Gradin, Curt Fraser, Ivan Boldirev, Ivan Hlinka, and Darcy Rota?

"That is one [trade] I wouldn't make again," said Milford to Tony Gallagher of *The Province* at one point. "It took me a week to make it and I wanted to trade [Jere] Gillis and Derlago, not Vaive. Derlago was never going to play for Harry [Neale], so that didn't bother me, but Vaive has come on and matured. We got the better of the deal for the first year and a half, with the way Tiger played, but Vaive would look good here now."

THE TRADE OF Vaive and Derlago gets overshadowed in Canucks history by a trade widely considered to be one of the worst in NHL history: Cam Neely to the Boston Bruins. After going to the Stanley Cup Final in 1982, the Canucks couldn't repeat the magic in 1983 and were bumped in the first round. On the positive side, that gave the Canucks the ninth-overall pick in the 1983 draft, which featured a wealth of talent. That included a local kid, Cam Neely, who happened to be ranked ninth overall by NHL Central Scouting.

Cam Neely was born in Comox and grew up in Maple Ridge cheering for the Canucks and idolizing Stan Smyl.

"The Steamer is my favourite player, ever since he presented me an MVP trophy in a midget tournament a year ago last Christmas," said the young Neely. "It's a great feeling, getting the chance to play in your own backyard and for the team you've been cheering for."

Neely was a force as a 17-year-old winger for the Portland Winterhawks in his draft year, putting up 56 goals and 120 points in 72 games in the regular season, then another 9 goals and 20 points in 14 playoff games. He kept rolling at the Memorial Cup, scoring five goals and nine points in the four-game tournament, including a hat trick in the final.

"All our scouts liked him," recalled Canucks scout Mike Penny. "Everybody did."

It's a wonder Neely wasn't ranked higher by Central Scouting, but he had some stiff competition in the 1983 draft, including Pat LaFontaine and Steve Yzerman.

Even though Neely was ranked ninth, the Canucks were concerned that he wouldn't be there by the time they picked. They had Neely ranked fifth on their own list and knew that other teams were just as high on the powerful young forward. They were mostly worried about the Buffalo Sabres, who were picking fifth. Their general manager, Scotty Bowman, loved Neely.

"Bowman thought [Neely] was one of the finest two-way hockey players he has seen," said Winterhawks general manager Brian Shaw to Jack Keating of *The Province*.

The next players on the Canucks' list, if the Sabres took Neely, were Russ Courtnall, Dave Gagner, and Normand Lacombe. Both Courtnall and Gagner played for the Canucks later in their careers and were solid players, but neither one was Neely.

Fortunately for the Canucks, Bowman had another plan: build the Sabres from the net out. The top prospect goaltender was a 6'3" high school kid named Tom Barrasso. Bowman liked Barrasso's size and his scouts liked his puck handling and competitive nature. When Sabres scout Bucky Kane came back from the 1983 World Junior Championship with a glowing report about Barrasso facing 50 shots from the Soviet Union to keep Team USA in a game, Bowman was sold.

"The big reason we drafted [Barrasso] was because Bucky saw him over there," said Bowman to Jim Matheson at the *Edmonton Journal*. "It was the game against the Russians that convinced him and convinced us."

The pick caught a lot of people off-guard—a goaltender had never before been picked that high in the draft—but Barrasso made Bowman look like a genius when he made the jump directly from high school to the NHL at 18 and won the Vezina Trophy as the best goaltender in the league in his rookie year.

As soon as Buffalo picked Barrasso, the Canucks were gleeful, knowing that Neely was likely to slide to them at ninth overall. They knew that the New Jersey Devils and Toronto Maple Leafs wanted John MacLean and Russ Courtnall and that the Winnipeg Jets were not high on Neely. Instead, they happily selected the highly ranked Andrew McBain instead.

"I can't believe McBain was left until the eighth pick or that Neely was left for us," said Harry Neale to Arv Olson of the *Sun*. "Almost all of the teams had rated both of them to go much earlier. It took a couple of weird drafts to open things up."

Neely was the Canucks' first-ever first-round pick from British Columbia. In fact, it was the first time the Canucks picked someone west of Brandon, Manitoba, where Derlago and fellow first-round pick Rick Blight played their junior hockey.

"I just think he's a complete hockey player," said George Wood, the Canucks' western scout. "He's a good worker, a goal scorer who plays just the same on the road as he does at home."

Neely was the big, powerful right winger the Canucks had been searching for—so, of course, just like Dale Tallon before him, they tried to turn him into a centre.

To be fair, Neely had played centre until the Winterhawks moved him to right wing, so it wasn't outrageous that Canucks head coach Roger Neilson tried him at centre at training camp. He dreamed of a one-two-three punch up the middle of Thomas Gradin, Patrik Sundström, and Neely in the near future.

Neely found his way to where he belonged on the right wing in short order and made the Canucks out of training camp. He was sent back down to the Portland Winterhawks for 19 games but was recalled again and finished the season in Vancouver. The 18-year-old winger chipped in 31 points in 56 games and added two goals in four playoff games. It seemed like Neely and the Canucks were a perfect fit.

NEELY'S SECOND SEASON was when things started to go awry. While Neely scored 21 goals and was continuing to progress, it wasn't the major leap forward that some were expecting. Then his third season was a disappointment, with just 14 goals. It didn't help that he was stuck on the third line behind fellow right-wingers Stan Smyl and Tony Tanti and given limited opportunities on the power play.

The Canucks' new head coach, Tom Watt, didn't take a shine to the young power forward either, criticizing his defensive play and giving Neely little direction.

"I don't know what the reason was, but Tom just didn't have a lot of confidence in me and I began to lose confidence in myself," said Neely to Mike Beamish of the *Sun*. "I went to him a few times to talk about it, but I could never read him. He never really told me what he wanted me to do, never really gave me an explanation why I wasn't being used as much as I was before."

Just like with Derlago and Vaive, the Canucks grew impatient with the development of the young player and looked to turn their fortunes around by trading for veteran help. Neely wasn't even the only first-round pick that new general manager Jack Gordon moved in a short period of time. Defenceman J.J. Daigneault, their 1984 first-round pick, was moved to the Philadelphia Flyers with a pair of draft picks for Rich Sutter and Dave Richter shortly before the Neely trade.

Gordon and the Canucks had a target in mind: Barry Pederson, a talented 25-year-old centre who racked up goals and assists in his first few seasons in the NHL with the Boston Bruins. As a rookie, Pederson scored 44 goals, then bettered that total in his sophomore season with 46 goals. In his third year, he had a career-high 116 points.

The young centre had proven himself in the postseason too, scoring 14 goals and 32 points in 17 games as a 21-year-old in the 1983 Stanley Cup playoffs. He was a legitimate star, and the Canucks believed he would immediately be the best player in franchise history.

The only reason Pederson was even available is that he was a "free agent with compensation"—similar to a restricted free agent in today's NHL. That meant any team could offer Pederson a contract and, if he signed, the Bruins could either match the offer or receive compensation. In Pederson's case, the compensation would be a first-round pick and their pick of any player on the signing team's roster after that team had protected four players—including Pederson.

The Canucks wanted Pederson badly enough that they were willing to pay him a lot more money than the Bruins, but they were also nervous about the compensation rules. If the Canucks could only protect three players in addition to Pederson, the Bruins might claim a talented young player like Patrik Sundström, a bruising defenceman like Garth Butcher, or even Canucks captain Stan Smyl. So, instead of signing Pederson as a free agent, the Canucks negotiated a trade.

The Bruins got a first-round pick, just like they would from the free agent compensation, but instead of the Bruins selecting whichever player on the Canucks roster they wanted, the Canucks gave them Cam Neely.

The trade looks terrible in hindsight but it didn't look much better at the time.

Pederson was no longer the same player that had scored 116 points in 1983–84. Shortly after that season, doctors discovered a benign tumour in Pederson's shoulder. That led to multiple operations, which included removing parts of his shoulder muscle. While he returned to the ice and was still effective, he was nowhere near the dominant player he was before the surgeries.

In the season before he was traded, Pederson put up 29 goals and 76 points in 79 games—good, but still just 42nd in league scoring in the high-flying '80s. Trading a former first-round pick in Neely and a future first-round pick was a high price to pay for someone that might not be a star anymore.

In addition, the Canucks weren't even trading for Pederson; they were trading for Pederson's free-agent rights. They still had to get him to sign a contract, with no guarantee that he would. If they didn't get him signed before June 30, he would become a full free agent, meaning the Canucks would have traded Neely and a first-round pick for literally nothing.

Certainly, the Canucks were confident Pederson would sign their generous contract offer—they essentially had a handshake deal ahead of the trade—but there was still risk involved. Pederson's agent, Bill Watters, even joked about seeing how far the Canucks would go to sign his client—"But I don't want to be too nasty," he said shortly after the trade.

Pederson wound up becoming the highest-paid player in Canucks history up to that point.

It gets worse. The first-round pick in the trade could have been either the Canucks' 1986 pick, which was seventh overall, or their as-yet-undetermined 1987 pick. The Bruins chose to postpone their pick, betting that the Canucks—who had just mortgaged two pieces of the team's long-term future to get better in the short term—would be even worse in the 1986–87 season and give them a higher pick than seventh overall.

They were completely right.

THE TRADE WAS a disaster immediately. Neely was given all the opportunities in Boston that he didn't get in Vancouver and thrived, putting up 36 goals and 72 points in 75 games in his first season with the Bruins. He would only get better in the coming years. He became the NHL's premier power forward, scoring 50-plus goals in three separate seasons, including an incredible 50 goals in 49 games in the 1993–94 season.

Thomas Gradin added some extra salt in the wound by signing with the Bruins. Disappointed by what he saw as a low-ball offer from the Canucks, Gradin signed in Boston as a free agent—without compensation—before the trade. In his first season with the Bruins, he centred none other than Cam Neely, the winger that Watt wouldn't play him with in Vancouver.

The legendary Howie Meeker didn't mince words in the midst of the 1986–87 season at a Burnaby sports awards banquet.

"Cam Neely for Barry Pederson was a terrible trade," said Meeker. "Neely plus a first-round draft pick for Pederson was ridiculous."

Pederson, meanwhile, repeated his pre-trade season almost exactly, putting up an identical 76 points in 79 games. He followed that up with 71 points in 76 games the following season—serviceable numbers in that era, but not the superstar that the Canucks were hoping for.

The Canucks as a team crashed and burned, falling to the bottom of the standings. They nearly finished dead last, which would have given them the first-overall pick for the first time in franchise history, only for that pick to instead go to the Bruins.

Fortunately, the Canucks rattled off a late-season rally, winning three straight games to climb past both the New Jersey Devils and the freefalling Buffalo Sabres. The Canucks scored 19 goals in those final three games—Pederson didn't score any of them.

The first-overall pick in 1987 was Pierre Turgeon, another player projected to be the next Gilbert Perreault. Turgeon went on to score 515 goals and 1,327 points in 1,294 career NHL games. It would have been just too painful if the Canucks had missed out on yet another Perreault.

The Bruins instead got the Canucks' third-overall pick and it still hurt—they selected defenceman Glen Wesley, who went on to play 1,457 career games in the NHL.

JACK GORDON GOT torn to shreds in the media for the Neely trade, but Canucks scout Mike Penny suggests he wasn't entirely to blame.

"I remember Jack Gordon calling me, saying we were doing the Neely deal," said Penny. "I said, 'Jesus, Jack, why would you want to even think about doing something like that?' And he said, 'It's out of my hands.' I'm not quite sure what that was supposed to mean."

Some have suggested Watt was the driving force behind trading Neely. Considering the short shelf life of coaches, that would not have been a smart decision—Watt was out as Canucks coach after the 1986–87 season.

"I had no idea we were considering trading Neely," insisted Watt to Patrick Johnston of *The Province* in 2022. "That was done by the owner, I think."

Watt isn't the only one who thinks that ownership was involved.

"I think Jack Gordon gets a bad rap for that deal," said Penny. "There was more than Jack Gordon involved with this—I think it went up to the ownership level."

The Canucks were in turmoil at the time, with ownership seeking the right general manager to right the ship—Pat Quinn took over a year after the Neely trade—and Gordon was essentially a placeholder.

"I remember basically saying to Jack, 'Will you do this for us?'" Canucks owner Arthur Griffiths recalled years later to Ed Willes of *The Province* about hiring Gordon. "We needed to find a long-term solution."

But even if Gordon was only a short-term general manager, Griffiths has insisted that ownership didn't make any hockey decisions in those years. He has said that he was too busy with the business operations of the Canucks—he had just negotiated the arena lease—and had limited hockey knowledge to bring to the table.

"My hockey exposure was pretty minor," said Griffiths to Johnston. "That said, when Jack came to me and said we have a chance to add Barry Pederson, who was so talented and also a local kid from Nanaimo, I certainly wasn't opposed. But, of course, we didn't know Pederson had had those health problems."

The Canucks definitely knew about Pederson's health. His operations were well known at the time and Gordon was certainly aware, saying, "I've had assurances that his arm is fine," when asked about Pederson's surgeries after the trade.

There's one other theory: that it wasn't Arthur Griffiths but his father, Frank Griffiths Sr., who got involved. That was the theory advanced by longtime sportswriter Tony Gallagher in a 2012 column in *The Province*.

"[Gordon] would no sooner have presumed to make that trade than leap off the Pacific Coliseum roof," said Gallagher. "If you must, blame former Canucks owner Frank Griffiths Sr., who actually made the Neely deal happen with his insistence the team sign Pederson as a free agent requiring compensation."

Everyone involved washed their hands of the Neely trade, so who is really to blame? It's hard to say after so many years. What is certain is that any time a top-tier draft pick like Neely gets traded away, it's tough to take for the scouts that invested so much time in drafting him in the first place.

"All that work goes out the window," said Penny. "You've got to believe in the people you have working for you and what they're doing—that they can assess talent and project professional potential to a point where they can say, 'This guy's got a chance to be an elite player in the National Hockey League.' Which he turned out to be."

Unfortunately, he turned out to be an elite player for a team other than the Canucks.

STEFAN NILSSON: DRAFTED BY FOUR TEAMS, PLAYED FOR NONE OF THEM

One of the more unusual draft stories in NHL history is the tale of Stefan Nilsson: he was drafted by four NHL teams and never played for any of them.

In 1986, the same year Cam Neely was traded, Stefan Nilsson was a promising young prospect out of Sweden. He played a few games in the Elitserien, Sweden's top men's league, and had five points in five games at the European Junior Championships.

The Washington Capitals selected Nilsson in the sixth round of the 1986 draft, but they couldn't get him signed in the following two years, so he went back into the draft in 1988. That's where things get weird.

By the 1988 draft, the 20-year-old Nilsson had proven himself in the Elitserien, scoring 10 goals and 21 points in 31 games in the 1987–88 season. That caught the attention of NHL scouts for at least two teams: the Calgary Flames, who selected Nilsson in the seventh round, and the Vancouver Canucks, who selected Nilsson in the 12th round.

Wait, what?

When the Canucks announced the selection of Stefan Nilsson, the Flames immediately protested, and seemingly had a rock-solid argument: you can't pick a player who has already been picked by another team, and the Flames had already picked Stefan Nilsson. There was just one problem—the Flames had picked the wrong 20-year-old Stefan Nilsson out of the Elitserien.

There were two of them. The Stefan Nilsson that the Flames and Canucks wanted played for Luleå; the other Stefan Nilsson played for HV71. The Flames accidentally picked the one from HV71 in the seventh round.

Adding to the confusion, there was a third Stefan Nilsson who was also eligible for the 1988 draft. That Stefan Nilsson was 19 years old. All three Stefan Nilssons—or should that be Stefans Nilsson?—played together for Sweden in the 1988 World Junior Championship.

It's no wonder Flames general manager Cliff Fletcher got things confused.

So, Nilsson was essentially picked twice in the 1988 draft after already being picked by the Capitals in the 1986 draft. While the "real" Stefan Nilsson never came over to Vancouver to play for the Canucks, he wasn't done getting drafted by NHL teams.

NHL expansion in 2000 added two new teams—the Columbus Blue Jackets and Minnesota Wild—and held an expansion draft to fill out their rosters. The expansion draft rules allowed teams to protect up to 15 players: nine forwards, five defencemen, and one goaltender. That left little for the two expansion teams to choose from, but two players still had to be picked from every team.

The first player selected from the Canucks was Darby Hendrickson by the Minnesota Wild. The 28-year-old centre was from Minnesota, giving him a hometown connection, and the Wild gave him an "A" as one of their first alternate captains. To give you an idea of the limited talent available, Hendrickson was legitimately one of the best players to come out of the 2000 expansion draft, and he had spent 20 games in the AHL the previous season.

The second player the Canucks lost in the 2000 expansion draft was Stefan Nilsson.

There was no transfer agreement between European leagues and the NHL, so teams held the rights for older European draftees indefinitely. That meant Nilsson, 12 years after he was drafted for a third time, was still Canucks property and was on the team's unprotected list for the expansion draft.

The Nilsson drafted by the Canucks proved to be the best of the three Stefans Nilsson, with a long career with Luleå and serving as their captain for six seasons. He represented Sweden at the World Championship three times, captaining them to silver in 1997.

By the 2000 expansion draft, Nilsson was 32 and wasn't going to be coming over to the NHL. So, why did the Wild pick Nilsson? Did they somehow make a mistake like the Flames in 1988?

Nope. It was about money. The Blue Jackets and Wild were required to take two players from every team but late in the expansion draft, they had already picked every player they actually wanted. Eventually, the two teams started picking players they knew they wouldn't have to pay. The Wild picked Nilsson because he would stay in Sweden and therefore not cost them any money.

"We've put chicken wire over the hotel windows to stop anyone from throwing themselves out," deadpanned Canucks general manager Brian Burke about losing Nilsson. If the Wild weren't so worried about money, they might have instead picked 23-year-old Brent Sopel, who became a key part of the Canucks' blue line in the years to come. The biggest miss at the 2000 expansion draft, however, was Martin St. Louis. The future Hart and two-time Art Ross winner was left exposed by the Calgary Flames, but the 24-year-old had yet to break out, so neither the Blue Jackets nor the Wild picked him. Instead, the Flames bought out his contract and he signed as a free agent with the Tampa Bay Lightning—a bigger blunder by the Flames than picking the wrong Stefan Nilsson.

As for Nilsson, he never played a game for the Capitals, Flames, Canucks, or Wild. He eventually retired with Luleå in 2004 but returned again to the club as a coach in 2012, then became their general manager. In 2015, Luleå retired his No. 4.

6

THE CAPTAIN:
TREVOR LINDEN

———————

IT TOOK A LONG TIME FOR THE CANUCKS to draft a legitimate star in the first round of the NHL entry draft—or at least one who actually played his best years in Vancouver.

Trevor Linden was exactly two months old when the Canucks drafted Dale Tallon second overall in 1970. Eighteen years later, he was drafted in the exact same position, second overall, in the 1988 draft. For the Canucks, Linden became exactly what it was hoped that Tallon would be: a franchise-defining player.

No one epitomizes the Canucks more than Linden, who did everything he could to will the Canucks to the Stanley Cup in 1994. He was the quintessential captain, a two-way power forward who led by example by playing a hard, physical, yet clean game on the ice and by giving back to the community off the ice.

In many ways, he was the continuation of Stan Smyl in Vancouver—the same blue-collar, lunch-bucket effort but with more size and skill to go with it. As Smyl once said, "If you play a hard game consistently, people appreciate it." That was Linden: hardworking, consistent, and appreciated.

TREVOR LINDEN GREW up in Medicine Hat, Alberta—the Hat, as he called it—and when he wasn't playing sports, he was working on the family farm. He would always credit his parents and grandfather for passing down the work ethic that got him to the NHL. His father, Lane Linden, managed not just the farm but a gravel-hauling company to provide for his family.

Lane's hard work at turning a struggling business into a success resonated with Linden for the rest of his life, but it was his mother, Edna "Ed" Linden, who was primarily responsible for Trevor making the NHL.

"She was the gal who made sure the kids were at the rink and had the equipment and all the rest of it," recalled Lane. "She's the one who really made it all happen. She made the opportunities available and she covered for me when I was busy trying to earn the money it takes to have three kids in rep hockey."

"My mom was the athletic one and the real sports-minded person," said Trevor to the *Vancouver Sun*. "She was a real good fastball player. Our coach quit our baseball team one year and she coached our team.

"I do have a great appreciation for both my parents, how hard they worked in the '70s during tough times. We didn't have a lot, but we never needed anything more, either. My mom bought my first pair of skates from a second-hand store, and it was the best present I ever got. My equipment was from garage sales—I didn't care. I appreciate the sacrifices they made."

Linden didn't get his first pair of new skates until he was 15 and already a highly regarded prospect. Along with his on-ice prowess, Linden got good grades in school and was offered a scholarship to play hockey at Princeton. But Linden decided he'd rather stay closer to home and play for the Medicine Hat Tigers in the WHL. He became a regular in the lineup at just 16 years old, tallying 36 points in 72 games in the 1986–87 season.

"Ever since I can remember—and this was every kid's dream in the Hat—my dream was to play for the Medicine Hat Tigers," said Linden to Lee Bacchus of the *Vancouver Sun*. "Hockey was everything to me. It's all I thought about from when I was in grade two."

It wasn't the only sport at which he excelled. His grand-father, Nick van der Linden, was a speedskater in Holland before he immigrated to the Canadian prairies in 1929, and Linden picked up speedskating as a kid, which helps explain his long, smooth stride on the ice that propelled him to the puck a lot faster than the lumbering strides one might expect from a 6'4" winger. Linden also played his mother's favourite sport, baseball, as well as volleyball, basketball, and golf.

Linden got something else from his grandfather along with his skating prowess: a fiery determination in the face of any adversity. Before Linden was born, his grandfather got pinned under a tractor and was told his leg would have to be amputated; van der Linden refused, struggling through 34 surgeries on his crushed leg to will himself back on his feet. "He would pace around at night with a cane," said Linden to Lee Bacchus of the *Sun*, "repeating over and over, 'Bullshit! I can walk!'"

Years later, as Linden hobbled off the ice after Game 6 in the 1994 Stanley Cup Final, it's easy to imagine that his grandfather's words were echoing in his head while Canucks fans heard play-by-play announcer Jim Robson give the immortal call, "He will play. You know he'll play! He'll play on crutches!"

"Trevor is a lot like me," said van der Linden. "When he sets his mind on something, no one can stop him."

THE YOUNG LINDEN won the Memorial Cup in 1987 while playing in a depth role. Even at age 16, he was a clutch performer, scoring two goals in the final game of the tournament.

Those clutch performances would continue throughout his career. In nine Game 7 appearances in the NHL, Linden had six goals and 12 points, both of which are tied for third all-time in NHL history.

When he played for Team Canada in the 1998 Olympics, Linden scored only one goal, but it was a clutch one. Down 1–0 late in the semifinal against the Czech Republic, Linden tied the game with just 63 seconds remaining, scoring one of the few goals that anyone got past Dominik Hasek in that tournament. It proved to be the only goal for Canada in that game, as Hasek stopped all five Canadian shooters in the shootout for the stunning upset. Hasek then went on to shut out Russia in the gold medal game, while a reeling Canadian team fell 3–2 to Finland in the bronze medal match.

Ten years before that, a 17-year-old Linden was named the Tiger's captain for the 1987–88 season and he led the team back to the Memorial Cup. He racked up 45 goals and 110 points in 67 games during the regular season, while also providing strong defensive play and mucking it up along the boards. He then added a league-leading 13 goals and 25 points in 16 playoff games to win the WHL Championship.

The 1988 Tigers became the first team to win back-to-back WHL Championships since Stan Smyl's New Westminster Bruins in 1978.

Just like Smyl, Linden captained his team not just to back-to-back WHL Championships but back-to-back Memorial Cups, scoring three goals and seven points in the five-game tournament, after which he was named to the tournament All-Star Team.

Linden finished behind a couple of other first-time draft-eligible players in WHL scoring. One was Glenn Goodall, who had 53 goals and 117 points, but whose small stature limited his chances of making the NHL. The other was Mike Modano.

Modano had been even better than Linden a year earlier as a 16-year-old in the WHL, putting up 32 goals and 62 points in 70 games with the Prince Albert Raiders. Linden kept tabs on Modano throughout his draft year, knowing that he was his primary competition for going first overall in the 1988 draft.

"There was no internet or all-sports television in those days," recalled Linden years later to Ed Willes of *The Province*. "I had to listen to [Tigers broadcaster] Bob Ridley's sportscast in the morning and wait for *The Hockey News.* I was super interested in what was happening in Prince Albert, and I knew Mike was my main rival."

Linden was ranked first early on in Central Scouting's draft rankings, then slipped to second behind Modano in the middle of the season. It might have been because of Modano's stronger World Junior performance for Team USA, though it was Linden's Team Canada who won gold. By the end of the season, Modano was well ahead of Linden in scoring, putting up 127 points to Linden's 110 points. He also had a strong playoff performance, putting up 18 points in 9 games, but when the two top prospects went head-to-head in the second round, Linden's Tigers came out on top.

By the time of the draft, Modano was seen as the clear-cut No. 1 pick, but there were still some who thought Linden might prove to be the better player.

Doug Sauter, head coach of the WHL's Regina Pats, told the *Star Tribune*, "I'd take Linden. He plays great under pressure and if you're going to be the number-one pick overall, you better be able to handle pressure. Linden has proven he can."

Still, the prevailing sentiment was that Modano was the obvious pick, and Linden seemed to agree with that assessment in his typically humble way.

"Mike's a great player and I'm more of a gamer," he said. "I just do what I can out there."

Linden was described by scouts as a "prototypical NHLer" who combined size, skating, and skill with all of the intangibles that coaches love: leadership, determination, and coachability. Modano had more offensive upside but wasn't as strong defensively.

"Modano's the jet and Linden's the bomber," said one NHL scout quoted in the *Windsor Star*. "Modano is the playmaking specialist, while Linden is a good, up-and-down, grinding winger."

The Canucks knew they were getting either Modano or Linden. Even though they had the third-worst record in the NHL at the end of a dreadful 1987–88 season, the Canucks still held the second-overall pick because of the NHL's playoff format at the time.

The North Stars and Toronto Maple Leafs had worse records than the Canucks but they both played in the five-team Norris Division. Since the top four teams from each division made the playoffs, one of the Leafs or North Stars would compete for the Stanley Cup; the other would get the first-overall pick.

In their final game of the regular season, the Leafs faced the Detroit Red Wings—the only team in their division with a winning record. After going down 3–0 early, they stormed back with five unanswered goals for a 5–3 come-from-behind victory. The win landed the Leafs one point ahead of the North Stars, who lost their final game of the season to the Calgary Flames.

That meant the Leafs made the playoffs despite a dreadful 21–49–10 record and faced the Red Wings in the first round. The Leafs even won a couple of games, including the series opener. But they also suffered an embarrassing 8–0 loss on home ice, with disgruntled Leafs fans pelting the ice with garbage and souvenirs after the eighth goal.

Besides leading to that embarrassment, that final win of the regular season also cost the Leafs a chance to draft either Modano or Linden. They were bumped all the way from first overall to sixth overall—behind the five teams that missed the playoffs—and picked Scott Pearson, who played 292 games in the NHL and just 63 of them for the Leafs.

It's not like that win was the only thing that cost the Leafs a franchise player, as some better scouting might have helped. The next four players drafted after Pearson—Martin Gelinas, Jeremy Roenick, Rod Brind'Amour, and Teemu Selanne—all went on to play more than 1,200 NHL games.

All that mattered for the Canucks is that the wonky playoff system gave them the second-overall pick behind the North Stars and they were happy to take whoever the North Stars didn't. Linden's general manager with the Tigers, Russ Farwell, had a strong opinion of who the Canucks wouldn't get.

"Vancouver won't get Trevor Linden," said Farwell to Elliott Pap of the *Sun*. "It's our feeling, from what we've seen and what we've heard, that Trevor has cleared up who is going to go number one. I really think if you're a struggling team like Minnesota or Toronto, you need the things Trevor can do for you both on and off the ice. He's going to be an NHL captain one day and you just can't pass up a guy like that."

THE 1988 NHL Entry Draft was the first for the Canucks' new general manager, Pat Quinn, though he was a familiar face to longtime Canucks fans as one of the original defencemen on the Vancouver blueline when they entered the NHL.

He was also not that new to the Canucks organization by the time of the 1988 draft. Quinn had been hired by the Canucks as president of hockey operations and general manager back in December 1986, but there was just one issue: he was still head coach of the Los Angeles Kings when he signed his contract with the Canucks.

Quinn contended that he had the legal right to sign with the Canucks as the Kings had not exercised the option on his contract, leaving him free to negotiate with other teams. Considering Quinn had spent the time since retiring from his playing career earning his law degree, he was likely right about the legalese in his Kings contract allowing him to sign with the Canucks.

He didn't, however, take into account how the NHL might feel about it.

NHL commissioner John Ziegler called the situation "a serious threat to the integrity of the league." In his view, because Quinn remained the head coach of the Kings after signing a contract with the Canucks, it represented a conflict of interest. Ziegler admitted there was "no evidence" that Quinn actually acted unethically at any point, but said that coaching the Kings while signing a deal with the Canucks damaged the trust the fans had in the league.

"This trust must be zealously guarded and protected at all times," said Ziegler in an official statement. "This trust obligation includes not only guarding against actual threats to the integrity of the game but, equally important, making sure the perception of integrity is not tainted in any fashion."

It didn't help that Quinn signed his contract with the Canucks the day after his Kings had faced the Canucks and lost 6–4—their third loss to the Vancouver Canucks that season. To Ziegler, the "perception of integrity" was definitely under threat.

Accordingly, Ziegler came down hard on Quinn, the Canucks, and even the Kings.

The Kings had made a crucial error of their own. They wanted to file a tampering charge against the Canucks for signing away their head coach but discovered they were unable to do so: they had never actually filed Quinn's coaching contract with the league. Technically speaking from the NHL's perspective, there was no contract to tamper with.

Theoretically, that put Quinn on even firmer legal ground, but Ziegler and the NHL didn't care. He levied heavy fines against both teams: the Kings were fined $130,000 and the Canucks $310,000—the largest fine ever levied against an NHL team at the time.

As for Quinn, he was expelled from his position as coach of the Kings and barred from acting in any capacity with the Canucks or the Kings until after June 15, 1987—the date of the 1987 NHL Entry Draft—and was banned from coaching anywhere in the NHL until the 1990–91 season.

Quinn and the Canucks appealed the suspension and fines. The Canucks were able to reduce their fine to $10,000, with the judge asserting that Ziegler "exceeded his jurisdiction." The $300,000 reduction in fines—as well as a ruling that awarded the Canucks $500,000 in court costs—was a black eye for Ziegler.

Quinn's suspension was upheld, however, so he wasn't able to take over the Canucks until after the 1987 NHL Entry Draft, especially with the NHL watching the situation closely.

Instead, Quinn kept an eye on the Canucks from the stands like any other fan.

"As far as I know, I haven't been restricted from going to hockey games," said Quinn to Robert Fachet of the *Washington Post*. "[Ziegler] can't stop me from buying a ticket."

It was a frustrating situation for Quinn, who always asserted that he had acted both legally and ethically in signing with the Canucks.

"As far as I'm concerned the NHL made a [mess] of the situation," said Quinn later to the Chris Baker of the *Los Angeles Times*. "And it didn't have to be that way."

Perhaps it was for the best. The Canucks didn't have a first-round pick in the 1987 draft, as their pick was part of the Cam Neely trade for Barry Pederson. Instead, Quinn's first draft for the Canucks was a year later in 1988, where he had the opportunity to pick a franchise player.

The Canucks flew Linden out to Vancouver in the spring of 1988, with Quinn inviting him into his house. The two quickly connected, with Quinn seeing something of himself in the teenager, who was far more mature than his years.

"My dad always had a great respect for Trevor—his work ethic, his values—even when he was 18," said Quinn's daughter, Kalli, to Ed Willes of the *Sun*. "I think Trevor had a lot of the same qualities my dad had."

Linden was supposed to make a second trip out to Vancouver before the draft but it never happened. It became a favourite story for Brian Burke. As he recalled, Linden was supposed to undergo a series of physical and psychological tests, but Linden said he couldn't make it.

"Could you make it any other weekend?" he asked. "We're branding this weekend."

Burke asked for clarity on what that meant and Linden explained: when it came time to brand the cattle on the Linden family farm, Lane did the ear-tagging, Ed inoculated the calves, and Grandpa Nick handled the branding iron. Trevor's job, along with his brothers, was to wrestle the hefty bovines to the ground and hold them down while the elder Lindens got to work.

"We do the hard part. I love it," said Linden later to *Sports Illustrated*.

That was good enough for Burke.

"I said, 'Kid, you can skip these tests.' And you know what? We never tested him," said Burke.

The Canucks viewed Linden as a more complete player than Modano, the exact type of leader they needed. In fact, Quinn was so high on Linden that he compared him to an all-time great.

"He's the type of kid you want on the ice in any situation, whether it's the power play, penalty killing, or last minute of the game," said Quinn. "When I watched him and met him, I thought at least from the work habits that his focus and dedication were those of a Bob Clarke."

Quinn wasn't the only one who compared Linden to Bud Poile's great draft find with the Philadelphia Flyers. His Tigers general manager saw the same thing.

"I don't see how [Linden] can miss," said Farwell to *Sports Illustrated*. "He's got the work ethic of a Bobby Clarke, but I think he may be more talented than Bobby was."

AS THE DRAFT approached, it became clear that the North Stars were going to go with the consensus and pick Modano first overall. The Canucks couldn't have been happier.

"When I heard they were taking Modano, as far as we were concerned that was the best news we could have gotten," said Burke to Jack Keating of *The Province*. "And that's not knocking Mike Modano, because we like him plenty too.

"Mike Modano probably has a little higher skill level than Trevor, but if you've got to go to war, Trevor's got skill and a lot of heart and a lot of leadership. And we felt we have to develop some players with leadership ability and this is one of them."

In fact, Quinn claimed the Canucks ranked Linden ahead of Modano on their draft board and would have picked him even if they had the first-overall pick.

"We had him rated on the top of our list," said Quinn to Keating. "Modano is a tremendous physical player and has the potential of maybe being a star in our game, but from the intangible sides, we thought this young man would be best suited for our club at this particular time."

Canucks scout Mike Penny said the Canucks would have been thrilled to get Modano if the North Stars had taken Linden, but they were just as happy to get Linden, who Penny said didn't play a single bad game in his draft year.

"We had the two of them one-two," said Penny, though he wouldn't say which was one and which was two. "Trevor was gritty, grinding, hard to play against, very competitive. They picked Modano and we ended up with Trevor and I don't regret it for one moment. This guy was fantastic for us every game. And he's a wonderful person, great in the community."

Plenty of other teams wanted to take Linden as well. Quinn said that he turned down three trade proposals for the second-overall pick and Burke made it clear that, although they would listen to offers, it would take a lot for the Canucks to walk away from picking Linden.

"It would have to be a trade where the other general manager would practically get fired for it," said Burke to Keating. "I mean, it's got to be a trade that anyone in the world would take."

Linden's head coach with the Tigers, Barry Melrose, made a bold prediction at the draft.

"Vancouver made an excellent pick," said Melrose. "He leads the kids in the room in the way he plays—he plays so hard, he embarrasses other people into playing harder. I think you'll see that Vancouver got the best player in the draft."

That prediction didn't come true. The 1988 draft turned out to be a strong one, with four Hall of Famers, including Modano, as well as three other players who topped 1,000 points but are not in the Hockey Hall of Fame in Jeremy Roenick, Rod Brind'Amour, and fifth-round pick Alexander Mogilny.

Still, Linden is eighth in scoring among all players selected in the 1988 draft and Canucks fans likely wouldn't trade him for anyone else from that draft year because of how much he came to mean for Vancouver.

IT DIDN'T TAKE long for Linden to make an impression after he was drafted. While many thought the gangly 18-year-old would need another season in the WHL—including Farwell, his general manager with the Tigers—Linden had his sights set firmly on making the Canucks. He embarked on a tough off-season regimen of running, cycling, swimming, and weight lifting, along with a calorie-heavy diet to get his weight up to where he thought it needed to be to survive the rigours of the NHL.

"I didn't want to disappoint," he said to *Sports Illustrated.* "If I was going to fail, it wasn't going to be because I wasn't in shape."

Canucks head coach Bob McCammon was impressed immediately.

"With his attitude, it's going to be tough to keep him off the team," said McCammon early at camp, making the same comparison as Quinn and Farwell. "I call him Bobby Clarke with talent." McCammon had actually coached Clarke with the Philadelphia Flyers, so there was some authority behind his assessment.

Linden's efforts were noticed not just by the coaching staff but by his fellow prospects. Dan Woodley, taken seventh overall by the Canucks two years earlier in 1986, saw Linden's arrival as a wake-up call.

"I see Trevor Linden with his gung-ho attitude and I realize that's the way I should have been," said Woodley to Mike Beamish of the *Sun*. "I was callow, I wasn't in great shape. I didn't realize what it takes to prepare yourself for a pro camp."

Linden may not have outperformed Modano in their careers, but he was first to sign an NHL contract between the two. Linden signed a four-year deal worth an estimated $700,000, a cheaper deal than other high draft picks. While Modano held out for a bigger contract, playing one more season in the WHL with the Raiders, Linden was happy to get a deal done so he could hit the ice.

"My goal had always been to play in the NHL," said Linden, "not to own three houses or six fancy cars."

Not that Linden didn't like cars. He just preferred them to be of a certain vintage. His one big purchase with the money from his first contract was Garth Butcher's 1965 Ford Mustang for $2,000. Unlike Linden, it wasn't in the best shape, but he eagerly took it to the streets of Vancouver, typically with his captain in the passenger seat. He and Smyl lived around the corner from each other, so Linden volunteered to carpool with Smyl to the Pacific Coliseum.

"Have you ever driven with Trevor? He likes to drive," recalled Stan Smyl years later to Iain MacIntyre of the *Sun*. "You could always hear him because he had the bad muffler. He always picked me up to go to games and my daughter Jillian would say, 'Dad, Trevor's on his way,' because you could hear him."

As always, Linden was willing to put in the work, fixing up the classic muscle car. Back in "the Hat," Linden had helped his dad restore a 1956 T-Bird, so it was right up his alley.

While Linden tried to avoid stalling in downtown traffic, he had no issues hitting top speed on the ice. In his rookie year, Linden broke the team record for most goals by a rookie with 30 and was a point away from Ivan Hlinka's rookie points record of 60, though Hlinka was 32 years old in his rookie year compared to Linden at just 18.

"Usually with a rookie, you're waiting for some sign of maturity," said Harold Snepsts, who roomed with Linden on the road. "With Trev, you wait and wait for him to show some sign that he's still only a kid."

Linden made an impression off the ice as well. Burke asked Joanne Robinson, the ex-wife of Bobby Hull and mother of Brett Hull, to take in Linden for the season. He fit right in with the family.

"You couldn't ask for a nicer young man," said Robinson. "He has so much character for a boy his age. He won't just be a leader in hockey; someday he'll be a leader in the community."

Robinson's comments proved prescient. Linden's work in the community became a key component of his legacy in Vancouver. He was particularly known for his work with children. Linden would drop by the B.C. Children's Hospital at all hours. His father, Lane, shared a story with the *Vancouver Sun* that was passed along by a nurse at the hospital.

"She told us how Trev used to come up there at the end of a game or just unannounced," said Lane. "He used to stop by the nurse's station and ask if there was a kid that was having trouble sleeping and he would just go in there and talk to them and maybe read a book."

Linden set up a private box at Canucks games to bring kids to games who would otherwise be unable to afford to go. When he brought the idea to Canucks leadership, they wanted to attach a sponsorship to the idea but Linden said he would only do it without sponsors. He only wanted what was best for the kids and didn't want any company gaining publicity from them.

That only scratches the surface of Linden's charitable contributions to the community, which earned him the NHL's King Clancy Memorial Trophy in 1997, given annually to the player "who best exemplifies leadership qualities on and off the ice and has made a noteworthy humanitarian contribution in his community."

AS A ROOKIE at camp in 1988, Linden was handed the number 49 by the training staff, but he had his eyes on one specific number.

"All my life I've worn only two numbers—16, because that was the number Bobby Clarke, my favourite player, wore—and No. 9, after I got to Junior," said Linden in a camp diary feature in the *Sun*. "I guess every player has a special number he'd like to have. But, look: I'm just happy to have a sweater! I'll take any number they give me. It's the player who makes the number, not the other way around. It was Clarke who made No. 16 great."

In Vancouver, Linden made 16 great. On June 11, 2008, exactly 20 years after he was drafted, Linden's number 16 was retired by the Canucks.

ALEK STOJANOV

The Canucks drafted a future captain in 1988 when they took Trevor Linden second overall. A few years later at the 1991 draft, they picked Alek Stojanov seventh overall, who ultimately led to the next great Canucks captain.

To be blunt, Stojanov had no business being a top-10 pick. Multiple players with 1,000-plus game careers went shortly after he was picked in the first round, like Bryan Rolston, Alexei Kovalev, and, ironically enough, Markus Näslund.

Among first-time draft-eligible players in the OHL in his draft year, Stojanov was 23rd in scoring with 25 goals and 45 points in 62 games. Eric Lindros, taken first overall in 1991, had 71 goals and 149 points in 57 games in the OHL that year—more than three times as many points as Stojanov.

These days, teams wouldn't think of using a top-10 pick on a forward who isn't even close to being a point-per-game player in major junior. Coming out of the fight-happy '80s, however, teams were eager to find the next Bob Probert.

The 6'3" Probert had just 28 points in 51 games when he was drafted in the third round by the Detroit Red Wings in 1983, but he developed scoring talent to go with his pugilistic prowess. In the 1987–88 NHL season, Probert was a threat with his gloves on or off—he led the regular season in penalty minutes with 398 but also scored 29 goals and 62 points in 74 games. In the 1988 playoffs, Probert led the Red Wings in scoring with 8 goals and 21 points in 16 games before the Red Wings were struck down by the dynastic Edmonton Oilers.

Every team wanted their own Probert—a player who could put the fear of God in opponents but could also put the puck in the net.

The 6'4" Stojanov was seen as exactly that type of player, and not just by the Canucks. NHL Central Scouting ranked Stojanov 14th overall in their 1991 draft rankings. Peter Forsberg, taken a pick before Stojanov by the Philadelphia Flyers, was ranked 25th.

"He's not ranked low on a lot of lists," said Pat Quinn. "I was up to three in the morning trying to defend our position because teams were trying to move into position to take him."

If the Canucks didn't take Stojanov, he wouldn't have made it out of the top 10. The Minnesota North Stars, picking eighth, were also high on Stojanov. The Hartford Whalers, picking ninth, wined and dined Stojanov in a pre-draft meeting. The Detroit Red Wings, picking 10th, tried to trade up to take him but "couldn't work out a deal," said Red Wings general manager Bryan Murray. Stojanov lived in Detroit's backyard across the border in Windsor and Murray wanted him badly. The Red Wings ended up with Martin Lapointe instead, who went on to play 991 NHL games.

Stojanov cemented his reputation as a tough guy when he took on Eric Lindros in their rookie OHL seasons and fought him to a draw. Not many players were able to go toe-to-toe with the 6"5" Lindros, and scouts liked Stojanov's hands and skating too.

"He's as good as anybody," Mike Penny said of Stojanov to Beamish. "He's a big kid with some skill. He's no stumblebum."

Stojanov welcomed the comparison to Probert, minus the off-ice issues. While Probert was getting into legal trouble—he was arrested for cocaine possession in 1989 and temporarily suspended from the NHL—Stojanov was praised for his character. On the ice, he could be mean and nasty; off the ice, he had a cheerful demeanour and affable nature.

"When people say I'm a clone of Bob Probert, I think they mean on the ice," said Stojanov after he was drafted. "I've never gotten into any trouble. But that's a pretty accurate comparison. I love it. They say I'm so much like Bob Probert it's uncanny. That's very flattering, but again I feel like I am my own player."

Stojanov believed he could be a legitimate power forward rather than just an enforcer and that's how the Canucks felt too.

"He's a hockey player who can fight, not just a fighter who plays hockey," said Brian Burke, then the Canucks' director of hockey operations, according to Mike Beamish at the *Sun*. Burke compared Stojanov to the likes of Rick Tocchet and Cam Neely.

"He's not just a tough kid, but a player with ability who's also tough," said Burke. "We project him as a 20-goal scorer, possibly 30. He's not a goon."

When Stojanov played for the Canucks, however, that's exactly how he was used: as a goon. He was given limited ice time and was expected to drop the gloves with the toughest enforcers in the NHL. In 62 games with the Canucks, Stojanov didn't score a single goal and had just one assist, but he managed to pile up 136 penalty minutes, including fights against tough customers like Bob Boughner, Tony Twist, and Probert himself.

THINGS COULD HAVE been different for Stojanov in Vancouver if his career hadn't been derailed by injuries. At his first Canucks training camp, Stojanov separated his right shoulder, ending any chance of making a quick jump to the NHL.

"I was prepared to play with the Canucks or at least show them what I could do," said Stojanov to Beamish, "but I never got the chance."

The following season in the OHL was a nightmare for Stojanov. He suffered further injuries to both shoulders, as well as ankle and wrist injuries, limiting him to just 33 games. Stojanov required surgery on his right shoulder—his second on the same shoulder. To add insult to literal injury, he was the captain of one of the worst teams in major junior history.

It was the first season for the newly named Guelph Storm and they won just four of their 66 games. In his final year in junior, however, Stojanov started to show some serious potential. He tallied 36 goals and 71 points in 49 OHL games in the 1992–93 season, then joined the Canucks' farm team in the AHL, the Hamilton Canucks, for their final four games and scored four goals. He looked like he had a chance to live up to his top-10 draft billing.

But in a prospect game against the Calgary Flames in 1993, Stojanov suffered another shoulder injury in a fight, this time to his left shoulder. Sent down to Hamilton again, he reinjured his left shoulder twice more, playing just four games before it was determined he needed another shoulder surgery to end his first professional season.

"I don't have any bone in front of the cup," Stojanov said to Gary Kingston of the *Sun* to explain his shoulder issues. "The only thing holding my shoulder in the front is muscle and tendon. I'm learning to deal with it almost as an everyday thing but it's getting a little bit ridiculous."

With multiple surgeries on both shoulders behind him, Stojanov struggled to find his scoring touch again. It came in flashes, like when he set a franchise record with the Syracuse Crunch with goals in seven-straight games in the 1994–95 season, but he couldn't find any consistency. When he finally made the Canucks' NHL roster in 1995, it was as a fourth-line enforcer, but Stojanov still believed he could be more than just a tough guy with the right opportunity.

That opportunity came in 1996 with a surprising trade: the Canucks sent Stojanov to the Pittsburgh Penguins in a one-for-one deal for Markus Näslund.

Stojanov was stunned—he had no inkling that a trade was coming.

"I'm going home to Ottawa to get my head screwed on," said Stojanov to MacIntyre of the *Sun*. "I can't even think of anything to compare with this. Some of the best times in my life were here. I love Vancouver. I didn't want to leave. It's a great bunch of guys and I'll miss them all. But life goes on. I wanted to stay here for 10 years."

THE TRADE WAS one of the most lopsided deals in NHL history. When it was made, however, the reviews were not entirely positive in Vancouver. Canucks fans, gun-shy after seeing Cam Neely get traded and blossom into a dominant power forward, were nervous about trading Stojanov for a finesse player like Näslund.

Even Quinn was skeptical, wondering why the Penguins were so willing to give up on a forward with 52 points in 66 games for Stojanov, who had one point.

"Pittsburgh saw a potential Neely in big Alek and they were willing to give up this skill guy," said Quinn to MacIntyre. "You're always concerned about doing another Neely deal and giving away a guy too soon, especially some of these big kids."

But Mike Penny, now the Canucks' director of player development, was thrilled. When Penguins general manager Craig Patrick called Quinn asking about Stojanov, Quinn turned to Penny and received some direct advice.

"Craig says, 'I've got this kid here and I've had enough of him: Markus Näslund,'" recalled Penny. "Pat turns to me and says, 'Who's he?' And I said, 'Take him!'

"That's how we ended up with Markus Näslund."

Penny had passed through Pittsburgh about a week before the trade on a scouting trip and took in a Penguins game. He noticed that Näslund had talent but wasn't getting used much by Penguins head coach Eddie Johnston. That observation and some subtle inquiries let him know that Johnston was not a fan of Näslund but Penny never thought he would be available in a one-for-one deal for Stojanov.

Patrick had a reason to move Näslund beyond his head coach not liking him: Näslund asked for a trade. Stuck behind the likes of Mario Lemieux, Jaromir Jagr, Ron Francis, and former Canucks pick Petr Nedved, Näslund felt stifled and wanted to play a bigger role for another team.

"I really wanted out of here and I'm happy to be in Vancouver," said Näslund to MacIntyre after the trade. "I've been asking for a trade now over two months. It took a while. I'm looking forward to getting more chance to play and a fresh, new start."

There was some consternation in Vancouver when Stojanov scored his first career NHL goal in his very first game with the Penguins, especially since Näslund failed to tally a single point in his first nine games with the Canucks. But then Näslund scored a hat trick in the final game of the season against the Calgary Flames.

Näslund went on to score a lot more in the years to come. In 12 seasons with the Canucks, Näslund set franchise records in goals (346) and points (756). He came two points shy of winning the Art Ross Trophy in 2002–03 season with 104 points. He finished just behind the player taken a pick before Stojanov: Peter Forsberg.

With Todd Bertuzzi and Brendan Morrison, Näslund formed the West Coast Express and revitalized hockey in Vancouver. More than that, Näslund became a leader in Vancouver. On September 15, 2000, in the midst of a preseason trip to Sweden, Näslund was named the ninth captain in Canucks history. On December 11, 2010, the Canucks retired Näslund's No. 19, raising it to the rafters alongside Stan Smyl's No. 12 and Trevor Linden's No. 16.

WHILE NÄSLUND BECAME one of the greatest Canucks of all time, Stojanov struggled to become the player he believed he could be with the Penguins. He played a total of 54 games in Pittsburgh, putting up two goals and six points. Any chance of becoming more than a tough guy was ended by a serious car accident that left him with a fractured skull. Though he toiled in the minors for several years after, he never played in the NHL again.

It's hard to blame Stojanov for his disappointing career. He never would have been drafted in the top 10 without the '90s obsession with finding the next Bob Probert. He never would have played 58 games for the Canucks in 1995–96 without the era's desire for heavyweight enforcers. He might have been able to do more than just fight if not for his serious injuries.

Stojanov had the potential to do something more with his NHL career, even if he could never match the heights of Näslund's. Instead of being the protagonist in his own story, he was relegated to a footnote in someone else's, which isn't fair—everyone deserves to be the main character in their own narrative.

7

PAVEL BURE AND THE CASE OF THE MISSING GAME SHEETS

PAVEL BURE WOULD NEVER have played a game for the Canucks if not for the 1987 Canada Cup, the 1988 Winter Olympics, a Soviet sportswriter, and a completely honest mistake.

The Canucks' first-round pick in the 1989 draft was Jason Herter, a defenceman out of the University of North Dakota. Herter was a point-per-game player in the NHL. The only problem was he played just one NHL game, where he had a single assist for the New York Islanders.

That's not ideal for an eighth-overall pick, and it was a tough way to follow up drafting Trevor Linden the year before. At the time, however, the Canucks thought they had a steal. Herter was the top-ranked defenceman in the draft according to NHL Central Scouting and was expected to battle to go first overall heading into his draft year. When the Minnesota North Stars went off the board by picking Doug Zmolek seventh overall, Herter fell to the Canucks.

"There were three defencemen we liked a lot and it turned out we got the one we liked the best," said Canucks general manager Pat Quinn after drafting Herter. It took until the third round for the best defenceman in the draft to actually get picked—an unheralded "defensive defenceman" out of Sweden: Nicklas Lidstrom.

Herter might not have worked out, but the 1989 NHL Entry Draft was still a massive success for the Canucks. The Canucks got a superstar, just not with their top-10 pick. Instead, they got him in the sixth round: Pavel Bure, the Russian Rocket.

Bure was a once-in-a-lifetime player, a brilliant talent who combined lightning-quick skating with equally fast hands. Despite playing in one of the lowest-scoring eras in NHL history, Bure was a prolific goalscorer. He led the NHL in goals three times and his 0.62 career goals per game is behind only Mike Bossy and Mario Lemieux in the modern era.

It wasn't just the goals—Bure was electric to watch. Every shift was a marvel, as he blazed the length of the ice at a speed that seemed impossible, blasting past even the best defencemen in the league as if they were standing still. He was the most exciting player in the entire league and Canucks fans were lucky enough to see him start his NHL career in Vancouver.

Bure was inducted into the Hockey Hall of Fame in 2012. A year later, the Canucks retired his No. 10. When the NHL named the greatest 100 players of all time in 2017 to honour the 100th anniversary of the league, there was Bure, where he belonged among the greatest players in NHL history. Not bad for a sixth-round pick.

BUT WAIT—HOW IN the world did a player as good as Bure get picked that late in the draft? It's not like Bure was an unknown. Bure was considered one of the top three prospects in the draft with Mats Sundin and Bobby Holik.

"Brilliant talent, clearly the best 18-year-old in the world," said a scouting report in the *Philadelphia Daily News* ahead of the draft.

"He may be the top player in this year's draft," said Barry Fraser, the Edmonton Oilers' chief scout, to Matthew Fisher of the *Globe and Mail*. "But because he's from the Soviet Union, we don't analyze him the same way as a kid from the West."

"If Bure were from the West, he'd be a number one choice for sure," said Montreal reporter Marc Lachapelle. "He's a hell of a prospect."

Sundin famously became the first-ever European player to go first overall in the NHL draft, while Holik fell to 10th overall because of the uncertainty of getting him out from behind the Iron Curtain in Czechoslovakia.

But if there was uncertainty surrounding a Czech player like Holik, there was far more surrounding players from the Soviet Union like Bure. The Soviets had only just allowed some of their older veterans to join the NHL, with the three members of the famed KLM line—Vladimir Krutov, Igor Larionov, and Sergei Makarov—set to make their NHL debut in the 1989–90 season. For a younger star like Bure, NHL teams doubted whether the Soviet Union would ever let him leave.

"I was told they're not going to let their top players go," said Pittsburgh Penguins general manager Tony Esposito to the *Pittsburgh Press*.

"I don't think you will see an influx of players from the Soviet Union," said Minnesota North Stars general manager Jack Ferreira to the *Star Tribune*. "Many think he is the best 18-year-old in the world, but we won't be drafting him."

The Hockey News, in their 1989 draft preview, put it this way: "Bure is, without question, the best player available in this draft. He is not, however, the best available player."

THE NHL HAD some odd rules for the draft at the time that further complicated Bure's situation.

The first three rounds of the draft were open to any player who was at least 18 years old by September 15, 1989. After that, players had to meet at least one of the following eligibility requirements:

- Be born in 1969, meaning they would turn 20 in 1989.
- Have three seasons of major junior experience.
- Have three seasons of experience in a high school in the U.S.
- Have played at least one year of college hockey in the U.S.
- Have two seasons of "European Elite or First Division" experience.

That last point is the relevant one for Bure. Vitally, a "season" only counted if the player appeared in more than 10 games. Bure could only be drafted outside of the first three rounds if he had appeared in at least 11 games in at least two seasons in a "European Elite or First Division" league.

According to NHL Central Scouting, Bure played 32 games with CSKA Moscow, also known as Central Red Army, in the 1988–89 season. That's one season. But in the 1987–88 season, he had only played five games in the top Soviet league. That was not enough to count as a season, which meant he wasn't eligible to be drafted outside of the first three rounds.

Any team, however, could have drafted Bure in the first three rounds and every team knew it. They just had to be willing to take a chance on him coming to North America.

In retrospect, it seems insane that not a single team took a gamble on drafting Bure with a third-round pick. Thirteen of the 21 players drafted in the third round in 1989 didn't even play 100 games in the NHL—and five of them never played a single NHL game.

Any one of the teams that failed to get a legitimate NHL player in the third round could have drafted Bure and not lost a thing even if he never left the Soviet Union.

The Canucks weren't planning on picking Bure either—at least not according to their chief scout, Mike Penny.

"Bure is a great player, but would he be willing to come out?" said Penny to *The Province* ahead of the draft. "I know the situation we're in with the Soviets trying to get Larionov. We're not likely to be taking him."

Penny knew Bure as well as anyone in the NHL. He had been keeping an eye on him for two years.

Media mogul Frank Griffiths, who bought the Canucks in 1974, wanted to pry Soviet players out from behind the Iron Curtain in the '80s. The Canucks drafted Soviet star Igor Larionov in the 11th round of the 1985 draft, then his linemate, Vladimir Krutov, in the 12th round in 1986, and then another Soviet national team player, Viktor Tyumenev, in 1987.

Griffiths and his family—he transferred ownership of the team to his son Arthur Griffiths in 1988—established connections with Soviet hockey in multiple different ways. One was a coaching exchange, seen as a chance to share hockey knowledge between Canada and the Soviet Union. Legendary Soviet national team coach Anatoli Tarasov came to Vancouver to observe practices and conduct coaching clinics, with the Canucks sending two of their own to the Soviet Union to do the same.

It was more than just a hockey exchange. Griffiths and the Canucks even paid for Tarasov to have hip replacement surgery in Vancouver.

"The Russian doctors didn't want to touch him. He could have died on the operating table and the Russian doctor probably would have never been heard from again," said Arthur Griffiths in a 2014 feature on the Canucks' website. "Tarasov was a demigod in hockey there, and rightfully so. So I said, the Vancouver Canucks will bring you back, we will pay for your surgery, we'll get you back on your feet. Sadly for him, he was very overweight. It was a really dicey situation.

"The reality is, that was an attempt to create a bit of a bridge."

Canucks assistant coach Jack McIlhargey and prospect goaltender Troy Gamble, selected in the second round in the 1985 draft, went to the Soviet Union in the summer of 1987.

The pretext was their half of the hockey exchange, but they also wanted to connect with Larionov, Krutov, and Tyumenev and figure out how to get them to Vancouver. Gamble underwent the strenuous training methods of the Soviet national team, while McIlhargey wined and dined with Tarasov. More visits followed, as the Canucks continued to pull at threads in the Soviet sweater to see which would unravel and give them their Soviet draft picks. Penny, who did most of the Canucks' scouting in Europe, was visiting Moscow and watching a Central Red Army practice in 1987 when a small forward flying around the ice caught his eye.

"I see this guy and I'm thinking, 'Geez, this guy's pretty good—a little small,'" Penny recalled, so he grabbed Larionov and asked, "Who's that guy?"

"Oh, he's a young kid they brought up. His name is Bure," replied Larionov. "He's only 16."

Stunned to see a 16-year-old kid practicing with the senior Red Army team, Penny filed that information away, promising to himself that he'd keep an eye on the kid in the future. That was tough to do at the time, as the only chance to watch Soviet players play was typically when they traveled outside of the Soviet Union.

One of those opportunities came purely by chance. Penny was in Finland in December 1987 to do some scouting when he got wind from Göran Stubb, the NHL's director of European scouting, that the Soviet national team was traveling to Vierumäki to play two exhibition games against the Finnish national team. Penny got into a borrowed car and drove through the snow to Vierumäki on Christmas Day to watch the Soviets play.

Sure enough, Bure was there and, besides the two teams and the referees, Penny seemed to be the only person in the rink.

"If somebody else was there, I didn't see them," said Penny. "I actually went down and got a guy to go get Bure—that was the first time I met him. Just, 'Hi, how are you,' but [Soviet coach] Viktor Tikhonov didn't like that. You could see the scowl on his face, like 'What's he doing in the rink?' Well, you don't own the rink, so I'm staying."

After the game, Penny grabbed the official International Ice Hockey Federation (IIHF) game sheet and left. That game sheet, acquired through a little luck and some old-fashioned, hit-the-road scouting, ended up being an essential part of the Canucks drafting Bure.

By the time the 1989 draft came around, Bure wasn't a secret anymore. NHL teams couldn't miss his two outstanding performances in the Under-18 European Junior Championships. If they did, Bure was also the Soviet Union's top player at the 1989 World Juniors, scoring eight goals and 14 points in seven games.

But Mike Penny was one of the few people who believed that Bure was actually eligible to be drafted in 1989 outside of the first three rounds, believing he had played enough games in the 1987–88 season. He had his game sheet from that Christmas game in Finland, as well as information about other games he had played for the Soviet national team, all games sanctioned by the IIHF.

Even as he slyly suggested ahead of the draft that the Canucks wouldn't be picking Bure, Penny was lobbying general manager Pat Quinn to draft the young Soviet star.

Penny wasn't quite alone in his conviction. According to Brian Burke, then the Canucks' director of hockey operations, the Edmonton Oilers' chief scout Barry Fraser shared Penny's belief that Bure was eligible and the Oilers were planning on selecting Bure late in the draft. The Detroit Red Wings nearly took him a lot sooner.

The Red Wings had already drafted Bure's older Red Army teammate Sergei Fedorov in the fourth round, believing they could entice him to defect from the Soviet Union. According to Ken Holland, who was a Red Wings scout at the time, the team's chief European scout, Christer Rockström, also urged the team to draft Bure in the fifth round.

"Christer was convinced that he could prove Pavel Bure had played enough games so that he was eligible to be picked after the first three rounds," said Holland in 2021. Red Wings assistant general manager Neil Smith decided to check first with NHL vice president Gil Stein.

"Gil told Smith that Bure wasn't eligible and that if we picked him, we'd lose the player," said Holland. "So Neil comes back, scared off. But Christer kept pushing."

Instead of Bure, the Red Wings picked Shawn McCosh in the fifth round, but Rockström refused to let up, finally convincing Smith and general manager Jim Devellano to take Bure with their sixth-round pick, 116th overall.

Three picks earlier, the Canucks took Bure, 113th overall.

"We were just about to pick Bure when the Canucks announced his name," said Holland. As other teams stormed the stage to protest, the Red Wings were not among them. They could only tip their cap to the Canucks.

The Red Wings ended up just fine—1989 was their best draft in franchise history; they selected Nicklas Lidstrom, Sergei Fedorov, Mike Sillinger, and Vladimir Konstantinov. Even the player they selected 116th after Bure was gone was Dallas Drake, who played more than 1,000 games in the NHL.

But they nearly had Bure too.

If Penny hadn't insisted to Quinn that Bure was eligible to be drafted, Bure would have started his NHL career in Detroit. While the Red Wings asked the NHL if Bure was eligible before drafting him, the Canucks didn't bother asking—they just made the pick.

YOU CAN TRY to pick anyone you want in the NHL Entry Draft. The NHL has the right to reject the pick of any player they determine to be ineligible or, if the player is determined to be ineligible after the draft, the pick is voided. That has really only happened once, when "Punch" Imlach simply made up a player in the 1974 draft, selecting the fictional Taro Tsujimoto from the equally fictional Tokyo Katanas in the Japan Ice Hockey League—the league, at least, actually existed. The pick is now listed as an "invalid claim."

In the case of Bure, the NHL allowed the pick to stand at the draft, even though he wasn't listed as eligible by Central Scouting. The Canucks, led by Penny, insisted that Bure was eligible, so the NHL accepted the pick.

"When it came time for us to pick, Bure was still there and we said, 'Heck, we've got to do something,'" said Quinn. "Nobody else had jumped on it. Apparently, there was a kerfuffle over it but we had it verified and we took him. He's one of the finest players in the draft."

"Kerfuffle" was putting it lightly. Representatives from several teams protested, irate that the Canucks had seemingly broken the rules to snag a superstar in the sixth round. One of the teams most vociferous in their protests was the Washington Capitals, with Jack Button, their director of player personnel, calling it "a coup."

"Everybody would have taken him earlier. We assumed he was not eligible," said Button, before grudgingly adding, "You've got to give the Canucks credit for doing their homework."

After the draft, the Capitals rescinded that credit. Both they and the Hartford Whalers filed formal protests with the league. Bure had not played the required 11 games with CSKA Moscow in the 1987–88 season, they said, and therefore was ineligible to be drafted in 1989. They called for the NHL to void the pick and put Bure back in the NHL draft for 1990.

It went under review by NHL president John Ziegler and vice president Jim Gregory. If the pick was overturned, the Canucks would be left with nothing, but "nothing" was a pretty typical outcome for sixth-round picks.

"You draft at your own peril," said Burke at the time. "We think he was worth the pick."

The protest was correct—Bure had only played five games in the regular season of the 1987–88 USSR Championship, the top Soviet league. It was Mike Penny's understanding, however, that Bure's games with the Soviet national team, such as the one he watched on Christmas Day in Finland, counted toward his total of 11 games, as long as they were IIHF-sanctioned games.

That's how it was reported in 1989, with Elliott Pap of the *Vancouver Sun* saying, "In Bure's case, his eligibility hinges on whether he's made six international appearances with the Soviet senior national team."

That was also the understanding of others around the league, such as North Stars general manager Jack Ferreira. According to a 1989 report from Mike Beamish of the *Sun*, Ferreira was told by league officials that "Bure had to be picked in the first three rounds because of his limited international experience."

That understanding was wrong.

It didn't matter whether or not Bure had played international games with the Soviet national team. The rules of the draft were that an 18-year-old prospect like Bure had to play two seasons in a "European Elite or First Division" league. International games didn't qualify—they had to be games with his club team, CSKA Moscow.

When Penny insisted to Pat Quinn that Bure was eligible to be drafted because he knew that Bure had played international games that weren't listed by NHL Central Scouting, he was mistaken. It was an honest mistake—the NHL's communication of the draft rules was haphazard and confusing—but it was still a mistake.

The Canucks drafted Pavel Bure based on faulty information.

On May 21, 1990, Ziegler ruled against the Canucks and voided the pick of Pavel Bure. An 11-month investigation of the Whalers and Capitals' protest determined that Bure was ineligible to be drafted in 1989 and he was removed from the Canucks' reserve list.

The 1990 NHL Entry Draft was on June 16 in Vancouver. The Canucks had less than four weeks to prove that Bure had played enough games in the 1987–88 season or he would go back into the draft and another team would surely take him, possibly even early in the first round.

One of the voices lobbying hard for the pick to be voided was Capitals' general manager David Poile. The son of Bud Poile, who had watched the Canucks lose Gilbert Perreault to the spin of the wheel, was now hoping to wrench another superstar out of Vancouver's hands. While he expressed his sympathy for the Canucks' position, thinking it was a matter of mistaken statistics, it seems likely that he also wanted the chance to draft Bure himself, with the Capitals holding the ninth-overall pick in the 1990 draft.

"It's unfortunate that people were operating on two different sets of statistics," said Poile to the *Sun*. "The Russians don't keep stats with the same accuracy that we keep stats."

The Canucks needed to act quickly.

"The burden of proof is on us," said Quinn. "We thought we'd done enough checking with the proper authorities but the president has made his ruling and, at this time, I don't know if there is even an appeal process."

Before they could appeal, the Canucks needed to gather some evidence. They turned to their inside man in Soviet hockey: Igor Larionov.

The connections the Canucks made over the years with Larionov had paid off and the Professor was on his way to play for the Canucks in the 1989–90 season. The

Canucks asked Larionov if he could find evidence that Bure had played more than five games for CSKA Moscow in the 1987–88 season.

Larionov knew exactly who to call for help: a Soviet sports journalist named Igor Kuperman.

Kuperman was the hockey editor for *Sportivnye Igry— Sports Games* magazine—and the daily sports newspaper *Sovietsky Sport*. He was also an official statistician for Soviet hockey, making him the ideal person to locate any missing game sheets that could prove Bure played enough games.

While Bure had only played five games in the 1987–88 USSR Championship season, CSKA Moscow played in various tournaments throughout the year that qualified as "European Elite or First Division" hockey.

There was the 1987–88 Soviet Cup, which was actually played from 1986 to 1988. This was a tournament played between teams in the USSR Championship and the Pervaya Liga—the second division of Soviet hockey. CSKA Moscow also played in the 1987–88 European Cup. Similar to the Champions League in soccer, the European Cup saw the top teams from various European leagues face off to determine who was best.

CSKA Moscow dominated the European Cup, finishing on top for 13 straight years from 1978 to 1990. Pavel Bure won the European Cup in the 1988–89 and 1989–90 seasons, but he wasn't on the team for the 1987–88 tournament, so that was no help.

But Kuperman was able to find evidence that Bure played in two other tournaments.

Pavel Bure with one of the men responsible for
him coming to the Canucks, Igor Kuperman.
(Courtesy of Igor Kuperman)

"Larionov asked me to find any games," said Kuperman,
putting emphasis on the word "any," so he started digging. "I
went to the Soviet Ice Hockey Federation office and I found
scoresheets of a couple of tournaments, all domestic, not
international."

The first find was a preseason tournament that took place
in September 1987. While Russian sources say that Bure made
his CSKA Moscow debut on March 5, 1988, Bure himself
remembers first playing for CSKA Moscow much earlier,
remembering that the team was initially nervous about putting an undersized 16-year-old rookie on the ice.

"They said, 'We'd better wait another year because Pavel
might get killed.' They didn't want to take a chance on me
getting hurt," said Bure in an interview with the NHL's
Stan Fischler. "But I said to them, 'You have to put me in
because I can play with them.' Finally, my chance came when

a bunch of guys from the Red Army squad went to play in the Canada Cup. While they were away, the coaches put me on the fourth line."

The 1987 Canada Cup was a six-team tournament featuring the best players from around the world, which took place from August 28 to September 15, 1987. Since NHL players did not compete in the Olympics until 1998, international tournaments like the Canada Cup were one of the few chances to see the top NHL players face the top players from the Soviet Union.

The best-of-three final series from the 1987 Canada Cup is still legendary. Canada had Mario Lemieux and Wayne Gretzky playing on the same line, along with other legends including Mark Messier, Paul Coffey, Ray Bourque, and Larry Murphy. They faced the best of the Soviet Union, including the KLM line of Krutov, Larionov, and Makarov. Lemieux's tournament-winning goal on a pass from Gretzky is etched into hockey history.

The tournament also plays a small part in Canucks history. Twelve players on the Soviet side were from CSKA Moscow—with them gone, Bure got his chance to make his debut for CSKA Moscow. Kuperman found that Bure played four games in that preseason tournament, held at the same time as the Canada Cup, bringing him up to a total of nine games with CSKA Moscow. He still needed two more to be eligible for the 1989 draft.

There was one last tournament to check: the Trade Union Cup, a tournament that was played in February 1988. Once again, many of Bure's Red Army teammates would have been with the Soviet national team, this time at the 1988 Winter

Olympics in Calgary, where Krutov and Larionov led the tournament in scoring and led the Soviet Union to the gold medal. Perhaps, just like when his teammates were away at the Canada Cup, Kuperman reasoned, Bure would have gotten in the Red Army lineup.

"I clearly remember that when I was looking through Trade Union Cup scoresheets in the summer of 1990, my hands were literally shaking," recalled Kuperman. "There were still just nine games with Pavel's participation and only two CSKA games left to check."

Soviet game sheets at the time had a "Yes" or "No" column to indicate if a dressed player actually played in the game. Kuperman scanned the game sheets and saw Bure's name on both of them. He looked across and breathed a sigh of relief that they both indicated "Yes"—Bure had played in both games.

Five games in the regular season; four games in a preseason tournament in September; two games at the Trade Union Cup in February—Kuperman could hardly believe it: "It summed up to exactly 11."

WITH JUST A few days remaining before the 1990 draft, Kuperman and Larionov rushed to the Canadian embassy to fax their evidence to the Canucks. They faced just one more unexpected obstacle.

"I wrote the document in English that these scoresheets were legit and it was signed by a USSR hockey federation representative, by CSKA assistant coach Boris Mikhailov, and Vladimir Bure, Pavel's father," said Kuperman. "But the policeman at the door of the Canadian Embassy didn't let us in."

It took some convincing because they didn't have an appointment. Fortunately, the policeman recognized the name Pavel Bure and he definitely knew who Igor Larionov was.

"It was funny," recalled Kuperman. "I had to try to explain to the policeman the rules of the NHL draft."

It must have been a lengthy conversation.

The Canucks quickly forwarded everything to the NHL and, just two days before the 1990 draft, Ziegler reversed his previous decision.

"The advice I now have from the USSR Ice Hockey Federation certifies that Mr. Bure played in the necessary 11 games with the Central Red Army Team in the 1987–88 season," said Ziegler in a press release. "My original decision was made after significant and repeated attempts to obtain all relevant information from the Soviets and in the belief that the information provided was full and complete.

"Apparently, the USSR Ice Hockey Federation did not completely understand our previous requests for a listing of all games played by Mr. Bure and excluded the six additional games which he had played in separate tournaments."

Opposing general managers and owners howled in outrage, not just at the decision but at the timing, coming so close to the start of the draft.

There were even accusations of skulduggery. Tony Gallagher of *The Province*, citing an anonymous NHL owner, governor, and general manager as sources, reported that the Canucks made a backroom deal with Ziegler. Supposedly, the Canucks convinced him to rule in their favour in return for letting go of a grievance Pat Quinn had with Ziegler and the NHL after he was fined and suspended from coaching for signing with the Canucks while still under contract with the Los Angeles Kings. Everyone involved adamantly denied that such a deal took place.

In any case, such a deal wasn't necessary. According to Kuperman, the USSR Ice Hockey Federation, and Bure's own assistant coach with CSKA Moscow, Bure had played 11 games in the 1987–88 season. He was eligible to be drafted in 1989 after all, even if it wasn't for the original reason the Canucks believed he was eligible.

Even though the Canucks won the battle to keep Bure, they didn't think he would play for them for several years. It was thought that the Soviets wouldn't release Bure to play in the NHL until after the 1994 Olympics, at the very least. But the Soviet Union was collapsing far more quickly than anyone anticipated and Soviet players started leaving in droves.

On November 5, 1991, Bure made his Canucks debut just two and a half years after the team took a chance on drafting him in the sixth round. Over the next seven seasons with the Canucks, Bure scored 254 goals and 478 points in 428 games, including two 60-goal seasons.

The Canucks can thank Igor Kuperman for those seven seasons, though Kuperman's next employers were not too happy about it—a few months before Bure joined the Canucks, Kuperman came to Canada, hired by the rival Winnipeg Jets as their director of hockey information and hockey operations.

"I got a hard time from the Jets office staff in those days," recalled Kuperman to Beamish. "We played the Canucks a lot and the Winnipeg people never let me forget I was the guy who helped get Pavel Bure to Vancouver."

IGOR "THE PROFESSOR" LARIONOV

Pavel Bure wasn't the first Russian star to play for the Canucks. The Russian Rocket was preceded by one of the other great nicknames in hockey history: the Professor.

Igor Larionov wasn't your typical draft pick; he was already 24 years old and one of the best hockey players on the planet.

Before he was drafted by the Canucks in 1985, Larionov already had an Olympic gold medal, two World Championship gold medals, and two World Junior gold medals. He was one of the top scorers in the Soviet league with CSKA Moscow on the feared KLM line with Vladimir Krutov and Sergei Makarov, a line that also dominated in international play for the Soviet Union, including the best-on-best Canada Cup tournaments.

As befitting his professorial nickname, Larionov was incredibly intelligent both on and off the ice. On the ice, Larionov took a cerebral approach to the game, with hockey sense that rivaled Wayne Gretzky's.

"In the eighties, he was arguably the best centre in the world," said Gretzky when Larionov went into the Hockey Hall of Fame in 2008.

Off the ice, Larionov was an avid chess player, devoured books, and already had a strong grasp on the English language at a young age. He was thoughtful and analytical even as a teenager, with a maturity far beyond his years.

"He was one of the smartest people I've talked to on this earth," said Sergei Federov to ESPN's Pierre LeBrun.

Larionov wanted to control his own destiny, a privilege not afforded to him by the authoritarian control of the Soviet government and the Soviet hockey system, which were often intertwined. Multiple trips to North America with the national team and tournaments against top NHL players convinced Larionov that he wanted to play in the NHL, something he expressed publicly, much to the consternation of his coach, the dictatorial Viktor Tikhonov.

"It depends on the team," said Larionov about his desire to play in the NHL during the 1983 Super Series, a tour of exhibition games against NHL teams. "Montreal, yes; otherwise, I cannot say."

His teammate, Sergei Babinov, quipped via an interpreter, "He wants to know if there are any teams close to Miami." Fortunately for the Canucks, Florida wouldn't get any NHL teams until the early '90s.

The Canucks already had success with luring Czech players Ivan Hlinka and Jiri Bubla out from behind the Iron Curtain and were optimistic they could do the same with players from the Soviet Union. The Canucks decided to target Larionov, knowing he wanted to play in the NHL.

"I was quoted in the media and expressing myself quite openly that the day would come where I would play in the NHL, but I wasn't sure when," said Larionov. "It took us a while to get the doors open for many of us to come to the National Hockey League."

Canucks general manager Jack Gordon drafted two more players out of Czechoslovakia—Robert Kron and Martin

Hrtska—before drafting Larionov in the 11th round in the 1985 draft, 214th overall. To a certain extent, it was a coup, as Larionov was easily the best player selected in the draft, but it wasn't clear if they would ever actually see him don a Canucks jersey. It led to questions of why the Canucks would even use a pick on the Soviet star.

"Why bother drafting a guy like Larionov?" said Gordon. "Because he's a player and that's what this is all about. We've drafted him and put him on our list and sure, we'll try to get him out. We've got some people to do that and hopefully, we can. No one has been able to get a Soviet player to play for them but we're the team that hopes to do it."

It was so obvious that Larionov wanted to play in the NHL that when Tikhonov left him out of the lineup of the Central Red Army team for the 1986 Super Series, there was wide speculation that it was for fear that he might try to defect while touring North America.

Larionov didn't want to defect. Instead, he aimed to open the door for those that came after him. If he could leave the Soviet Union and play in the NHL with the blessing of the Soviet government, then that would lead the way for others to do the same.

The Canucks made overtures to Soviet hockey with their hockey exchange program and paying for Anatoli Tarasov's hip replacement surgery. Meanwhile, Larionov was applying pressure within the Soviet Union. In 1988, Larionov published an open letter to Tikhonov in *Ogonyok*, a popular Soviet magazine that leaned toward a pro-capitalist position. In it, he harshly criticized the Red Army coach over the course of three pages and 7,000 words.

"I published the letter to the coach to open the society's eyes to what really was being done in this system," said Larionov. "I wasn't doing it for myself—I was doing it for the whole team."

Larionov ripped into Tikhonov's harsh training regimen that had the entire team stay in dormitories together while training for 10 to 11 months of the year, quipping, "It's a wonder our wives manage to give birth."

"I have a daughter, Elena, one year, nine months, whom I cannot see every day because of this arrangement," said Larionov to Sports Illustrated. "I love hockey, but it's too much. It's hard to live like this."

Along with Slava Fetisov, Larionov led the charge for getting Soviet hockey players clearance to decide their own futures. As Tikhonov cut Larionov from Central Red Army for the Super Series and the Soviet national team in retaliation for his letter, Fetisov sat out too in solidarity.

Even if he wasn't allowed to leave the Soviet Union for the NHL, Larionov had no intention of playing again for Tikhonov and Central Red Army. Instead, he planned to return to his hometown team of Khimik Voskresensk, who he played for before Tikhonov recruited him eight years earlier.

"Hockey players are treated like human beings on Khimik's team," said Larionov to Sports Illustrated at the time. "Tikhonov has to realize that hockey players are people and not robots."

As the 1988–89 season came to a close, Larionov and Fetisov continued to push to be allowed to play in the NHL and permission was finally granted, on the condition that both play one more time for the Soviet Union, at the 1989

World Championship in Sweden. They agreed and the Soviets swept the tournament, going undefeated in 10 games to win the gold medal.

After the tournament, Buffalo Sabres draft pick and future Canuck Alexander Mogilny became the first Soviet star to defect, bolting when the team was granted a day of shopping at a local mall in Stockholm after winning gold. More players would defect in the coming years, including Sergei Fedorov and Vladimir Konstantinov.

Larionov was determined to get to the NHL without defecting. Pat Quinn made it happen, flying to Moscow and negotiating his release, along with his KLM linemate, Vladimir Krutov, who the Canucks drafted a year after Larionov. It didn't come cheap to either the Canucks or Larionov, as part of his deal saw a large chunk of his NHL paycheck go back to Soviet hockey.

"Those guys paid high taxes to the Russian sport government agency in order to leave," said Fedorov. "Their salaries were minimized by 65 percent. I just defected. But they couldn't do that. They were older and wiser and they had to be responsible. I respect them for that."

By the time Larionov made his NHL debut with the Canucks he was already 29, but his cerebral approach to the game meant he had many good years left in his career. His KLM linemate didn't fare as well. Freed from the strict training regimen of Central Red Army, Krutov embraced the excesses of the West and fell out of shape.

When Larionov went through medical testing at his first NHL training camp, the Canucks were surprised to discover that the Professor, renowned for his vision on the ice, couldn't see very well. He needed glasses.

"He'd never had his eyes tested before," said Canucks physician Dr. Ross Davidson to Beamish. "Do you know what his medical was at the Red Army? The doctor asks him, 'Igor, how are you this year?' 'Good,' he says. That was his medical."

Larionov's best year with the Canucks came alongside the young star he helped get to Vancouver, Pavel Bure. Larionov welcomed Bure into his home when he first came to Vancouver and the Russian Rocket helped revitalize the Professor, who had just four points in 11 games when Bure arrived. Lined up with Bure, Larionov put up 18 goals and 61 points in his remaining 61 games, while helping usher in the Bure era in Vancouver.

It was the only season he would play with Bure.

While Larionov likely would have played longer than three seasons for the Canucks, he grew disillusioned with the Canucks' agreement with the Russian Federation that sent a large portion of his contract back to Russia. When it came time to re-sign with the Canucks, Larionov wanted to remove that "tax."

"When I was signing the deal with Soviet authorities, one of my conditions or requests was that this money would be used for youth programs for development of Russian hockey players," said Larionov to LeBrun. "But every year, I went home to Russia and never saw any trace of money spent on youth programs."

Unable to escape that agreement, Larionov left the NHL for Switzerland to play for HC Lugano. After he left, the Canucks didn't protect his rights in the waiver draft because they weren't sure if he would return, and he was claimed by the San Jose Sharks ahead of the 1993–94 season.

Finally able to secure a contract that wasn't taxed by the Russian Federation, Larionov returned to the NHL and played 11 more seasons, eventually joining the Detroit Red Wings to form the Russian Five with Fetisov, Fedorov, Konstantinov, and Slava Kozlov.

It seems a shame that the Canucks, who put in so much legwork to get Larionov out of the Soviet Union, only got to have him on their roster for three seasons. But ultimately, all of that work also led to the Canucks getting Pavel Bure.

There's still a "what if" that hangs over the team: What if the Canucks still had Larionov during the 1993–94 season? Would they have won the 1994 Stanley Cup if the Professor was still setting up Bure for goals?

8

DRAFTING THE 1994 CANUCKS

"**P**AT QUINN'S PHILOSOPHY** is to build through the draft and that can be a slow, painful process," said Canucks chief scout Mike Penny to Mike Beamish of the *Vancouver Sun* in 1991. "You've got to sit and wait and take some heat while you're waiting for your kids to develop."

It's with some irony, then, that the Canucks team that went on a run to the 1994 Stanley Cup Final wasn't built through the draft at all. In fact, it's almost astounding how few Canucks draft picks were on the 1993–94 team.

Sure, Trevor Linden and Pavel Bure were the best players on the team, but only two other Canucks picks played even a single game in the 1994 playoffs: Shawn Antoski and Gino Odjick. The contributions of the four drafted players could not be more wildly diametric. Linden and Bure led the Canucks in playoff scoring with a combined 56 points; Antoski and Odjick combined for one point, a single assist.

Of course, scoring points wasn't really their role. Antoski was a speedy fourth-liner whose job was to throw hits and punches, while Odjick's job was to send a message to opposing teams that if they touched Pavel Bure, they'd be eating their teeth.

The draft was still involved in acquiring the core of the 1994 Canucks, however, as general manager Pat Quinn used former picks to execute a series of significant trades.

THERE WERE THREE major trades that built the team around Linden and Bure. Two of them involved a former first-round pick for the Canucks; the third, a former ninth-round pick.

That ninth-round pick was Patrik Sundström, the second Swedish player ever drafted by the Canucks—175th overall in 1980. Sundström was a talented centre who was already playing in Sweden's top men's league, the Elitserien, at 18 years old, putting up 12 points in 25 games.

At the time, that was the eighth-most points ever by an 18-year-old in the Elitserien, but that wasn't enough to get Sundström drafted in the first eight rounds. General manager Jake Milford was only too happy to get Sundström late in the draft.

"The Swede could turn out to be a heckuva hockey player in the next few years," said Milford to Arv Olson of the *Sun*. "I scouted him on my last trip to Sweden and he was very impressive. He has a twin brother who also plays hockey but who excels at soccer. I'll bring him over here for the Whitecaps."

That's right, the Canucks drafted a Swedish twin before Daniel and Henrik Sedin were even born.

Milford never brought over Patrik's twin brother, Peter Sundström, for either the Whitecaps or the Canucks. Instead, Peter was drafted a year later by the New York Rangers at 50th overall.

Though his brother was the higher draft pick, Patrik was the better player and the first of many Swedish draft picks to make a major impact for the Canucks. His career high of 91 points in the 1983–84 season led the Canucks in scoring. Peter, on the other hand, had two seasons with 44 points with the Rangers and never did better. Maybe things would have been different if the Sundström twins played their entire careers together like the Sedins later would.

The Sundströms did play one season on the same team after the Canucks traded Patrik to the New Jersey Devils in 1987 but, by that point, Peter was more of a depth player.

That deal with the Devils was one of the first moves Pat Quinn made after he was finally allowed to act as general manager of the Canucks. It was a doozy. Quinn sent Sundström and a fourth-round pick in the 1988 draft to the Devils and brought back Kirk McLean and Greg Adams.

Arguably the last of the great stand-up goaltenders, McLean became the Canucks' starting goaltender for the next decade. During that time, he was a two-time Vezina finalist as one of the best goaltenders in the NHL, while his finest hour came in the 1994 playoffs, where he put up a marvelous .928 save percentage. One of the saves contributing to that percentage was The Save: a stupendous pad-stacking kick save on what looked like a sure goal by Robert Reichel in overtime of Game 7 in the first round against the Calgary Flames. It's one of the greatest saves in playoff history.

Meanwhile, Adams became a key top-six forward, scoring 30-plus goals three times for the Canucks. He may have only been sixth on the team in scoring in the 1994 playoffs with 14 points in 23 playoff games in 1994, but he scored some of the team's most important goals, including the tying goal in the third period against the Flames to send Game 7 to overtime. That set the stage for The Save, then Bure's eventual game-winner.

Adams scored two more massive goals in Game 5 of the Western Conference Final against the Toronto Maple Leafs. First, he scored the tying goal to get the game to overtime, then, in the second overtime period, he went hard to the net and banged home a Dave Babych rebound to send the Canucks to the Stanley Cup Final.

The Devils couldn't complain too much about their end of the deal. Sundström had several strong seasons in New Jersey and led the Devils in scoring in the playoffs the year after the trade in 1988, with 20 points in 18 games to bring them one game away from reaching the Stanley Cup Final. But the Canucks got a decade-long starting goaltender and a clutch scorer—not a bad return for a player originally drafted with a ninth-round pick.

A FEW YEARS into his tenure as general manager, Quinn added two key pieces to the blue line in separate trades with the

Montreal Canadiens, sending them a pair of picks in the 1991 draft and bringing back Jyrki Lumme and Gerald Diduck.

He then added two more defencemen via trade, getting Dana Murzyn from the Calgary Flames for Kevan Guy and Ronnie Stern, and Dave Babych from the Minnesota North Stars for Tom Kurvers. That series of trades completely reshaped the Canucks' defence corps.

That made former 10th-overall pick Garth Butcher expendable. While Butcher was never able to score in the NHL like he did in Juniors, he was respected for his physical defensive game, as well as his heart and character. He left the Canucks as their all-time leader in penalty minutes with 1,668 in 610 games, which would eventually be surpassed by Odjick.

The 29-year-old Butcher was packaged up for a trade to the St. Louis Blues with the Canucks' captain, or at least one of them. Dan Quinn shared the "C" with Linden and Doug Lidster in the 1990–91 season, helping to transition the team from the captaincy of Stan Smyl to that of Linden. Quinn was a savvy centre who was one of the team's top scorers, but there were question marks about his consistency and defensive game.

The Blues, led by Adam Oates and Brett Hull, were a legitimate Stanley Cup contender, but they wanted more bite on the back end. General manager Ron Caron was set on Butcher to provide the size and toughness he craved and also wanted Quinn to fill a hole at second-line centre.

Pat Quinn played hardball, refusing to give up Butcher.

"I tossed in a few more names to make it more pleasant," said Caron after the trade to Tom Wheatley at the *St. Louis*

Post-Dispatch. Caron was willing to pay handsomely to acquire Butcher and Quinn, which Butcher appreciated.

"If I did have to go someplace, St. Louis was my number-one choice," said Butcher to David Banks of *The Province*. "Winning is what it's all about and St. Louis has found a way to win. It's through hard work and effort and that's something I look forward to. The losing is frustrating."

The Canucks did a lot of losing in the 1990–91 season, with a 28–43–9 record that still somehow got them into the playoffs in the Clarence Campbell Conference. Their terrible record got them the seventh-overall pick in the 1991 draft, which they used unwisely on Alek Stojanov. Stojanov didn't help turn the Canucks around, but the trade return from the Blues certainly did as the "few more names" that Caron tossed in proved to be key pieces for the Canucks.

The package started with winger Geoff Courtnall, who was third on the Blues in scoring behind Oates and Hull at the time of the trade. The veteran Courtnall didn't exactly fit the youth movement that Pat Quinn was building in Vancouver but he was a legitimate top-six winger. In addition, he was born and raised in B.C. and thrived playing for his hometown team, with several solid seasons with the Canucks. That included the 1993–94 season, where he was second on the Canucks in scoring behind Bure with 70 points in 82 games.

Courtnall was a clutch playoff performer, with 61 points in 65 playoff games in his five seasons with the Canucks and he played a key role in the 1994 playoff run, with 9 goals and 19 points in 24 games. His biggest goal came in Game 5 of the first round against the Calgary Flames. Down 3–1 in the series, the Canucks pushed the game to overtime, when

Courtnall blasted a slap shot past Mike Vernon on a break-away to keep the Canucks alive.

Getting Courtnall was crucial, but the biggest piece of the trade return might have been the smallest player, as Pat Quinn got Cliff Ronning from the Blues as well. Ronning's small size and style of play didn't mesh with Blues head coach Brian Sutter, who favoured a crash-and-bang, dump-and-chase game. While he got some time on the top power-play unit, Ronning was primarily used as a fourth-line centre in St. Louis.

Let loose in Vancouver, Ronning became an offensive force. Like Courtnall, Ronning was a local kid, born and raised in Burnaby, and eagerly performed for the local fans. In six seasons with the Canucks, Ronning put up 328 points in 366 games, essentially proving that he could have been the second-line centre the Blues were looking for when they traded him away.

Ronning was a spark plug for the Canucks in the 1994 playoff run and was frequently one of the best forwards on the ice. He was tenacious on the forecheck to go with his ability to stickhandle in tight quarters and find open wingers in stride with his excellent vision. He finished the playoffs with 15 points in 24 games, fourth behind Bure, Linden, and Courtnall.

Courtnall and Ronning would have been enough of a return for Butcher and Quinn by themselves, but Caron also tossed in Robert Dirk, Sergio Momesso, and a fifth-round draft pick.

A 6'4" defenceman, Dirk made up for some of the size and nastiness the Canucks lost in Butcher, while Momesso combined his 6′3″ stature with a bit of skill and surprising speed. Momesso slotted into the Canucks' middle-six forwards, sometimes playing with the smaller Ronning on the second line.

"All three of us have the same feeling—that St. Louis made a mistake," said Dirk to Elliot Pap of the *Sun* early in the 1991–92 season. Dirk never got to fully see how true that was; he was traded to the Chicago Blackhawks during the 1993–94 season and missed out on the Canucks' run to the Stanley Cup Final.

Momesso, however, made an impact in the playoffs. The big, physical winger even came through with an overtime game-winner in the playoffs of his own, ending Game 4 against the Dallas Stars.

Ultimately, what the Canucks got for drafting Garth Butcher 10th overall in 1981 was 10 years of hard-nosed, heart-and-soul hockey, then two top-six forwards and some key depth for a run to the 1994 Stanley Cup Final.

On the Blues' side, the trade was blamed for their quick ouster in the second round of the 1991 playoffs, as it decimated their depth. Quinn put up 11 points in 13 playoff games, but that wasn't able to make up for the loss of Courtnall, Ronning, Dirk, and Momesso.

IN 1990, VANCOUVER hosted the draft and the Canucks were hoping to select a future star in front of their hometown fans. A dreadful 1989–90 season had landed the Canucks at the bottom of the Western Conference, though they couldn't compete in futility with the Quebec Nordiques in the Eastern

Conference, whose 12–61–7 record was one of the worst in NHL history.

Accordingly, the Nordiques got the first-overall pick, and the Canucks, for the third time in their history, picked second. The 1990 draft wasn't a bad time to be picking second instead of first. It was generally thought that there were four different prospects all worthy of going first overall, with no clear winner among the quartet: Mike Ricci, Owen Nolan, Keith Primeau, and Petr Nedved. Ricci was ranked first by NHL Central Scouting after racking up 52 goals and 116 points in 60 games in the OHL, but the Nordiques had their hearts set on the second-ranked Nolan, seeing him as the prototypical rugged NHL winger. That left the Canucks with the choice of Ricci, the third-ranked Primeau, or the fourth-ranked Nedved.

The Canucks chose Nedved.

Nedved was 6'4", but with a slight build that made some NHL scouts nervous. The Canucks, however, simply saw the centre's elite skill that helped him score 65 goals and 145 points in 71 games with the Seattle Thunderbirds in the WHL.

"We think he's the best offensive talent, a real threat," said Brian Burke, then the Canucks director of hockey operations. "He sees the ice well and he's a great passer. We think he's an offensive dimension that this club has been lacking for 20 years."

"Petr's not afraid of the traffic, but his game is the perimeter game," said Canucks scout Ken Slater to *The Province* columnist David Banks. "He's a darter, going in and out, moving and thinking. He's got great natural ability, skating, sees the ice, and is very creative."

The hockey world had also fallen in love with Nedved's story, as he courageously defected from his home country of Czechoslovakia at the age of 17 to escape communist rule and follow his dream of playing in the NHL like his idol, Wayne Gretzky. In fact, Nedved was directly compared to Gretzky, as the hype reached a fever pitch heading into the draft.

"If the Vancouver Canucks take Nedved in Saturday's NHL Entry Draft, they'll get nothing less than an apprentice to Gretzky's genius," raved Banks. "Considering the kinship of upbringing, philosophy, and talent, he might come close."

There was no way for Nedved to live up to those expectations. He made the jump directly to the NHL after the draft but clearly wasn't ready and likely would have been better served going back to the WHL for one more year. Nedved played primarily on the fourth line as a rookie and had minimal impact.

Still, Nedved steadily progressed and, at the age of 21, was one of the team's top scorers, with 38 goals and 71 points despite limited power play time. That was good for second in goalscoring behind Bure in the 1992–93 season but, instead of playing a major role in that critical 1993–94 season for the Canucks, a contract dispute led to him leaving the Canucks entirely.

Nedved felt the Canucks' initial contract offer was far too low and then felt insulted when the Canucks came back with a second offer that was $50,000 less than the first. The relationship was fully severed when Canucks vice president George McPhee wrote a letter to Nedved's agent, Tony Kondel, telling him that Nedved might never play in the NHL again unless Kondel stopped being his agent.

"That was the biggest reason," said Nedved to Tony Gallagher of *The Province*. "It was so low and underhanded. How could he say something like this? It blows my mind." When Nedved defected at 17, Kondel took him in, first becoming Nedved's legal guardian before he became his agent. In other words, Kondel was practically family and trying to tear the two apart became the last straw for Nedved.

"I don't care if it takes one week, one month, or two years, I'm not going to play in Vancouver anymore," said Nedved. "I have a lot of friends on the team and I wish them very well. I don't have a problem with any guy there. I have a problem with the management there and a personal problem with Pat Quinn."

As Nedved sat out, Quinn looked to trade him and was about to pull the trigger on a deal with the Hartford Whalers, sending them Nedved and Gerald Diduck in exchange for Michael Nylander, Zarley Zalapski, and James Patrick. Those plans were scuttled, however, when Nedved suddenly signed an offer sheet with the St. Louis Blues just two weeks before the trade deadline.

While Quinn and the Canucks weren't happy about losing the chance to trade Nedved, the upshot is that they were due compensation from the Blues, as Nedved was a Group One free agent—similar to a restricted free agent in today's NHL. When the two teams couldn't agree on the compensation for Nedved, an independent arbitrator stepped in and awarded the Canucks playmaking centre Craig Janney and a second-round pick.

It's a decision that no one liked. The Canucks had boldly asked for the Blues' leading scorer, Brendan Shanahan, as compensation and were disappointed to get Janney instead, especially because the centre had a knee injury and wouldn't be available to help the Canucks' playoff push. The Blues weren't happy, even though they had offered Janney in arbitration, as they felt that Janney was a better player than Nedved, making the entire process unbalanced and unfair.

"They win. Petr wasn't playing with them, and now they get a second-round draft pick and a 100-point guy," said Blues star Brett Hull. "The team that wants to improve themselves always seems to get the short end of the stick."

Least happy of all was Janney, who wanted to stay in St. Louis and refused to report to Vancouver. He went as far as threatening to challenge the NHL's arbitration system in court.

In the end, the Canucks and Blues worked out a deal. The Canucks sent Janney back to the Blues in exchange for defencemen Jeff Brown and Bret Hedican, as well as forward Nathan Lafayette.

The trade filled a key need for the Canucks, giving the team an entire defence pairing in Hedican and Brown, with Brown stepping in to quarterback the power play. Brown led all Canucks defencemen in scoring in the 1994 playoffs with 15 points in 24 games, including a vital assist on Bure's Game 7 winner against the Flames. Lafayette provided important depth on the third line and chipped in nine points in 20 playoff games. He also came achingly close to scoring the biggest goal of his career when he rang the puck off the post late in the third period of a one-goal Game 7 against the Rangers in the Stanley Cup Final.

The addition of Hedican and Brown also left another Canucks draft pick in the press box for the playoffs. The Canucks drafted Jiri Slegr 23rd overall in 1990 and he played a major role on the blueline during the 1993–94 regular season, but he didn't play a single game in the playoffs. As fate would have it, the trio of Nylander, Zalapski, and Patrick that Quinn had tried to acquire from the Whalers for Nedved were instead traded as a package to the Calgary Flames and faced the Canucks in the first round of the 1994 playoffs. They combined for zero goals and four assists in the seven-game series.

WHILE THE PICK of Nedved ultimately gave the Canucks some key players for their 1994 playoff run, they might have instead picked a legitimate legend if they had looked a little further afield in the 1990 draft. Nedved's fellow Czech, Jaromir Jagr, went fifth overall to the Pittsburgh Penguins and was undoubtedly the best player in a very strong 1990 draft. Nedved eventually played with Jagr on the Penguins for two seasons, including a career-high 99-point season in 1995–96.

The Canucks were nervous about whether Jagr, who had stayed in Czechoslovakia while Nedved defected, would come to the NHL. There were even reports that Jagr had to complete two years of compulsory military service unless certain "dispensations" were made—not something the Canucks wanted to deal with after navigating their way through the bureaucracy of Soviet hockey to extricate Igor Larionov and secure Pavel Bure.

"That's why we backed off," said Mike Penny. "There was fear that he would stay in Czechoslovakia. But Nedved was already here."

The Canucks could be forgiven for being hesitant to pick Jagr. According to Craig Patrick, then the general manager of the Penguins, Jagr cleverly manipulated his way onto exactly the team he wanted to play for.

"I found out years later that when he was interviewed by teams ahead of us, he told them all that he wasn't coming over right away," said Patrick to Penguins reporters in 2016. "When we asked him that question, he said, 'I'll be here tomorrow if you draft me.' I think the other teams backed off because of that."

Jagr idolized Mario Lemieux and dreamed of playing with Lemieux on the Penguins. He knew exactly what to say to make that happen. If Jagr told the Canucks that he wouldn't be coming over to the NHL, it's no wonder they went in another direction. The Canucks had taken a chance on drafting Bure in the sixth round a year earlier but weren't going to risk a second-overall pick on a player that might never play for them, especially with the dazzlingly talented Nedved already in North America, playing just down the road in Seattle.

Still, it remains one of the most tantalizing hypotheticals in Canucks history: What if the Canucks had Jaromir Jagr to play alongside Trevor Linden and Pavel Bure in the '90s?

THE CANUCKS HAD two first-round picks in the 1990 draft, as they held the Blues' pick from an earlier trade. If the selection of Nedved over Jagr was understandable, the Canucks' second pick was disastrous, even if it did get the Canucks a player who actually contributed to the Canucks' 1994 playoff run.

Shawn Antoski was already 20 years old by the time of the 1990 draft and was in his third year of draft eligibility. In his first year, Antoski had just seven points in 52 OHL games, then followed that up with 27 points in 57 games. As an over-aged player at 20, Antoski had broken out with 56 points in 59 games, but that was still only 68th in OHL scoring.

These days, a 20-year-old winger who scored less than a point per game in major junior would be lucky to get drafted at all, let alone in the first round. In 1990, however, scouts were salivating over Antoski, who was 6′4″ and 220 pounds but could also skate like the wind. That combination made him a terrifying opponent in junior hockey. Antoski was like if a brick wall could chase you around the ice and smash you into the boards at 30 miles per hour.

Antoski could forecheck and he could fight—the trouble was that he couldn't do much of anything else. He lacked the hockey sense and skill to be anything more than a fourth-line forward at the NHL level. His jump in points in his over-age season, however, convinced scouts that he was a late bloomer who would rack up as many points as he would hits.

Pat Quinn was enthralled by Antoski's size and powerful skating and pushed hard to draft him 18th overall, seeing him as exactly the type of player the Canucks needed to strike fear into the hearts of their opponents. Canucks head coach Bob McCammon was inclined to agree.

"Antoski is not a guy who goes into the corner and just comes out with the puck," said McCammon at the draft. "He goes into the corner and comes out with the corner."

Not everyone in the Canucks organization, however, agreed with the pick.

"Antoski was no good," said a blunt Mike Penny, who said he instead advocated for drafting Keith Tkachuk, who went one pick later to the Winnipeg Jets. "[Tkachuk] had only played a few games, had a bad ankle injury. Pat said, 'I'm gonna overrule you here, we're gonna take Shawn Antoski.' I said to him, 'Are you sure you want to do this?' He said, 'Yep.'

"About two years later, Pat says to me, 'Don't ever let me do that again.'"

Tkachuk's ankle injury limited him to just six games of high school hockey in his draft year but he scored 12 goals and 26 points in those six games. Tkachuk went on to score 1,065 points in 1,201 career games in the NHL and also racked up 2,219 penalty minutes—exactly the type of tough power forward that Quinn had wanted. Antoski finished his NHL career with eight points in 183 games.

In his defence, Quinn wasn't the only one who badly overrated Antoski. NHL Central Scouting ranked Antoski 17th overall heading into the draft, viewing him as ready to immediately jump to the NHL and contribute. He was likened to Bob Probert, much like Alek Stojanov would be a year later at the 1991 draft.

Antoski did play in the NHL in the season following the draft, but just for two games. He spent most of his time in the minors before the 1993–94 season, when he finally found a home on the Canucks' fourth line.

While Antoski managed just three points in 55 games that season, he piled up 190 penalty minutes, second behind another Canucks pick from the 1990 draft: Gino Odjick.

NO ONE COULD have imagined the impact that Gino Odjick would have on the city of Vancouver when Pat Quinn drafted him in the fifth round, 86th overall, in 1990. Odjick was an unlikely candidate to get drafted into the NHL, let alone become a beloved legend, greeted with standing ovations and crowds chanting his name. He was never a high-level prospect—four years before he was drafted, Odjick was playing house hockey on outdoor rinks in the First Nations community of Kitigan Zibi in Quebec. He was coached by his father, Joseph Odjick, a residential school survivor. When Odjick made it to the NHL, he chose No. 29 in honour of his father—it was his registration number at the residential school in Spanish, Ontario.

Odjick was spotted by Bob Hartley, who would go on to coach the Colorado Avalanche to the Stanley Cup in 2001. Hartley was looking for a tough customer to play for his Junior A Hawkesbury Hawks and the burly Odjick fit the bill. Odjick had no illusions about why he was recruited for the Hawks.

"They needed somebody to fight because they lacked toughness," said Odjick before he was drafted by the Canucks. "But I really wanted to play. Once I got there, I was willing to do anything."

The following year, Hartley got Odjick a tryout with the Laval Titan in the QMJHL, taking him from house hockey to major junior in two years. Odjick's ability to fight got him in the door but he also began to refine his game. Originally a defenceman, Odjick was moved up to the wing by Laval coach Paulin Bordeleau, who had been a centre with the Canucks in the '70s. Gradually, Odjick became more and more reliable over his two seasons with the Titans, learning from Bordeleau and Pierre Creamer, who replaced him as head coach.

Odjick caught the attention of Canucks scout Ron Delorme, who connected with the big, tough hockey player from a First Nations background.

"I saw myself in him," said Delorme to Iain MacIntyre of the *Sun*. "It's hard to take a native person and put 'succeed' beside his name—in all facets of life, not just hockey. Native kids have grown up all their lives on reserves. All of a sudden, you have to put these kids in the mixed world, the white world. Nineteen white kids and one native kid on a hockey team: that's culture shock."

Delorme was—and is—a tireless advocate for First Nations people, opening doors in hockey that might otherwise remain closed. He opened the door for Odjick in Vancouver.

"After the draft, [Canucks coach] Bob McCammon came over to me and said, 'That damn Ron was bugging us to pick you after the second round,'" said Odjick in 1990. "'He bugged us so much we had to pick you in the fifth round.'"

The Canucks weren't opposed to adding another big body to their prospect pool, least of all Brian Burke, a longtime fan of truculence in hockey.

"He's not just tough, he's scary tough," said Burke in the *Sun*. "We feel he has legitimate big-league potential. He'll play in the minors or as an over-age junior next season."

That was the plan. Instead, Odjick caught the Canucks off guard at training camp because he showed them something they didn't expect: the enforcer could play.

"He's really played well defensively and makes the right play along the boards," said McCammon. "What surprises me is he has good hockey sense. He knows his limitations and he plays within them."

Odjick spent only a brief stint in the minors with the Milwaukee Admirals, where he piled up a whopping 102 penalty minutes in just 17 games but also put up 10 points, showing he had more dimension to his game than anyone expected.

"He was a smart player," recalled Milwaukee head coach Mike Murphy to Patrick Johnston of the *Sun*. "People don't give him credit; he had excellent hockey IQ."

Called up to the NHL, the 20-year-old Odjick took on both Dave Manson and Stu Grimson in his first game, electrifying the fans. It wasn't long before fans were chanting "Gi-no! Gi-no! Gi-no!" with the same fervor they'd chanted "Har-old! Har-old! Har-old!" for Harold Snepsts. But Odjick knew that he needed to do more than just fight.

"Pat Quinn, as soon as I got here, said, 'I don't want a goon, I want somebody who can play. I don't want you just coming off the bench to fight; you have to contribute. You have to be part of the leadership group. I'm going to give you an opportunity every night to do something special,'" recalled Odjick in an interview on Global BC. "And true to his word, that's what he did, and I grew as a player from the first day that I walked in as a 20-year-old and when I left as a 32-year-old, I was still getting better as a player."

Odjick's fists got him drafted and into the Canucks lineup, but it was his hockey sense that allowed him to play with talented linemates like Pavel Bure. Odjick was assigned the task of protecting the Russian Rocket in his rookie season and the two became fast friends, bonding over their shared outsider status.

"He came from the reserve and I came from the Soviet Union," recalled Bure to The Athletic in 2019. "We both couldn't speak English well, but we learned to understand each other, you know?"

Odjick's best season came alongside Bure in 1993–94, when he tallied 16 goals and 29 points while also making sure Bure had the space he needed on the ice. Perhaps because his goals were rare, Odjick celebrated each of them with unrestrained exuberance, further endearing himself to the Canucks faithful.

Beyond the fans, Odjick was also beloved by his teammates, who appreciated his specialized role.

"Gino was like a big brother," said Ronning to the BC Sports Hall of Fame. "As a smaller player trying to survive playing against giants, I always knew Gino had my back. That alone gave me confidence to perform at my best."

In the 1994 playoffs, however, Odjick was a frequent healthy scratch behind a deep Canucks forward group. Antoski was the better skater, so he got into more games on the fourth line with John McIntyre and Tim Hunter, a line designed around hard forechecking and mucking it up along the boards. Odjick was limited to just 10 games and didn't make a single appearance in the Stanley Cup Final.

Would it have made a difference if the heart-on-his-sleeve Odjick had gotten into more games? He didn't manage any points in his 10 games, but then Antoski only had one assist in 16 playoff games. The seven-game series against the Rangers was a tough, physical bout—would Odjick's presence have evened the odds in the Canucks' favour?

Fans certainly wanted to see more of Odjick. More than anything else, Odjick connected with people. He always made time to talk, sign autographs, and, like Delorme before him, work with First Nations youth. He was earnest, honest, and unfiltered, with a disarming and charming personality. Most of all, he cared deeply—about his teammates, his city, and his community.

"He is a hero," said Delorme after Odjick's first season. "I stress to put something back in the game. Never walk by a kid who asks for an autograph. Remember where you came from."

Odjick never forgot. He was one of the Canucks most heavily involved in their community and charity work. During the 1995 off-season, he ran 800 kilometers through 20 Indigenous communities from Calgary to Vancouver in what he called a "Spiritual Journey of Healing" to raise awareness among Indigenous youth of the dangers of alcohol and drugs.

"On the ice, he did what he had to do," said Stan Smyl. "But off the ice, he was one of the kindest human beings that I have met and played with."

Smyl made those comments after Odjick's passing in 2023. It seemed achingly cruel that a man with a heart big enough to encompass the entire city of Vancouver was afflicted with cardiac amyloidosis, a rare disease that attacks the heart.

Odjick was a giant in Vancouver, a larger-than-life hero. He was inducted into the BC Sports Hall of Fame in 2021 and he marveled at the honour.

"I was just a fifth-round draft choice," he said. "No one expects you to play in the NHL your first year. Twenty games into the season I'm called up and stayed in the NHL for 12 years. That was quite the ride."

DOUG LIDSTER

Doug Lidster was one of the Canucks' best draft picks of the '80s. Selected in the seventh round in the 1980 NHL Entry Draft, Lidster went on to play 897 NHL games, 666 of them with the Canucks. Just 11 players from the 1980 draft played more games in the NHL than Lidster.

Ironically, Lidster ended up being part of the Canucks' downfall in the 1994 Stanley Cup Final.

Before he was drafted, Lidster was a star for the Kamloops Chiefs and Rockets in the BCJHL, leading all BCJHL defencemen in scoring in the 1978–79 season with 36 goals and 83 points in 59 games. He built up his strength and conditioning in the summer by working five days a week at the Afton Mine in Kamloops, then the other two days at a lumberyard.

Lidster then went to Colorado College and put up 43 points in 39 games as a freshman in the 1979–80 season. That was enough to convince the Canucks that he was worth a chance in the seventh round, even if it was understood that he was a long-term project. Lidster wanted to complete his education, meaning he was at least three years away from playing in the NHL.

"The draft didn't cross my mind when I was finishing high school while playing junior in Kamloops," said Lidster to Arv Olson of the *Sun* a few years later. "The most important thing to me at that time was that I was getting a free college education and playing hockey as well."

Lidster was an honour student, graduating with a business degree, while also skating miles for Colorado College. In his senior year, Lidster led CC in scoring with 56 points in

34 games and reportedly would play as much as 40 minutes per game with little offensive help. Unfortunately, that also led to some bad habits that he had to unlearn before he could make the NHL.

"Basically, I've had to learn how to play without the puck because at college, I was used to handling it all the time," said Lidster. "I had to think offensively, to create or get the goals. I was constantly up ice."

Lidster got a crash course in defence during a stint with Canada's Olympic team after he graduated and before signing with the Canucks. While Canada finished just off the podium in fourth place at the 1984 Olympics, Lidster learned lessons he could apply with the Canucks.

"I've been far better off with the Olympic program rather than turning pro last fall," he said. "We practice daily, and in the practices, with at least two and sometimes as many as four coaches on the ice, we have more skill-type drills."

The Olympic detour worked out well. Lidster became one of the Canucks' best defencemen for the next nine years. Just like at Colorado College, he sometimes was asked to do too much for a weaker team, but he proved capable at both ends of the ice. He was one of their most stalwart defensive defencemen but also set a franchise record for points by a defenceman with 63 in the 1986–87 season. The record stood for 35 years before it was finally broken by Quinn Hughes.

Unfortunately, Lidster's tenure with the Canucks ended right before the 1993–94 season, through an unusual trade.

1993 saw the NHL continue to expand in the south, adding the Florida Panthers and Mighty Ducks of Anaheim to the league. That meant an expansion draft, with teams able to protect nine forwards, five defencemen, and one goaltender above players who were exempt, such as first-year pros.

The Canucks were able to protect most of the players they wanted to keep but were worried about losing 26-year-old goaltender Kay Whitmore, who had proven himself as a reliable backup to Kirk McLean. Bizarrely, Whitmore even received a single third-place vote for the Vezina Trophy after the 1992–93 season despite playing in just 31 games.

Meanwhile, across the continent, the New York Rangers weren't just worried about losing a goaltender; they were certain they were going to lose a goaltender.

The Rangers had an enviable goaltending tandem in Mike Richter and John Vanbiesbrouck but the rules of the expansion draft allowed them to protect just one of them. Whichever goaltender they left exposed was certain to be picked, especially since the expansion draft rules required the Panthers and Ducks to select three goaltenders each.

Forced to choose between the two, the Rangers went with Richter, who was three years younger. The Rangers didn't want to lose Vanbiesbrouck for nothing, however, so they worked out a side deal with the Canucks to trade Vanbiesbrouck for "future considerations" with the understanding that Vanbiesbrouck would be exposed in the expansion draft and claimed by either the Ducks or the Panthers.

Since only one goaltender could be claimed from a single team, Whitmore would be safe. With the very first pick of the 1993 expansion draft, the Panthers selected Vanbiesbrouck, the first of a run of six straight goaltenders. Vanbiesbrouck went on to have the best season of his career for the fledgling Panthers; he posted a career-high .924 save percentage and finished second in Vezina voting behind Dominik Hasek, third in Hart voting, and was named a Second Team All-Star. He went on to almost single-handedly carry the Panthers to the Stanley Cup Final in 1996.

Whitmore remained the Canucks' backup goaltender for two more seasons, then spent the rest of his career in the minors, appearing in just six more NHL games for the Boston Bruins and Calgary Flames.

The "future considerations" in the deal turned out to be Lidster, who had been attached to the deal in the media from the start. Pat Quinn, with his emphasis on getting younger on the blue line, saw the need to move on from the veteran. By structuring the trade as a "future considerations" deal, the Canucks and Rangers avoided the possibility of Lidster getting claimed in the expansion draft from the Rangers.

Lidster didn't play a major role for the Rangers in the 1993–94 regular season, playing in just 34 games and not always getting a regular shift from Rangers head coach Mike Keenan. In the playoffs, however, Lidster was inserted into the Rangers lineup when injuries struck, appearing in 10 games. That included all seven games of the Stanley Cup Final, as Lidster faced off against his former teammates on the Canucks.

Lidster's only points in the 1994 playoffs were two goals, both scored against the Canucks in the Final, including opening goal in the Rangers' 3–1 win in Game 2. Considering that was a one-goal game until an empty-net goal in the final seconds, things might have been different if the Canucks had never traded Lidster and the Rangers had to rely on a less experienced, less talented defenceman instead.

As for Lidster, he felt a strange mix of emotions after winning the Stanley Cup against his former team.

"Once we won and we were shaking hands, I realized that I knew the Canuck players better than I knew my own teammates," recalled Lidster to Andy Radia for Canucks.com years later. "One of the advantages of being a West Coast team, because you travel so much, you have the opportunity to really bond with your teammates. I felt a real camaraderie with [the Canuck players].

"To win the cup against them was a very bittersweet moment for me."

9

THE SEDIN COUP

IN MORE THAN 50 YEARS as an NHL franchise, the Vancouver Canucks have never picked first overall in the NHL Entry Draft.

But that doesn't mean that the Canucks have never held the first-overall pick. In 1999, the first overall pick belonged to the Canucks, even if it was only for a few minutes. It was part of a sequence of events that led to the Canucks drafting the two best players in franchise history: Daniel and Henrik Sedin.

THE SEDINS' DRAFT story starts more than a year earlier, when the Canucks made their most controversial trade ever. On February 6, 1998, nearly a decade after he was drafted by the Canucks, Trevor Linden was traded to the New York Islanders.

Linden was the Canucks captain for seven years before handing over the captaincy to Mark Messier at the beginning of the 1997–98 season, signaling the beginning of one of the darkest eras in Canucks history. It was meant to be a bold new direction—the addition of Messier to a core that already included Pavel Bure and Alexander Mogilny was supposed to get the Canucks back into Stanley Cup contention after missing the playoffs for the first time in seven years. The team even went through an extensive rebrand, with the new ownership group—dubbed Orca Bay Sports and Entertainment—introducing an orca logo and a new navy blue, maroon, and silver colour scheme.

The Canucks did go in a bold new direction—straight down. The team went on a franchise-record 10-game losing streak early in the season and never recovered, finishing the season with a 25–43–14 record. General manager Pat Quinn and head coach Tom Renney were fired and the mercurial Mike Keenan was brought in to whip the team into shape. Instead, he exacerbated divides in the dressing room and the team was dismantled piece by piece, with the few remaining fan favourites from the 1994 playoff run shipped out the door.

That included Linden, who was struggling with injuries and scoring. He was the main target of Keenan's ire, as Iron Mike belittled Linden both in private and in public. But even as he was the target of Keenan's scorn, Linden was still highly regarded around the league and was even named to Team Canada for the 1998 Olympics. As a result, Linden brought back impressive value when he was traded to the Islanders.

The Canucks needed defensive help, so the main piece of the trade was young defenceman Bryan McCabe, who had just been named captain of the Islanders at the age of 22 and didn't see the deal coming.

"I'm shocked. I'm totally shocked," said McCabe. "I guess I'm stupid to think like that but I figured I was just named captain so I'd stick around for a while."

Along with McCabe came a third-round pick—used on agitator Jarkko Ruutu, who played 267 games with the Canucks—and a 23-year-old power forward who had worn out his welcome with Islanders general manager Mike Milbury. Todd Bertuzzi was heavily criticized by Milbury for his lack of intensity and for failing to improve in his second season with the Islanders.

"If I ever felt he was going to fulfill his potential, I would have been a fool to make the deal," said Milbury about Bertuzzi in the *New York Daily News*.

With that, Milbury gave everyone permission to call him a fool. Bertuzzi scored 449 points in 518 games with the Canucks, including a 46-goal, 97-point season in 2002–03 where he was named a First-Team All-Star. Bertuzzi formed the West Coast Express with Markus Naslund and Brendan Morrison, becoming one of the best lines in the NHL.

It was McCabe, however, that would help deliver the twins.

KEENAN TOOK THE blame for the Linden trade—and, eventually, the credit when it panned out favourably for the Canucks—but he wasn't entirely responsible for the deal, according to Mike Penny, by that time promoted from head scout to assistant general manager.

"It was [director of player personnel] Steve Tambellini and myself, we basically laid the groundwork for it," said Penny. "I'd been to the Island a couple of times and I'd seen Bertuzzi and I knew people that knew him from the Sudbury and Guelph area. The guy that was going to be part of the deal was Travis Green but the Islanders traded him to Anaheim, so we took the draft pick instead, which turned out to be Jarkko Ruutu."

"Mike Keenan had nothing to do with the thing," added Penny. "I said, 'Mike, you're like the guy that came through the door and paid the bill after everyone had eaten.'"

Penny made it clear that it was tough to move on from Linden—"I love Trevor"—but that the timing was right to move on.

"What do you do with a player whose career was in decline?" said Penny. "Well, we got a pretty good player in Todd Bertuzzi, Jarkko Ruutu played just short of 700 games in the NHL, and Bryan McCabe became one of the Sedins. It worked out pretty well."

How did McCabe become one of the Sedins? It's all because of the man who became the next general manager of the Canucks: Brian Burke.

"THE 1999 FIRST round is the worst first round in the history of the National Hockey League," declared Burke in an episode of Sportsnet's "Hey Burkie" series.

It's hard to argue with Burke's point. Just three players from the 1999 first round scored more than 500 points in their careers and 12 of the 28 players selected in the first round failed to play 100 NHL games. Two of the three players who scored more than 500 points, however, scored more than 1,000 points and both were selected by Burke and the Canucks.

The Tampa Bay Lightning, headed up by president Rick Dudley, held the first overall pick heading into the 1999 draft. The expansion Atlanta Thrashers, with Don Waddell as general manager, held the second-overall pick, much like the expansion Canucks 29 years earlier. Burke and the Canucks had the third-overall pick and the Chicago Blackhawks, with general manager Bob Murray, had the fourth-overall pick.

The top tier of the 1999 draft class consisted of four players: Daniel Sedin, Henrik Sedin, Patrik Stefan, and Pavel Brendl. Stefan and Brendl were both Czech imports, with Stefan considered the best pure talent in the draft and the player most ready for the NHL. He would have been the obvious lock to go first overall if not for a pair of concussions and some caginess around releasing his medical records.

Brendl utterly dominated the WHL in his draft year, with 73 goals and 134 points in 68 games, leading the league in scoring as an 18-year-old. There were questions, however, about his defensive game and his work ethic, with hockey pundits cracking jokes about his love for hot dogs.

Then there were the Sedins, who posted two of the greatest seasons of all time by 18-year-olds in the top Swedish league, then called the Elitserien. Daniel scored 21 goals and tallied 42 points in 50 games, with Henrik not far behind with 34 points in 49 games. In an unprecedented move, the Elitserien gave both Sedins the Guldpucken award as co-MVPs.

The only 18-year-olds who had put up similar numbers in the Elitserien in the previous decade were Markus Näslund and Peter Forsberg.

Daniel and Henrik Sedin changed the course of the Canucks franchise when they were drafted in 1999.

Despite comparing favourably with such elite players, there were concerns about the Sedins. Could their unique style translate to the NHL? Were they strong enough to protect the puck and take a beating from NHL defencemen along the boards and in front of the net? Most importantly, could they be as good individually as they were together?

That last question was a stumbling block for the teams picking at the top of the draft because it seemed almost impossible that a team could pick both Daniel and Henrik—they had to pick one or the other. Publicly, the teams at the top of the draft were quick to say they didn't mind having one Sedin instead of two.

"I don't buy that they have to play together," said Murray to the *Chicago Tribune* ahead of the draft. "They want to play together, which I respect. But they don't need each other. There is too much talent there."

"They're very good players. They're special players, independently or together," said Waddell to *Sports Illustrated*. "I'm very high on both players, I've seen both players many times."

"I think if you ever got both Sedins you could set your franchise up for a long time," he added. "I think they're going to be great players individually, but together, what a marketing ploy you could have for 10 to 12 years."

The uncertainty surrounding all four of the players at the top of the draft created an environment where teams were more willing than usual to trade a top pick. That included the Lightning at first overall—they had already taken Vincent Lecavalier with the first-overall pick in 1998 and were eager to make more immediate improvements after reaching the playoffs just once in their first seven seasons.

The unique situation with the Sedins meant that Dudley was in a good spot; if a team wanted both Sedins, they would have to go through Dudley and the Lightning. If they didn't make a deal with Dudley, the Lightning could take one of the Sedins first overall and spoil any plans to keep them together.

"There's a lot of hanky-panky going on for the two of them to end up on the same team," said Dudley. "But we're in the driver's seat."

TWO MONTHS BEFORE the draft, Brian Burke had every intention of trading away the Canucks' first-round pick. He wasn't impressed with the quality of the draft class. In his mind, the only player worth anything in the first round was Patrik Stefan, and the Canucks were not quite bad enough to finish last in the NHL and get the first-overall pick to take him.

On the other hand, Thomas Gradin, who had become the Canucks' head European scout, was convinced that the Canucks had to pick the Sedins—both of them. By that point, Gradin had been scouting the Sedins for years and believed they could be stars in the NHL.

"Mike Penny, the boss of the scouting at the time, and I were in Sweden and we were staying in my farmhouse because the tournament was played in the village area around there," recalled Gradin in a feature on the Canucks' website. "On the way down to Stockholm, we were supposed to stop at one of the smaller towns to see this tournament with these unbelievable twins.

"So, we went there and they were only 16 years old playing for the under-18 Swedish National Team and they were unbelievably good. You could see it at that time that they were unbelievable players. That was the first time we ever saw them."

Gradin repeatedly tried to convince Burke that the Canucks had to find a way to draft both Sedins, but Burke came away from the 1999 World Junior Championship unimpressed. Although the Sedins were among the tournament's leading scorers, Burke felt they piled up points against lesser competition and wilted against Canada in the semifinals. They were too easily knocked off the puck and couldn't score on Canadian netminder Roberto Luongo.

"I joked to our scouts that they spent more time on the ice surface than the Zamboni," said Burke in his book, *Burke's Law*. "It was hard to imagine them being impact players in the NHL."

So, Burke told Gradin and the rest of his scouts to wave goodbye to their first-round pick.

Then the rosters for the World Hockey Championship in Norway were announced. Surprisingly, the 18-year-old Sedins were both on Team Sweden. Burke assumed that there must have been injuries that forced the twins onto the roster but a phone call to Gradin disabused him of that notion.

"Nobody got hurt," said Gradin according to *Burke's Law*. "They made the team. You've got to come over and watch them."

The Sedins didn't score any goals. Henrik finished the tournament with no points in eight games, while Daniel had just one assist in seven games. But their talent and their unique ability to find each other on the ice was plain to see, in a way it wasn't at the World Juniors.

"Good lord, now I get it," Burke recalled thinking as he watched them work their magic for Team Sweden. He had carpooled with the Blackhawks' front-office staff, including their director of player personnel, Dale Tallon, to Hamar, Norway, where Sweden was playing their games. After seeing them in action, Burke was in full agreement with Gradin—the Canucks absolutely had to have both Sedins.

Unfortunately, Blackhawks general manager Bob Murray was also on that trip and saw exactly what Burke saw. He wanted the Sedins just as badly as Burke, even as both tried to play it cool in the car ride back from Hamar. Fortunately for the Canucks, Burke had the upper hand: he had the third-overall pick and Murray had the fourth. After the World Championship, Murray reached out to Burke, asking if he was willing to trade the pick.

"No," said Burke in *Burke's Law*. "But you're going to trade me the fourth pick."

Murray had no choice but to concede defeat. Even if he stubbornly held onto the fourth-overall pick, he had no way of getting both Sedins. What he could do was exact some pain on his way out.

"Okay, you smart Irish bastard," said Murray according to Sportsnet's Marc Spector. "But it's going to cost you."

The exact price was Bryan McCabe and a future first-round pick—either 2000 or 2001. McCabe, the linchpin of the Trevor Linden trade, was now part of the price to draft the Sedins.

AS MUCH AS it hurt Burke to trade McCabe, the truth was that he could spare a defenceman. What had been a position of weakness a year earlier for the Canucks when they acquired McCabe had swiftly become a position of strength.

Pavel Bure, citing years of grievances with Canucks management, forced a trade out of Vancouver by refusing to report for the 1998–99 season. Burke finally traded him to the Florida Panthers on January 17, 1999. One of the key pieces of the deal was Ed Jovanovski, a promising young defenceman who had gone first overall in the 1994 draft—making him the first-ever first-overall pick to play for the Canucks.

Burke used his first draft pick as general manager of the Canucks to select 6′5″ defenceman Bryan Allen fourth overall in the 1998 draft. The team's best defenceman was Mattias Öhlund, their 13th-overall pick in 1994, and next best was late-round gem Adrian Aucoin, picked in the fifth round by the

Canucks in 1992. Another later pick, 1995 sixth-rounder Brent Sopel, was on the verge of breaking into the Canucks lineup as well. The Canucks also had Jason Strudwick, acquired in 1998 from the Islanders for Gino Odjick.

That group of young defencemen made it easier to part with McCabe—but easier doesn't mean easy.

"We tried everything to avoid giving [McCabe] up," said Burke the next day in the *Vancouver Sun*. "We tried to offer more picks but they wanted a defenceman and they wanted him."

Murray was willing to move the fourth-overall pick because he wanted immediate help to get the Blackhawks back to the playoffs. Unlike the other teams picking at the top of the draft, the Blackhawks hadn't finished in the NHL's basement. Instead, they had the fourth-overall pick because they won the draft lottery that year, moving up four spots from eighth overall. Murray was all too happy to take the 24-year-old McCabe along with a future first-round pick, believing that McCabe was the key to drastically improving their defence corps.

"I always said if I could get a player who can help the hockey club immediately, I would do it," said Murray. "It was a matter of getting Brian interested enough to step up to the plate."

The Blackhawks made the playoffs just once in the next nine years after trading for McCabe.

THE DEAL WITH Murray and the Blackhawks was finalized a week before the draft but Burke requested the trade be kept a secret, hoping he could gain some leverage by not letting anyone else know he had two picks in the top four. The trade was only registered with the NHL the day before the draft and even on the day of the draft, the trade was still just a rumour.

"Did the Chicago Blackhawks give up their pick to the Vancouver Canucks?" said Greg Millen at the start of ESPN's broadcast of the draft. "We think they perhaps could have and, if they did, obviously Brian Burke for Vancouver has been very, very busy making sure picks one and two lay off their guys, so maybe they're after the Sedin twins."

That was the problem. Burke had picks three and four but that still didn't guarantee they could get both Sedins. The Lightning or the Thrashers could spoil everything if they took a Sedin first or second overall. Just hoping that the Lightning and Thrashers took Stefan and Brendl wasn't going to cut it—Burke had to be certain.

That meant convincing either Waddell and the Thrashers or Dudley and the Lightning to move down in the draft.

Waddell was a non-starter. The expansion Thrashers were looking for a franchise-defining player, just like the Canucks were in 1970. They weren't going to give up the second-overall pick in exchange for some short-term help and they didn't want to move down in the draft either. They needed a star.

That meant trying to make a deal with Dudley and the Lightning for the first-overall pick. The trouble was, the Canucks weren't the only team talking to Dudley and Burke had already used his biggest trade chip, McCabe, to acquire the fourth-overall pick. While Burke could offer that pick in a trade for first-overall, that didn't provide the Lightning with the immediate help they were seeking.

But something fell in the Canucks' favour.

The only reason for most teams to trade for the first-overall pick was to select a bona fide future star and the only one that fit the bill was Patrick Stefan. The Lightning were willing to move the pick, but teams were nervous about trading up to pick Stefan because his agent, Rich Winter, refusing to share Stefan's medical reports with any NHL teams. With Stefan's concussion history and no assurances he was fully recovered, teams were less willing to part with the quality players and prospects Dudley and the Lightning were looking for in a trade.

According to a report in the *Hartford Courant*, the Islanders' Mike Milbury called Winter a "slimeball" for putting him and other general managers at a disadvantage by not sharing Stefan's medical reports.

"He's a disgrace to the Mormon religion," said Milbury.

The Canucks might never have gotten both Sedins if not for a last-second decision by a meddlesome billionaire owner—Art Williams of the Tampa Bay Lightning.

An insurance magnate with a southern drawl and a forceful personality, Williams only owned the Lightning for one season and it was, in many ways, a debacle.

Williams was entirely unfamiliar with hockey by his own admission. He boasted that he had only ever watched one hockey game in his life before he bought the Lightning, but he believed he could not only rescue the Lightning from the depths of debt but also quickly turn them into one of the best teams in the league.

"We ain't building this team Phil Esposito's way or Jacques [Demers]' way or anybody else's way but my way," said Williams at his first press conference. "This team is going to adopt my personality. I am a tough, get-up-and-get-after-it, take-no-prisoners kind of dude. And that is the kind of team we're going to have. We're going to the playoffs every year. We're going to win championships. We're going to fill the Ice Palace."

Instead, the Lightning crashed to the bottom of the NHL standings with a 19–54–9 record. Williams couldn't take it, saying, "This team broke my heart," as he looked to sell the Lightning. The $20 million he claimed to lose in the 1998–99 season might have had something to do with the heartbreak.

Jacques Demers was coach of the Lightning and acted as general manager until Williams made a deal with the Ottawa Senators to hire their general manager, Rick Dudley, who had two years left on his contract. His hiring wasn't made official, however, until after the 1999 draft. The Lightning sent Rob Zamuner and a second-round pick to the Senators for Andreas Johansson and the rights to hire Dudley on June 30, 1999. The draft was on June 26.

Even if his position with the Lighting was unofficial, Dudley was already in a decision-making position and was expected to run the draft. Except Williams made things complicated.

Williams was overly involved in hockey decisions even after Dudley came on board. He nixed a trade the week of the draft that would have sent Darcy Tucker to the Dallas Stars for goaltender Roman Turek. It was a money matter—the man who had spent lavishly when he bought the Lightning was now pinching pennies as he looked to sell the team and Turek made $1 million more than Tucker. So, no deal.

Williams' interference left open the question—was Dudley really in charge of the Lightning? Was he going to be able to make moves at the draft without having to run everything through Williams?

According to a June 27, 1999, report in the *Tampa Tribune*, Dudley wasn't granted the authority to run the draft himself until the day before the draft.

"That's when current-but-outgoing Lightning owner Art Williams finally agreed to let Dudley run the draft as he saw fit," wrote Roy Cummings of the *Tribune*. "Once he was given that freedom, Dudley saw an opportunity to rebuild the Lightning in a hurry and he took advantage of it."

Williams didn't want to give up the reins until he was sure that the sale of the Lightning was certain. On Friday, the eve of the draft, the deal still wasn't done and the ownership of the team was up in the air, with no one sure who was calling the shots.

But late Friday night, Williams finalized the sale of the Lightning for $115 million to the Palace Sports and Entertainment group, headed up by Detroit Pistons owner Bill Davidson. Williams finally let go of the Lightning.

"It was not done [by Friday]," said Williams of the sale of the team to the *Tribune*. "It is not done yet, but it will be Monday, when they wire me the money. I commend everyone involved. They worked as late as they could Friday night and got all the papers signed....It was too late to send the money. They said it will be done Monday.

"So, I told them to proceed with the draft as if it were all done and they were the full-fledged owners. And they did. Hope they are good choices—you all there in Tampa deserve it."

If that deal didn't get done on Friday night or if Williams insisted that he still owned the team until the money came through on the Monday after the draft, the Canucks might never have drafted both Sedins.

Burke's plan relied heavily on getting a deal done with Dudley for the first-overall pick. Dudley was willing to trade the pick but might not have been able to if Williams had still been in charge, as Dudley himself admitted.

"The finality of this came very quickly," said Dudley. "If we had to run this by Art, it would have been hard to get it done."

Would Dudley have been granted the authority to trade the first-overall pick if Williams still owned the team? Williams loved the limelight and loved his star players—if Dudley wasn't given free rein at the draft, Williams might have vetoed any attempt to trade the first-overall pick and give up their chance at Stefan, Brendl, or one of the Sedins.

Tom Wilson, president of Palace Sports and Entertainment, made it clear that the Lightning's draft day trades likely wouldn't have happened if Williams hadn't let Dudley run the draft: "It freed us up to do the deals that we did and get these guys."

You can imagine the worst-case scenario: with the Canucks stuck with just the third and fourth-overall picks, there would have been nothing to prevent the Lightning from taking one Sedin first overall, then the Thrashers from taking the other Sedin second overall. Instead of leaving the 1999 draft with both Sedins, the Canucks could have left with neither of them.

WHILE ART WILLIAMS was negotiating to sell the Lightning, Burke was up until 3:00 AM on the eve of the draft trying to get a deal done for the first or second pick. Perhaps because of the Lightning's ownership confusion, Burke had to go to bed empty-handed that night. He slept just three hours, then was right back up at 6:00 AM to continue wheeling and dealing.

Burke couldn't accept the possibility that he had traded McCabe away to get only one Sedin or, worse, neither of them. With Waddell standing firm on keeping the second-overall pick, Burke focused all his attention on Dudley, offering up the fourth-overall pick and a package of other picks for first-overall.

According to Burke, what Dudley wanted to move back from first to fourth was a second-round pick and a fourth-round pick. Burke refused to give up a second-round pick and countered with two third-round picks.

The Canucks had a third-round pick to spare because the NHL handed out compensatory picks like candy at Halloween in those days. When teams lost veteran players to free agency, they would get a free compensatory pick added to the draft order. So, when Jyrki Lumme signed with the Phoenix Coyotes in the 1998 off-season, the NHL gave the Canucks the 75th-overall pick to make up for it. So, in a way, Lumme helped the Canucks draft the Sedins as well.

Dudley didn't want draft picks, but he finally said yes to Burke's offer of the fourth-overall pick and two third-round picks on the morning of the draft. He already had his next trade lined up with the New York Rangers, who were targeting Pavel Brendl. If Dudley couldn't get the immediate help he wanted by trading the first-overall pick, he'd get it by trading the fourth-overall pick.

That gave Burke the first and third-overall picks but he wanted two more things—assurances that Waddell and the Thrashers wouldn't spoil things by taking a Sedin with the second-overall pick and to be able to call up both Sedins to the stage at the same time.

So, Burke orchestrated one more trade. He approached Waddell with a compelling offer: why not give Thrashers fans the thrill of picking first overall at their first-ever NHL Draft? They could make a splash by getting the top player, Patrik Stefan, and Burke would sweeten the deal by tossing in yet another third-round pick. With that, the Thrashers could be the star of the draft.

"Watching you run around, I have a pretty good fucking idea who's going to be the star of this draft," replied Waddell, according to Burke. But Waddell agreed to the trade.

Just 15 minutes before the draft officially started, all of the deals were done. The Thrashers had the first-overall pick, the Canucks second and third, and the Lightning had traded their way right out of the first round, moving the fourth-overall pick to the New York Rangers in exchange for the immediate help they needed, including goaltender Dan Cloutier, who would wind up in Vancouver just over a year later.

Waddell was cagey with the media, saying, "I think you're going to see us move real quickly here," with a sly smile on the ESPN broadcast before the trades were announced. "In a few minutes, you're going to find out, but we'll be sitting right at the top of the board before the day begins."

Burke was significantly more forthright a few minutes later: "We've wired in a deal, actually, that will be announced in a short while and we will be picking the Sedin twins at two and three."

"I WOULD NORMALLY announce who has the first selection," said NHL commissioner Gary Bettman. "But we have three trades to announce before we get started.

"First, Vancouver trades Bryan McCabe and its first-round pick in 2000 to Chicago in exchange for Chicago's first-round pick in the 1999 draft—that's fourth overall.

"Tampa Bay trades its first-round pick, first overall, in today's draft to Vancouver in exchange for the fourth pick overall in '99, previously acquired from Chicago, and two third-round picks in 1999—the 75th and the 88th overall.

"The third trade—Vancouver trades to Atlanta the first pick overall in this year's draft in exchange for the second pick overall this year and a conditional third-round pick in 2000."

"Well, how's that for excitement?" said Jim Hughson after Bettman finished laying out the Canucks' array of deals.

Shortly after, Waddell took the stage to select Patrik Stefan, who ultimately failed to live up to the lofty expectations of being a first-overall pick. His career continued to be plagued by injuries and he became a depth scorer rather than the franchise forward the Thrashers hoped he could be.

Stefan's struggles only made Burke look more like a genius for wheeling and dealing his way to the only two stars in the first round of the 1999 draft, but Burke had to admit that the Canucks still had Stefan at number one on their draft board. As individual players, Burke and the Canucks thought Stefan was better than either Daniel or Henrik Sedin—the value in the twins was getting both of them.

In fact, Burke dreamed of getting all three players.

"Dave Nonis can vouch for me on this: we tried to get the top three picks," said Burke to Sportsnet's Ryan Dixon. "We liked Patrik Stefan very much. We tried desperately to pick one, two, and three in that draft."

Getting just the Sedins was a pretty good consolation prize.

IT'S ASTONISHING HOW much had to go right for the Canucks to get the Sedins. If they hadn't been named to Sweden's World Championship roster, Burke wouldn't have given them another chance and might have traded the third-overall pick. If another team that was higher on Pavel Brendl, like the New York Rangers, had the fourth-overall pick, Burke wouldn't have been able to trade McCabe for that pick.

If the sale of the Lightning had taken even a day longer to finalize, Art Williams might have killed any attempt to trade the first-overall pick. If Winter had been more forthcoming with Stefan's medical reports, another team could have made a more compelling offer to the Lightning to trade up to first overall. With Stefan gone, the Thrashers could have decided to pick a Sedin instead—Waddell had been adamant that he wasn't trading away the team's first-ever first-round draft pick.

It came down, as the draft so often does, to a combination of luck and hard work.

"Brian Burke orchestrated all of that and I've got to give him all the marks in the world for pulling it off," said Penny. "He was up to the wee hours of the morning—he worked night and day on it. I commend him, he was like a dog on a bone. He wasn't gonna let up until he had both Sedins."

Burke, meanwhile, gives the credit to Thomas Gradin, as he never would have put in those long hours without Gradin's influence.

"Thomas did all the work on these kids," said Burke to Sportsnet in 2011. "He pushed and pushed and pushed. When I came back and said I'd made those deals, I'd never seen a smile on a guy's face bigger than that. It's like he'd won the lottery."

In truth, Canucks fans were the ones who won the lottery. They got 17 seasons of two of the most unique players in NHL history, who won major awards with their play on the ice and made a difference in the community with their kindness and charity off the ice. Both broke franchise records, finishing with more than 1,000 points each, all with the Canucks. In February 2020, their Nos. 22 and 33 were retired and raised to the rafters of Rogers Arena. Nine months later, both were inducted into the Hockey Hall of Fame in their first year of eligibility.

Who says the Canucks are unlucky?

THE SWEDISH CONNECTION

After the Canucks lost out on Gilbert Perreault because of an errant spin of the wheel, Canucks president Tom Scallen, who had invested so heavily in acquiring the Canucks and getting them to the NHL, made a vow.

"I'm sad and I'm mad," said Scallen. "We received a setback here today but it makes us more determined than ever to go out and find our own talent. We'll go to Sweden, Finland, even Russia—but we'll get players."

It took eight years, but the Canucks eventually did go to Sweden to find some talent, although Scallen was long gone by then. Convicted of stealing money from a sale of Canucks shares to pay off Medicor debts and issuing a false prospectus, Scallen sold the team in 1974 to Frank Griffiths, a local media executive who owned the Western Broadcasting Company. Scallen maintained his innocence and was officially pardoned in 1982 by the National Parole Board.

Scallen's influence remains in the stick-in-rink logo he chose, which is still in use as an alternate logo for the Canucks and in that simple declaration that the team would "find our own talent" in Sweden.

THOMAS GRADIN WAS the first Swedish star for the Canucks, though he wasn't drafted by them. He set the stage for the likes of Markus Näslund, the Sedins, and Elias Pettersson in the decades to come.

Gradin made his debut in the 1978–79 season, but he wasn't alone. He was part of a wave of Swedish players on the Canucks: Roland Eriksson, Lars Lindgren, and Lars Zetterstrom also made their NHL debut for the Canucks that season and, at the 1978 draft, the Canucks selected their first-ever Swede, Harald Lückner, in the fourth round.

Lückner never played for the Canucks—he played with Färjestad BK in Sweden for his entire professional career—but he was the first of many Swedish draft picks for the Canucks, several of whom became some of the Canucks' best players.

Gradin, of course, plays a large role in the Canucks' history of Swedish draft picks, even if he wasn't one of them himself, in his decades as an amateur scout. He had a major influence in the drafting of Mattias Öhlund, Daniel and Henrik Sedin, and Alex Edler.

In total, 36 Swedes have been drafted by the Canucks to date, including four Swedish twins—Sundström, the Sedins, and Pathrik Westerholm—and two Elias Petterssons. Six of the 36 were first-round picks. Two of them are the top scorers in Canucks history, another two are the top scorers all time among Canucks defencemen, and the elder Elias Pettersson is likely to surpass them all if he stays in Vancouver his entire career like the Sedins.

With a Swedish general manager in the front office in Patrik Allvin—the first Swedish general manager in NHL history—the Canucks' connection to Sweden isn't likely to stop anytime soon. Here are all the Canucks' draft picks from Sweden thus far.

1. Harald Lückner (56th, 1978)
2. Patrik Sundström (175th, 1980)
3. Håkan Åhlund (151st, 1985)
4. Roger Hansson (213th, 1987)
5. Leif Rohlin (33rd, 1988)
6. Roger Åkerström (170th, 1988)
7. Stefan Nilsson (233rd, 1988)
8. Jan Bergman (248th, 1989)

9. Bert Robertsson (254th, 1993)

10. Mattias Öhlund (13th, 1994)

11. Jonas Soling (93rd, 1996)

12. David Ytfeldt (136th, 1998)

13. Daniel Sedin (2nd, 1999)

14. Henrik Sedin (3rd, 1999)

15. Nicklas Danielsson (160th, 2003)

16. Alex Edler (91st, 2004)

17. Daniel Rahimi (82nd, 2006)

18. Anton Rödin (53rd, 2009)

19. Peter Andersson (143rd, 2009)

20. Ludwig Blomstrand (120th, 2011)

21. Pathrik Westerholm (180th, 2011)

22. Henrik Tömmernes (210th, 2011)

23. Anton Cederholm (145th, 2013)

24. Gustav Forsling (126th, 2014)

25. Elias Pettersson (5th, 2017)

26. Kristoffer Gunnarsson (135th, 2017)

27. Nils Höglander (40th, 2019)

28. Arvid Costmar (215th, 2019)

29. Viktor Persson (191st, 2020)

30. Jonathan Myrenberg (140th, 2021)

31. Hugo Gabrielson (169th, 2021)

32. Lucas Forsell (201st, 2021)

33. Jonathan Lekkerimäki (15th, 2022)

34. Elias Pettersson (80th, 2022)

35. Tom Willander (11th, 2023)

36. Vilmer Alriksson (107th, 2023)

10

RYAN KESLER AND THE BEST DRAFT OF ALL TIME

THE 2003 NHL ENTRY DRAFT was a gold mine.

Even in the first round, the draft is always a gamble, but teams hit jackpot after jackpot in 2003. Just two players in the first round failed to play at least 100 NHL games—12th-overall pick Hugh Jessiman with the New York Rangers and 30th-overall pick Shawn Belle with the St. Louis Blues. Twelve of the 30 players picked in the first round have played more than 1,000 career games and goaltender Marc-Andre Fleury, picked first overall, will likely also reach that milestone.

The first round in 2003 didn't just produce NHL players—it produced stars. Seventeen of the 30 players selected in the first round went on to play in at least one All-Star Game. The players selected in the first round combined for 21 NHL awards, including a Hart Trophy for most valuable player, a Rocket Richard for most goals in a season, a Vezina Trophy for best goaltender, a Norris Trophy for best defenceman, and a Selke for best defensive forward.

That total doesn't even include Patrice Bergeron and his five Selke trophies—he wasn't picked until the middle of the second round.

The Canucks didn't miss the vein of gold in the 2003 draft. With the 23rd pick overall, the Canucks found the perfect player to complement the Sedins.

RYAN KESLER FIRST hit the ice in Livonia, Michigan at four years old. His father, Mike Kesler, played college hockey at Colorado College in the late '60s and, by the time Ryan came along, Mike had been coaching minor hockey for decades and ran a hockey school. It was only natural that Ryan would follow in his father's footsteps onto the backyard rink built by Mike complete with boards and lights for late-night hockey practices. It helped that Ryan's older brother, Todd Kesler, also played hockey.

"You always want to do what your brother does," said Kesler in a CBC interview in 2008. "So, I've had a stick in my hand since I was a baby."

Kesler also had a local NHL idol—Mike Modano, drafted one pick before Trevor Linden in 1988, was also from Livonia. While Kesler developed into a different type of player than Modano, he always had one thing in common with him: blazing speed.

Kesler's biggest influence as a young hockey player was his dad, particularly in his first year of bantam hockey, when he was cut from every AAA team in Detroit. His dad, however, got an opportunity to coach the Little Ceasar's major bantam team, giving Kesler the chance to play a year ahead of his age group. It was there that he started to learn the lessons that would turn him into one of the best two-way forwards in the NHL.

"It was drilled into my head that your own end is more important than the offensive end," said Kesler to Grant Kerr of the *Globe and Mail*. "My dad drilled it into me from day one that scoring more goals was not more important than getting the puck out of your own end."

Things did not always go smoothly, though. The agitating attitude that made Kesler such a pain to play against on the ice also made him a handful for his parents as a teenager and caused some clashes with his dad as a coach. After getting kicked off the ice for mocking his dad during his first practice, Kesler called his mom on a pay phone from the arena.

"Come and get me," said Kesler, according to *The Hockey News*. "I'm not playing for this asshole."

The father-son duo lasted just one season as coach and player. Still, the lessons his dad continued to drill into him about the importance of playing sound defensive hockey stuck with Kesler as he grew older and entered the U.S. National Team Development Program in nearby Plymouth.

"He stressed perfection," said Kesler to Ben Kuzma of *The Province*. "He was probably the hardest on me and I didn't understand it at the time. But now, you look back and understand why; he had to be."

In the years leading up to the 2003 draft, Kesler made a name for himself as a player who could be trusted in every situation. He led the Under-18 team with the U.S. Development Program in scoring in the 2001–02 season with 44 points in 46 games but earned the most praise from his coaches for his penalty killing.

"They kind of make you grow up fast in the organization," said Kesler in a 2016 interview with USA Hockey. "I went in as a scrawny kid and they teach you how to lift and work out and be a professional before you get to be a professional. I owe a lot to that program."

Kesler gave a lot back. He helped Team USA win gold in the World Under-18 championship in 2002, the first-ever gold medal for the Americans at that tournament. In total, he represented Team USA at eight major international tournaments, including two Olympics, and won World Under-18 gold, World Junior gold, and an Olympic silver medal.

In his draft year, Kesler played for Ohio State University, where he was one of the best 18-year-olds in the country, with 31 points in 40 games. That was already enough for NHL scouts to get excited but where he really leapt up the draft rankings was at the 2003 World Junior Championship, where he was second on Team USA in scoring with seven points in seven games and elevated his game against the toughest opponents.

"Kesler brought his A game against Canada in Halifax," said Canucks chief scout Ron Delorme to Kuzma. "We were very impressed. He had all kinds of special assignments against Canada."

In any other year, Kesler's résumé might have made him a top-10 pick. In the stacked 2003 draft, however, he was expected to go later in the first round. NHL Central Scouting ranked him 16th just among North American skaters, while TSN's Bob McKenzie ranked Kesler 19th overall on his list.

No one was worried about whether Kelser would play in the NHL—his speed and excellent defensive game would ensure that—but there was a sense that his offensive game might not translate.

"One word to describe this guy is 'solid'—solid in every single area, no weaknesses," said Bob McKenzie on TSN's broadcast of the 2003 draft. "Not expected to put a lot of points on the board at the National Hockey League level but a guy with character and grit and strength."

"I don't think he'll play as a first-line or second-line player, but he will be a great third-line player in the league," said Pierre McGuire.

The Canucks saw something different in Kesler—they saw someone who was already playing a pro-style game and was more NHL-ready than many of his fellow first-round picks. They also saw a familiar face.

While Kesler may have idolized Modano, he was more often compared to the player drafted right after Modano.

"When we watched him play, he reminded us of a young Trevor Linden in terms of his intensity and skating ability and hitting," said Canucks general manager Brian Burke. "We felt very strongly that if he was there or we had any shot of getting him, we were going to take him."

Steve Tambellini, then the Canucks' director of player personnel, did some scouting of Kesler himself and was convinced he was the right player for Vancouver.

"He's a very determined player every night," said Tambellini to Iain MacIntyre of the *Vancouver Sun*. "Competitive-wise, out of ten, he's usually at eight every night. You like that. He's going to be a big kid who can get to pucks, drive wide, and he's got a little bit of nastiness in him."

Vouching for Kesler was a tad bittersweet for Tambellini, who had to watch the Canucks pass over his own son, Jeff Tambellini, who was selected four picks later by the Los Angeles Kings. The Canucks were definitely interested in Tambellini, who outscored Kesler in college hockey that year, and even attempted to acquire another first-round pick to draft the fleet-footed winger, but it didn't work out.

"We're really consistent on our draft process. We cross names off our list and pick the best guy available," said Tambellini. "Jeff was a couple of players away on our list."

Burke said that he told his scouts to pretend that Jeff Tambellini was named "John Smith" to try to take out any personal bias.

"We've got to take the best player available, that's our philosophy," said Burke. "We like the kid a lot but we had Ryan Kesler ranked ahead of him. To be a forward in our league, you need proper levels of hostility, belligerence, and speed, and he's got those things. And, he's quite a bit bigger."

Even Kesler was surprised when the Canucks called his name, certain that they were going to take the nepotistic route.

"I thought they'd take Tambellini," said Kesler shortly after he was picked. "But this is a great feeling. All the pressure is lifted off you when you hear your name called."

Years later, Tambellini did end up in Vancouver with the Canucks. After signing a one-year contract as a free agent, Tambellini was part of the dominant 2010–11 Canucks that made a run to the Stanley Cup Final. At times, Tambellini would play on Kesler's wing on the second line. By then, Kesler was one of the best centres in the entire NHL.

THERE WAS AN added benefit to drafting Kesler in 2003—he already had chemistry with another of the Canucks' top prospects, R.J. Umberger.

The Canucks selected Umberger 16th overall in the 2001 NHL Entry Draft. They were thrilled to get him that late in the first round, as they had him ranked ninth overall. Just like Kesler, he was drafted out of Ohio State University and, just like Kesler, Umberger was compared to Trevor Linden.

"He's similar in that he's got size and he hits," said Burke. "He's not quite as tall as Trevor but that's the name that came up repeatedly in the process."

Umberger racked up points with Ohio State in his draft year, putting up 37 points in 32 games, though his World Junior performance wasn't quite as eye-catching as Kesler's. Heading into the 2001 draft, scouts loved everything about Umberger, as he combined exceptional skill with excellent skating and a projectable 6'2" frame.

The question mark for Umberger was his consistency.

"When the package comes together, it's scary—he's that good," said John Markell, his head coach at Ohio State, to MacIntyre. "It's how to get that strength and drive out of him each and every game."

"He is very good when he focuses," added Markell. "When he is on his game, he could be a second-line centre on most NHL clubs."

Umberger was aware of the criticism—not surprising given his own head coach was voicing it—and was intent on proving himself.

"I just want to keep seeing consistency from myself," said Umberger. "Everybody knows I have the offensive ability, but I also need to drive to the net, not just play on the perimeter the way I always have. I have this size and I need to use it more."

When Kesler joined Ohio State for the 2002–03 season, he and Umberger became linemates on the Buckeyes, with the older Umberger taking Kesler under his wing. While on the top line with Kesler, Umberger had a massive year, hitting career highs with 26 goals and 27 assists in 43 games to lead the Buckeyes in scoring. He was even a finalist for the Hobey Baker as the top college player of the year.

The potential of Kesler and Umberger playing on the same line for the Canucks in the future was a tempting proposition, as their combination of size and speed seemed like a great fit. It was expected that Umberger would sign ahead of training camp in 2003, joining the Canucks for the 2003–04 season.

But then Kesler signed with the Canucks first.

JOHN MARKELL ALSO coached Kesler at Ohio State and he claimed that Kesler was closer to NHL-ready than Umberger, with a well-developed two-way game that would more easily translate than Umberger's flashier offensive game.

"People tell me I play more of a pro game," Kesler said to MacIntyre at his first training camp. "I looked at R.J. Umberger. I didn't want to be [at Ohio State] three years. I wanted to start my pro career now."

That eagerness to jump to professional hockey might have led to him taking a lower contract offer than other recent first-round picks, with a signing bonus of around $825,000. This potentially hurt the bargaining position of Umberger as he stepped away from Ohio State to negotiate his first contract. He and his agent, Brian Lawton, made it clear—as a higher draft pick, a Hobey Baker finalist, and with more offensive upside, Umberger deserved a higher signing bonus and a bigger contract than Kesler.

Brian Burke disagreed. The signing bonus he offered Umberger was reported at the time as around $775,000, below that of Kesler and well below what Lawton and Umberger had asked for. According to Lawton, if he accepted Burke's offer, Umberger would have been the third lowest-paid player of the 27 that had thus far been signed from the first round of the 2001 draft.

"It's an embarrassment and to top it off with the fact the offer is less than the guy they just signed who was drafted 23rd in his draft, it makes no sense," said Lawton to Brad Ziemer of the *Sun*.

It was neither the first nor the last time Lawton would reference Kesler and his contract to the media. He used Kesler's deal to negotiate in public, perhaps hoping that fans would call for Burke to soften his stance and pay Umberger what he felt he was owed.

"They were teammates at Ohio State and Ryan is a terrific player, but for them to offer a significant amount less is wrong," said Lawton. "I look at it like this: one guy had 53 points and was an All-American."

Of course, Umberger put up 53 points when he was 20 years old, while Kesler was only 18 in his freshman year at Ohio State. In addition, the 2001 draft was not as deep as 2003, so it didn't mean much that Umberger was taken seven picks higher than Kesler. The Canucks felt strongly that Kesler was the better prospect.

Seeing and hearing his name repeatedly brought up by Lawton and Umberger rubbed Kesler the wrong way. To Kesler, it wasn't just business, it was personal. In his mind, they were calling him a lesser player. It felt condescending.

"We got along as linemates at Ohio State, everything was fine until I signed and then I think there was a little jealousy from his part," said Kesler to Ziemer. "He and his agent going on radio stations and talking down to me. I just didn't think that was very classy."

"I just don't understand why he'd do something like that," he added.

That same stubborn personality that made Kesler call his mom from a pay phone after his dad kicked him off the ice is likely a big reason why he took the comments of Umberger and Lawton personally. That animosity simmered under the surface for years, boiling over almost every time they faced each other.

Maybe the animosity would have been smoothed over if Umberger had signed with the Canucks and the two had become teammates—something that could have been hashed out in the locker room during training camp—but Umberger never signed.

Ultimately, the Canucks and Umberger were about $200,000 apart in contract negotiations. That doesn't seem like an insurmountable sum, but it was a representation of the miles apart the two sides were in how they saw Umberger's value. To the Canucks, Umberger wasn't a high-end, top-tier prospect the way Kesler was.

Umberger sat out the entire 2003–04 season and would have become a free agent in the 2004 off-season. Before that happened, the Canucks took what they could get on the trade market for the disgruntled forward, trading him to the New York Rangers for Martin Rucinsky.

It was a trade deadline rental—Rucinsky played 13 regular season games and seven playoff games for the Canucks, but that's 20 more games than Umberger ever would have played for the team that drafted him.

Umberger went on to have a solid NHL career, scoring 20-plus goals in five of his 11 seasons. His 392 career points rank 13th among players taken in the 2001 draft. Kesler, on the other hand, put up 573 points in 1,001 NHL games—it seems the Canucks were right about who was the better prospect.

IRONICALLY, KESLER WAS nearly reunited with Umberger just a few years later when he signed an offer sheet in 2006—the first signed by a restricted free agent in the NHL in nearly nine years. The offer sheet came from Bobby Clarke and the Philadelphia Flyers, where Umberger landed after refusing to sign with the Rangers.

The Canucks matched the offer sheet, however, even though it meant giving Kesler a much bigger raise than they originally intended. It's a good thing they did—in the following years, Kesler proved that he was a lot more than the two-way, third-line centre that analysts had projected him to be. Trevor Linden, who re-signed with the Canucks after stints with the New York Islanders and Montreal Canadiens, saw the potential right from Kesler's first training camp. Kesler stuck to Linden like glue at that camp, absorbing everything he could from the former Canucks captain.

"I'll never forget watching the draft," said Linden to MacIntyre. "When we drafted him, the commentator said he was a mature kid who played solid defensively and had average skills. That player is different than the one I see. I see the way he skates. He's got a good shot, good puck sense. They made him out to be a checker, but I see a much bigger upside than that."

Linden was right. As Daniel and Henrik Sedin stepped to the forefront of the Canucks, Kesler was exactly the right centre to anchor the second line behind them. Where the Sedins were calm and soft-spoken, Kesler was fiery and passionate. The Sedins were tough in their own way but played more of a finesse game, while Kesler provided a hard-checking, gritty two-way game.

That one-two punch at even strength was the foundation of the Canucks' attack as they won back-to-back Presidents' Trophies in 2011 and 2012 and went on a run to the 2011 Stanley Cup Final. Their two styles merged on the power play—Kesler provided the speed on zone entries and the gritty net-front presence, with the quick hands to finish off the chances created by the Sedins.

It all came together in the 2010–11 season, when Kesler scored a career-high 41 goals—15 of them on the power play—and was awarded the Selke Trophy as the best defensive forward in the NHL.

Not bad for a guy who wasn't supposed to be a top-six forward.

KEVIN BIEKSA'S KNOCKOUT BLOW

One of the most vital pieces of the dominant 2010–11 Canucks was Kevin Bieksa, a right-shot defenceman who joined with Dan Hamhuis to form the team's formidable shutdown pairing behind the top pair of Alex Edler and Christian Ehrhoff. Getting a top-four, right-shot defenceman in the fifth round of the 2001 draft was quite the find for Brian Burke and his scouting staff, especially since Bieksa was already 20 years old and in his third year of draft eligibility.

In his first two years of draft eligibility, Bieksa played for the Burlington Cougars in the Ontario Provincial Junior A Hockey League, doing a little bit of everything—putting up points, shutting down top forwards, and playing a physical game—but he didn't stand out enough to attract the attention of NHL scouts.

College hockey scouts, on the other hand, were all over Bieksa, as he attracted interest from multiple schools and received scholarship offers from St. Lawrence University,

Niagara University, University of Massachusetts Lowell, and Bowling Green University. He chose Bowling Green.

"I wanted a fallback plan," said Bieksa to the NHL's Mike Morreale. "I didn't want to put all my eggs all in one basket, so I thought I'd go to school and get an education. The college route was picking up then and if I could make the NHL out of college, great, and if not, I had a degree to fall back on. I'd always been a pretty good student, so I think I made the right decision."

Bieksa's general manager with the Cougars, Ralph Judge, was effusive with his praise for Bieksa when he committed to Bowling Green.

"He's very good under pressure. He doesn't get flustered... he's very, very cool and very, very quick when he's breaking the puck out of his end. He makes smart plays," said Judge to Kevin Gordon of the *Sentinel-Tribune*. "He's not a dirty player but he plays the game with an edge. He knows how to be physical without taking bad penalties."

Bieksa didn't blow the roof off in his freshman season at Bowling Green, scoring just 13 points in 35 games, but he was seen as one of the team's top defencemen for his solid shutdown game and ability to play in all situations. That attracted the attention of Canucks scout Dave Morrison, who Bieksa remembers interviewing him at a Shoeless Joe's in Burlington, Ontario.

It was only Morrison's second year as a scout for the Canucks after retiring from his playing career that included eight games with the Canucks. Bieksa provided an early feather in the cap of his career, which has taken him to a role as the Toronto Maple Leafs director of player personnel.

Despite knowing the Canucks were interested, Bieksa decided not to travel to Florida for the 2001 draft. For him, getting drafted wasn't the goal.

"My dad was going to be in Sunrise for work and asked me to come in case I got drafted," said Bieksa. "I refused and went camping with my three best pals at Six Flags Darien Lake in Buffalo for the weekend. I told him, 'It was never my dream to get drafted but instead to be a good player in the NHL.' I stand by that comment."

So, Bieksa didn't find out that the Canucks had drafted him in the fifth round until the following morning.

"I got a call Sunday morning telling me I was drafted [in the] fifth round to Vancouver and we celebrated with a beer shotgun at 9 AM and off we went to ride roller coasters all day," said Bieksa.

Twenty-year-old players drafted in the fifth round don't typically make the NHL, so there was very little hype for Bieksa, except from Brian Burke, who could never resist a good name-drop.

"Not to say he's going to be like [Chris] Chelios, but he hits a lot and finishes his checks," said Burke.

In many ways, Bieksa was ahead of his time. Bieksa didn't quite fit the mold of the big, shutdown defenceman that dominated the clutch-and-grab era when he was drafted, and he wasn't as smooth as the flashy offensive defencemen of that era either. By the time he reached the NHL, however, the rules had changed to crack down on hooking and holding. Suddenly his brand of calm, mobile, intelligent, yet still physical defending was far more effective than that of the lead-footed defencemen of the past.

The Canucks knew that Bieksa was a long-term project, as he was committed to finishing his schooling. He spent the full four years at Bowling Green, earning his degree in finance with a 3.42 GPA. In his senior year, he was an honourable mention to the All-CCHA Team and was his coaches' choice as his team's best player.

Still, the Canucks were unsure about signing Bieksa after he left Bowling Green. If they didn't sign him, Bieksa would become an unrestricted free agent in the off-season. To earn a contract, Bieksa would have to impress the Canucks in his brief audition with the Manitoba Moose, their AHL affiliate.

"I didn't know if we wanted to sign him, so we sent him to Manitoba on an ATO [amateur tryout]," said Burke on an episode of Sportsnet's "Hey Burkie" series. "We liked his heart, we liked his try, we liked his brains—we weren't sure about his feet. The skating was suspect."

Bieksa had a strangely upright skating stride that always stood out on the ice, as if he was constantly concerned about his posture, like an uptight butler.

"The issue he had coming in, his agility laterally was kind of—we weren't quite sure, as a midsize guy, how effective he was going to be in closing plays off the rush, and things like that, quickly," said Marc Crawford to Sportsnet. "We knew that he had the physicality and the junkyard dog mentality to him. But we needed him to handle rushes better and those types of things."

Before Bieksa could ever prove himself in a game with the Moose, however, a run-in with one of his teammates in an Earl's parking lot changed the trajectory of his career.

As Bieksa remembers it, he was playing with the straw in his rum and coke when he accidentally flicked an ice cube out of his glass. The ice cube hit Kirill Koltsov, the Canucks' second-round pick in 2002. Thinking it was intentional, Koltsov got in Bieksa's face. At first, Bieksa was apologetic, but when Koltsov wouldn't back down, Bieksa was blunt.

"I said, 'Sit down before I knock you out,' and that's when Fedor put his hand on my shirt," said Bieksa.

Fedor Fedorov was 6'4", 230 pounds—bigger than his older brother Sergei and far bigger than Bieksa—and he was quick to step in for his fellow Russian. He wasn't going to let the rookie Bieksa get away with talking tough without backing it up. Fedorov made it simple: let's take this outside.

Taking in the scene was future NHL head coach Dallas Eakins, captain of the Moose at the time in the final year of his playing career. As Fedorov went out to the parking lot, followed shortly by Bieksa, Eakins decided the best course of action was to stay inside out of the cold and finish his wine.

"When I went out there, I thought I was fighting just Fedor, but there were two Russians," said Bieksa on The Fan 590. "When we first squared off, I ate a couple of leg kicks from Kirill from the side while I was fighting Fedor."

Fedorov managed to tag Bieksa once, giving him a shiner, but then Bieksa laid out the big Russian with a single punch to end the fight. Then it hit him as hard as he had just hit Fedorov—he had gotten in a fight with a teammate when he didn't have a contract and had yet to even play a game with his new team.

"I was a little bit ashamed. I was worried," said Bieksa. "I didn't know what I was getting into. I didn't know who this guy was—I knew his brother was a pretty good hockey player but I didn't know anything about him."

Bieksa called his dad, saying, "Dad, I messed up. They're going to send me home." Instead, Burke heard the story and immediately signed Bieksa to an entry-level contract.

As for Fedorov and Koltsov, Bieksa quickly made amends. In fact, Koltsov only enhanced Bieksa's reputation as a tough guy.

"Fedor and I went out to lunch a couple of days later and Koltsov and I were really good," said Bieksa. "People would go up to Koltsy, like, 'Hey Koltsy, what really happened out there,' and he goes, 'He beat us both up.'

"Which is funny, because I never touched Koltsov. Maybe I beat his foot up because he kept kicking me in the leg, but I never touched him."

Bieksa's toughness got him a contract, but his skill is what caught the Canucks off guard as he developed. He had three 40-plus point seasons with the Canucks, providing far more offence than expected.

His job on the 2010–11 team, however, was to prevent offence for his opponents and he excelled at it alongside Hamhuis. Among the 123 defencemen who played at least 1,000 minutes at five-on-five that season, Bieksa had the seventh-lowest rate of goals against despite being matched up against the best players in the NHL and starting the vast majority of his shifts in the defensive zone.

In Game 5 of the Western Conference Final against the San Jose Sharks, Bieksa provided the knockout blow like he did to Fedorov. When the puck hit a stanchion along the glass and deflected into the middle of the ice, only a handful of players saw it and only Bieksa could get to it, slapping the bouncing puck into the net to send the Canucks to the Stanley Cup Final.

11

ALEX EDLER
AND THE LUCKY
PHONE CALL

E VERY HOCKEY SCOUT dreams of finding a hidden gem, something to make the long hours of travel and the nights spent alone in a freezing hockey rink in the middle of nowhere worth it: the chance to find that one player that no one else knows about.

That was a lot easier in the early years of the NHL draft. A limited number of NHL games were televised, let alone junior hockey or European league games—you had to be at a game in person to see a prospect play. NHL teams could gain a competitive advantage simply by sending scouts to games that no one else was watching. The Detroit Red Wings built a dynasty with the bold strategy of employing a European scout, leading to late-round finds like Tomas

Holmstrom, Vladimir Konstantinov, Henrik Zetterberg, and Pavel Datsyuk.

Other NHL teams would, at most, send a North American-based scout on European scouting trips or hope to catch a glimpse of a future star at an international tournament. The Canucks were more active in Europe than a lot of teams in the '80s and '90s but that largely just meant a scout like Mike Penny would make more frequent trips to Europe than most other teams.

By 2004, finding a hidden gem was much harder. Every NHL team had some sort of scouting presence in Europe and teams had more access to video from a greater variety of leagues. A scout was rarely alone in a hockey rink in the middle of nowhere—he was frequently joined by a handful of other scouts, all watching the same players.

"It's worldwide now," said Nashville Predators general manager David Poile, who has been in NHL front offices since 1972 and has seen how the draft has changed over the years. "I can't remember the exact number of scouts Vancouver had in 1970, but I think it was maybe three, and they were all located in Canada. There was no video, no analytics, and travel was limited.

"In the old days, there could easily have been a player that no one else would have seen, based on the depth of your scouting, the bird dogs that you might have had working for you, the tips you might have had from coaches. Now we have scouts everywhere—there's no excuse for not seeing a player because you can watch as much video as you want."

Unlike the early days of the draft, it seemed impossible to find a prospect that other teams didn't know about in the new millennium.

But that's what makes Alex Edler such a unique story.

THERE WERE 161 European skaters ranked by NHL Central Scouting for the 2004 draft. Alex Edler wasn't one of them.

Central Scouting didn't seem to know Edler even existed, and for good reason. He had never played at a single international tournament and didn't play in the system of one of the top teams in Sweden. Instead, he was just a guy playing for his local team.

Edler was born in Östersund, Sweden, in the province of Jämtland, far north and inland from the hotbeds of hockey in Sweden. Jämtland is the second-largest province in Sweden but also one of the least populated—only the island of Gotland has fewer people—and Östersund is the province's only city.

Jämtland is well known for its outdoor sports, particularly cross-country skiing, but hockey still has its place in the sporting landscape.

"It is a big cross-country and biathlon and skiing in general area, but I never did that other than we always did it in school. It was part of the P.E. program," said Edler. "I played soccer, I did some track and field—that's what my older siblings did and my family was into those things. It was around 15 that I [began playing] hockey only."

Edler remembers the transition from multiple sports to one sport happening naturally. His older sister played high-level soccer—"She played for many years and won a bunch of Swedish championships"—and his older brother played hockey but mainly focused on track and field. Perhaps hockey was Edler's chance to do his own thing apart from his siblings, though he joked that he simply started getting too slow for soccer.

That wasn't an issue on the ice, where Edler powered around the rink with strong strides for the youth hockey

program of Östersunds IK, which became Jämtlands HF as
he entered his draft year in the 2003–04 season. Not that the
NHL entry draft was at all on Edler's mind.

"They didn't really show much NHL on TV when I grew
up," said Edler. "You saw some highlights once in a while but
they mainly showed the Swedish Elite League. That was the
dream at the time, or the national team. And then the NHL
too, but it felt far away."

At 17, Edler already had the size and the skill to play up
with Jämtlands' men's team, but that still didn't attract much
attention.

"It was a great youth team and organization but the men's
team was never in a high division," said Edler. "You didn't
have a lot of eyes on you up there."

Jämtlands played in Division 1, which was, despite
the name, the third tier of men's professional hockey in
Sweden. Now known as the Hockeyettan, it sits below the
HockeyAllsvenskan and the Swedish Hockey League, then
known as the Elitserien—the Swedish Elite League.

In other words, Edler was playing in the middle of
nowhere for a third-division team in a league that didn't get
scouted. There was seemingly no reason for an NHL team to
scout Sweden's third division, as the odds of finding NHL
talent were low.

With that in mind, Canucks scout Thomas Gradin must
have been wondering what in the world he was doing taking
a four-and-a-half-hour train ride into the proverbial middle
of nowhere based purely on a tip.

GRADIN NEVER WOULD have made that trip if not for one fateful phone call. That one phone call cost the Detroit Red Wings the chance to draft Edler without anyone else knowing about him. It was all because of a rare mistake by the Red Wings' European super scout Håkan Andersson.

Andersson played hockey as a teenager but a knee injury ended his hockey dreams and he became a fishing guide in Sweden. He would later quip, "I was a better fishing guide than scout."

If that's true, Andersson must have been a brilliant fishing guide. Andersson was recommended to the Red Wings by his friend Christer Rockström—the same scout who had urged the Red Wings to draft Pavel Bure in 1989—to replace him as their European scout when he took a job with the New York Rangers. Andersson initially split his time between running fishing tours and scouting hockey, but it didn't take long for the Red Wings to ask him to go full-time.

Andersson's scouting résumé sounds too good to be true. The first time he was given a chance to use a draft pick by the Red Wings, he selected Tomas Holmström in the 10th round in 1994. Then he was responsible for the Red Wings drafting Pavel Datsyuk in the sixth round in 1998. A year later, he snagged Henrik Zetterberg in the seventh round.

At the 2002 draft, the Red Wings selected a slew of players scouted by Andersson: Jiri Hudler in the second round, Valtteri Filppula in the third round, and Jonathan Ericsson with the final pick of the draft in the ninth round. In 2004, he grabbed Johan Franzen in the third round. Most of the players he scouted were drafted outside of the first round by the Red Wings, but he also influenced a key first-round pick: Niklas Kronwall, taken 29th overall in 2000.

The Red Wings' 2008 Cup-winning roster was built on players scouted by Andersson. Their top five leading scorers in the playoffs—Zetterberg, Datsyuk, Franzen, Kronwall, and Hudler—were all Andersson picks.

As other NHL teams caught on to the Red Wings' competitive advantage of employing at least one European scout, those hidden gems became harder to find. But Andersson thought he had found another diamond in the rough playing in third-division hockey in the interior of Sweden, where no one else was looking.

Andersson was tipped off by a fishing buddy who lived in the area. The friend had previously tagged along at a hockey tournament and Andersson gave him a few players to watch and asked him to do some scouting reports.

"I realized he had some feel for it, he wasn't completely off," said Andersson on the Elite Prospects Podcast. So, when this friend called him about a young defenceman playing for the local team, Andersson asked him for a proper scouting report.

"He came back two games later and said, 'The kid is good. He can skate, he can handle a puck. He doesn't play that physical, but he just skates out to the forward and just takes the puck from them,'" recalled Andersson.

The next step was to find out how old "the kid" was. When Andersson heard Edler was born in 1986, making him eligible for the 2004 draft, he knew he had to see him play. But there wasn't much time left: it was already January and the Division 1 season only went through February.

"I go up to watch him play and realize I like the kid," said Andersson. "Now I'm back scratching my head. Where does he fit in? They only have a few games to go. What do I do now? I've got to see him again."

Andersson's philosophy was to never under-scout or over-scout a player. Watching a player just once wasn't enough to get a full view of a player's capabilities; watching a prospect too many times led to nitpicking his weaknesses. Andersson felt he needed at least one more viewing of Edler to be sure that he was as good as he believed after that first game.

The trouble was, it was a long journey to Jämtland and he didn't want to waste his time on such a long trip if Edler wasn't going to be in the lineup. He had to be sure.

So, he made a phone call.

"HERE'S MY MISTAKE," said Andersson. "I call the coach and I say my name is Andersson, I'm a scout, I'm going to drive almost seven hours to see you guys play. I just want to check if he's playing. And he said, 'Yeah, he's playing.'"

Andersson got the confirmation he was looking for but the head coach got an intriguing new piece of information: an NHL scout was interested in Edler. The coach, Roger Forsberg, happened to have a friend who was a hockey agent and connected him with Edler after Andersson's second trip to watch him play.

Knowing that an NHL scout was interested in him changed everything for Edler.

"When there was interest from NHL scouts, I started to think, 'Whoa, this could actually happen.' Maybe I can actually do this for a living," said Edler. "But it didn't happen until I was 17 that I realized hockey was something that I could do as a career."

Edler's agent wanted to drum up attention for his new client—it wouldn't do if just one team knew he existed.

"He sends out an email and said, 'This kid is playing, I represent him, he only has one more game to go.'" said Andersson. "We're now into late February. They're not going to make the playoffs and they're not going to have to qualify to stay. Their season is just over."

It's a moment that Andersson has been kicking himself about for years.

"The problem was I fucked up," said Andersson. "I should have asked my friend to find out if he was playing. He knew some people on the team and everything. That was just stupidity by me. If I hadn't made that call, nobody would have known about him.

"Who would have known that that coach was friends with an agent?"

Of all the NHL scouts contacted by Edler's agent, just one made the trip to Östersund: Thomas Gradin.

"Those two were the only people that knew about me," confirmed Edler about Andersson and Gradin.

It's not surprising that no other scouts made the trek. There might have been some doubt that a great prospect was hiding, completely unscouted, in Division 1. Also, according to Gradin, Edler's team was expected to go on a playoff run that would see them play games closer to Stockholm, making scouting him a little more convenient. But Gradin didn't care about convenience.

"My business is kind of the same as yours; if you hear a scoop, you want to check it out," said Gradin to Iain MacIntyre of the *Vancouver Sun*. "But I was not that optimistic. I took the train up to this town, a four-and-a-half-hour trip. I didn't have high expectations. Most of the time you hear these things and it doesn't turn out to be anything. Once in a while, it's something."

This was something. Gradin saw Edler just once and immediately grasped what Andersson and his fishing buddy had seen: Edler was a legitimate prospect, well worth a selection in the NHL draft. In addition, Jämtlands HF lost the game, which meant no playoff run and no more opportunities for NHL scouts to see Edler.

"Nobody thought his team would lose but it did," said Gradin. "Obviously, Alex was a prospect—very big and could skate and make plays with the puck."

Gradin didn't need to see Edler again. What he saw in that one game was enough to convince him that the Canucks had to have him and he couldn't wait to let the rest of the scouting staff know.

"He was so excited, he called me," said Ron Delorme, the Canucks' chief scout. "It was purely a gut feeling Thomas had."

Gradin had lucked into seeing Edler play but now he had to convince general manager Dave Nonis that he was worth taking in the draft—not just a flyer in the sixth or seventh round, but in the top half of the draft. It's unusual to draft a player in any round based on just one viewing, but to use a draft pick in the first three rounds on a prospect that only one scout had seen just once? That's unheard of.

"It's not the way we go about trying to draft guys," said Gradin. "You really want to see the guy more than one time. We had a lot of talk about that."

Fortunately, Gradin had earned a great deal of trust in his time as a Canucks scout. He was the man who convinced Brian Burke that he needed to draft Daniel and Henrik Sedin in 1999 and had a major influence on the Canucks picking Mattias Öhlund in 1994.

"If anyone knows Thomas, he's a pretty opinionated man," said Nonis. "He lets himself be known and if he feels strongly about something, there's usually a good reason for it. We trusted his judgment."

SINCE NO OTHER Canucks scouts had seen Edler play, they had no way of comparing him to the rest of their draft list. To simplify things, they never bothered ranking him at all.

"Edler was on a different list," said Nonis to MacIntyre. "He was on Thomas' list."

The only thing the Canucks had to worry about was the Red Wings. Both teams knew that they were the only ones who had seen Edler, so all that mattered was picking him before the other team did.

The Red Wings, in their perennial pursuit of the Stanley Cup, had traded away both their first- and their second-round picks, so they didn't have a selection until 97th overall in the third round. The Canucks had their first-round pick but then didn't pick again until the fourth round. They had traded away their second-round pick to the Pittsburgh Penguins for goaltender Johan Hedberg and their third-round pick to the Columbus Blue Jackets for Geoff Sanderson.

Nonis wasn't going to use his first-round pick on Gradin's gut feeling, but Gradin was insistent that the Canucks had to take Edler before the Red Wings picked in the third round. He was right to do so.

Just as Gradin was deciding with Nonis when to pick Edler, Andersson was having the same discussion with Red Wings assistant general manager Jim Nill, the former tough guy who had helped the Canucks scrap their way to the 1982 Stanley Cup Final.

"Jim says to me, 'Where do you think he fits?' Kind of third round for me," recalled Andersson. Nill decided he was willing to use the Red Wings' third-round pick, their first in the draft, on Edler, based solely on Andersson's word.

In order for the Canucks to get Edler, they couldn't wait until their own pick in the fourth round. Their own third-round pick would have been 93rd overall, four picks ahead of Detroit's, if they hadn't traded it for 20 games of Geoff Sanderson. Instead, the Canucks needed to trade up to get ahead of the Red Wings.

Nonis found a willing trade partner in Dallas Stars general manager Doug Armstrong, who traded down multiple times on the draft floor that day in Raleigh. Armstrong started the day with the 20th overall pick in the first round before trading down twice, winding up with the 28th overall pick, as well as two extra picks in the second round, and two more in the third round.

It turned out that Armstrong didn't actually want to use either of those additional third-round picks. What he really wanted was to swap them for picks in the 2005 draft, which was expected to be deeper. So, he first traded the 88th-overall pick to the Washington Capitals for their third-round pick in 2005, then made the same deal with the Canucks for the 91st-overall pick.

"As soon as the Canucks got that pick, I told everyone at our table I'd eat everything on it if Vancouver didn't take Edler," said Andersson, who could only sit there and rue the phone call he had made. It wasn't all bad for Andersson and the Red Wings, as he advised they take another hidden gem at 97th overall, Johan Franzen. But Andersson knew if he had never made that phone call, the Red Wings could have taken Edler with their final pick in the ninth round, with none the wiser.

THE 91ST PICK the Canucks used on Edler had its own story connecting it to one of the great villains in Canucks history: Mark Messier.

The pick originally belonged to the Sharks, but it wasn't one of the picks normally granted to every NHL team. Instead, the Sharks had acquired the pick by exploiting a strange quirk in the NHL's Collective Bargaining Agreement (CBA).

The CBA introduced after the 1994–95 NHL lockout introduced a new type of free agent to the NHL landscape: the Compensatory Free Agent (CFA). Much like an Unrestricted Free Agent (UFA), a CFA could sign with any NHL team, but his previous team received compensation in the form of a draft pick. The better the player signed by another team, the higher the draft pick received as compensation.

There was one twist: teams that lost one CFA but then signed another CFA in free agency who was as good or better than the one they lost did not receive compensation. The quality of each CFA was calculated by assigning each player points based on factors like age, salary, NHL awards, Stanley Cup wins, and even if he was a captain.

This compensatory draft pick didn't come from the team that signed the CFA. It was created *ex nihilo*, right out of thin air—an extra pick that didn't exist before.

The Canucks received one of these compensatory picks when Jyrki Lumme signed with the Phoenix Coyotes in 1998 and used it as part of their trade with the Tampa Bay Lightning for the first-overall pick in the 1999 draft, paving the way for the Canucks to get both Sedins.

Eventually, NHL teams figured out a loophole: the CBA didn't say that a CFA had to play games for the team that lost him. The Nashville Predators were the first to exploit this loophole, taking pending free agents Mike Richter and Uwe Krupp in the 1998 expansion draft with no intentions of re-signing either of them. Instead, they just wanted the compensatory draft picks that they would get when both players signed elsewhere.

In 2002, multiple pending free agents were traded to teams that didn't intend to re-sign them, granting them bonus draft picks out of the ether. Teams were willing to trade their pending free agents if they knew they would be active in free agency and wouldn't be able to claim the compensatory picks. Trading the pending free agent gave them an extra asset, typically a late-round pick, for free.

Curtis Joseph, Ed Belfour, Theo Fleury, Tie Domi, and Richter were traded this way, granting teams bonus draft picks in the 2003 draft. But the most absurd CFA trades would affect the 2004 draft.

First, the New York Rangers traded Brian Leetch to the Edmonton Oilers for Jussi Markanen and a fourth-round pick. The Oilers, as planned, didn't re-sign Leetch and received a second-round pick, 48th overall, as compensation. The Rangers then signed Leetch in free agency and, even more absurdly, ended up trading for the compensatory 48th-overall pick from the Oilers in a separate trade.

They did the exact same thing a few days later with Mark Messier, who the Rangers traded to the Sharks for a fourth-round pick. The Sharks "failed" to re-sign Messier, and received a third-round pick, 91st overall, as compensation. Then, Messier returned to the Rangers on a one-year deal in free agency to close out his career.

The Rangers added two fourth-round picks and a backup goaltender for absolutely no cost, as they re-signed both Leetch and Messier. Meanwhile, the Oilers and Sharks upgraded fourth-round picks to second or third-round picks for essentially no cost as well.

Similar deals didn't happen again, likely because the NHL cracked down in light of how overtly fraudulent the Leetch and Messier trades were. Free agency was overhauled in the 2005 CBA that came out of the 2004–05 NHL lockout, removing CFAs entirely.

Without the Rangers' sham Messier trade, the Sharks never would have received the 91st-overall pick in 2004 and never would have traded it to the Stars, making it available for the Canucks to acquire to select Edler.

In other words, without Mark Messier, the Canucks wouldn't have Alex Edler.

IT'S PRETTY UNUSUAL for a player not ranked by Central Scouting to make the trip to the NHL Draft, particularly if that means flying from Sweden to North Carolina. But Edler was there, making his way out of the stands to pull on a Canucks jersey after he was selected 91st overall.

"My agent just told me that there's great interest from Vancouver and Detroit and I think they even want to draft you the first day, so I went to the draft. I didn't really know when I was gonna get picked," said Edler. When the Canucks traded up in the draft to pick him, it didn't even click just how badly they wanted him. "I still was clueless."

The Canucks, however, were thrilled. Nonis and Delorme happily crowed about the "secret Swede."

"He's a player I think very few people saw," said Nonis. "He played in an obscure place, it's quite far north, but he's playing in MoDo next year. We're pretty happy to get him. Smooth skater, big guy. He needs some time for sure, but in terms of raw skill, he's got quite a bit of it."

Gradin and Nonis eventually referred to finding Edler in a "glorified beer league," which became part of Canucks lore. It's a label that raises Edler's hackles—as much as the staid Swede's hackles can be raised—because he has tremendous respect for his former teammates and other players in that league.

"It definitely is unfair," said Edler. "It was the third league in Sweden but, to be honest with you, the people that play in that league, they probably work harder than everyone else because they practice the same but they also have to work on the side. It's a grind.

"It was crazy because I went to school back then, but the other guys were all working. Some were working from seven to four and then they came to practice and on bus rides to away games."

That hard work paid off. In 2022, the club, once again named Östersunds IK, was promoted to the HockeyAllsvenskan, the second tier of men's hockey in Sweden. The man responsible, head coach Kjell-Åke Andersson, was one of Edler's early mentors in his hockey career.

"Our captain is now the head coach of the team and now they're actually higher up," said Edler. "He was a great captain and he's done everything for that organization. I'm very happy for him and thankful for what he did for me early on."

THE NEXT STEP for Edler was to leave Division 1 and his local team behind. Edler was sent to MoDo, where the Sedins and Markus Näslund honed their craft, then moved to North America to play a year with the Kelowna Rockets in the WHL.

"That was all Vancouver," said Edler. "They had something to do with me going to MoDo to finish my last year of school—kind of a hockey high school program—and then they asked me if I wanted to come over and play junior hockey. It wasn't an easy decision but there were a lot of other defencemen the same age as me in MoDo that were ahead of me to make the pro team, so I figured it was a good opportunity.

"I'm very happy I did, because I think I developed that year in Kelowna to get ready for the style over here."

The development path worked for Edler, who didn't even spend a full season in the AHL after finishing his junior career in Kelowna. He quickly found himself in the NHL at the age of 20 and continued his upward trajectory until he was on the Canucks' top pairing, setting new franchise records.

When his time with the Canucks ended, Edler was the all-time leader among Canucks defencemen in goals, assists, points, power play points, shots on goal, hits, and blocked shots. He did everything for the Canucks, playing in every situation, whether they needed a defensive stop or a goal.

Daniel and Henrik Sedin went out of their way to heap laurels on Edler after their final game in Vancouver, suggesting he was the unofficial "third Sedin" rather than all of the forwards they lined up with over the years.

"There's few players that meant more than him," said Henrik. "We talk about Näslund and Mattias and Trevor, but he's the guy that we played with for a lot of years.... He gets a lot of criticism, but he's a heart-and-soul guy and he shows up every game and he does the little things all the time. He's been our best defenceman every year. There's no question about it."

Edler set franchise records while wearing the No. 23, chosen in honour of the scout who drafted him, Thomas Gradin, who wore No. 23 when he played for the Canucks.

THE STORY OF how the Canucks drafted Edler is a perfect illustration of how the NHL draft isn't just about luck; it's not just about hard work; it's not just about scouting skill; and it's not just about making bold moves. It's all of the above.

Yes, Gradin was lucky that Andersson made that phone call, but he also put in the hard work of making the trek to Östersund to see Edler play. He had the scouting skill to recognize Edler's potential in just one viewing and the confidence to assert that the Canucks had to get him. And then Nonis made the bold move of trading up in the draft to select Edler, trusting in Gradin's gut feeling.

All of those aspects of the draft had to work in unison for the Canucks to get Edler, and the same is true of other draft picks; it takes luck, hard work, skill, and boldness to get a great player.

MATTIAS ÖHLUND

A couple of the franchise records broken by Alex Edler belonged to his mentor, Mattias Öhlund, who perhaps should have been the greatest defenceman in Canucks history. If you ask some Canucks fans, he still is.

Öhlund established himself as a top prospect for the 1994 NHL Entry Draft with fantastic performances in international competition for Sweden, complementing a strong season playing against men in Division 1—then the second tier of men's hockey in Sweden. Öhlund was named the best defenceman at the Under-18 European Junior Championships and held his own against older competition at the World Juniors, winning a silver medal.

The Canucks had Öhlund high on their draft board, partly on the recommendation of Thomas Gradin, who had just joined the Canucks as a scout a year earlier. Gradin had seen Öhlund excel with Piteå HC in Division 1 and felt he was even better with his club team than he was in international play. Gradin convinced general manager Pat Quinn that Öhlund could be a top-tier defenceman.

Quinn said he felt the quality of the 1994 draft dropped after the top seven prospects on their board, but they had Öhlund ranked in that top seven. When he slid to them at 13th overall, he and Gradin were chuffed.

"A lot of people are surprised he lasted so long," said Gradin. "I think he was rated higher than 13th by everybody."

"We had him rated a lot higher than that," confirmed Mike Penny. "I'd seen Mattias Öhlund many times, he was playing for [former Canucks defenceman] Lars Lindgren in Piteå."

Other teams soon grew jealous of the Canucks' young defenceman, as evidenced by Swedish legend Kent Nilsson, who was then scouting for the Edmonton Oilers.

"He's unbelievable," said Nilsson to Tony Gallagher of *The Province*. "He's big, great with the puck, he can shoot, and he's not afraid to hit guys. We wanted him, but everyone wanted him. You didn't have to be a genius to figure out that he was going to be good."

Ohlund was still just 17 when he was drafted and wouldn't turn 18 until September 9, 1994, a mere six days before the September 15 cutoff date for eligibility in the 1994 draft. If he had been just a week younger, Öhlund would have gone into the 1995 draft, where Gradin believed he could have been the top pick.

"Top three for sure and possibly number one overall," Gradin said to Elliott Pap of the *Sun*. "He has very good hockey sense and he's a pretty good skater. He's very good offensively and, for sure, he's tough enough to play in the NHL."

The latter was definitely true. Even at 17, Öhlund was intimidating at 6'3" and 209 pounds. In the years to come, he added more size and strength and played like a top draft pick. Even though he was a defenceman, he was the top-scoring 18-year-old in the Elitserien, Sweden's top league, in his post-draft year. He was named the best defenceman at the 1996 World Juniors and was named the Swedish Junior Hockey Player of the Year that same season, as he helped Luleå HF to the Elitserien championship.

Still without a contract from the Canucks, Öhlund played for Sweden at the 1997 World Championship, taking home a silver medal as he was named a Second-Team All-Star.

That's when the Toronto Maple Leafs tried to steal him away, signing Öhlund to a five-year, $10 million offer sheet. They timed the signing for shortly after the Canucks signed Mark Messier to a $20 million deal, hoping that the Canucks' budget would be stretched too thin to match Öhlund's contract.

"We're looking at this as a franchise acquisition," said Leafs general manager Bill Watters. "It doesn't require a great deal of observation to realize that this guy is a franchise defenceman."

The Canucks matched the deal and Öhlund slotted right into the Canucks lineup. He proved to be just as good as Watters suggested.

"He stayed in Sweden for another couple of years," said Penny. "It was his choice, he didn't want to come because he didn't feel he was ready. But when he came, he just stepped from one league right into the other."

Öhlund put up 30 points in 77 games while playing stifling, physical defence. He became an all-situations defenceman for the Canucks in his rookie year, averaging 22:30 per game in ice time, while playing on both sides of special teams. By the end of the season, he finished second in Calder Trophy voting to Sergei Samsonov.

No one hit harder than Öhlund, but he was a complete player who could impact a game at both ends of the ice. He was a defensive force but just one defenceman from the 1994 draft had more career points than Öhlund: his eventual teammate on the Canucks, Ed Jovanovski. Öhlund could do it all.

"Maybe he's not regarded as highly as [Nicklas] Lidstrom and those guys, but he's a top-five defenceman all time [in Sweden]," said Henrik Sedin to the NHL's Corey Long. "Maybe his numbers don't stand out as much, but his defensive play and the things he did to help the team win always stand out for me."

It seemed like Öhlund had the potential to be one of the best defencemen in the NHL before a devastating eye injury in his third season changed the trajectory of his career. Öhlund was struck by a puck that deflected off an opponent's stick and collapsed to the ice in a pool of blood. Öhlund recalled telling Canucks trainer Mike Bernstein to "Just get the blood away," so he could make sure that he could see.

"After a couple of minutes I realized I couldn't see anything," said Öhlund to Grant Kerr at the *Globe and Mail*. "It was scary. The first thought I had was I was going to be blind."

Öhlund had to have surgery on his right eye, then another surgery a couple of years later to relieve pressure behind that same eye. He was left with only partial vision in the one eye and fans had to wonder what could have been. He was still the Canucks' best defenceman year after year with only partial vision in one eye. What could he have done with full vision?

"He never had a bad game," said Edler, who connected to Öhlund when he joined the Canucks. "I had Mattias, who's from up north in Sweden, a defenceman—a player that I looked up to. I would look at his game and try to play like he did because he was so good, so consistent."

Öhlund was a mentor on and off the ice, leading by example with his hard work and leading in the community by giving selflessly of his time with the Canucks' charities. He set new Canucks franchise records for a defenceman with 93 goals and 325 points in his 11 seasons in Vancouver, both records which would go on to be broken by Edler. In 2016, Öhlund was the sixth player added to the Canucks' Ring of Honour at Rogers Arena.

12

DRAFTING THE 2011 CANUCKS

THE CANUCKS' FIRST two trips to the Stanley Cup Final featured a few star players that were selected in the NHL Entry Draft, such as Stan Smyl, Trevor Linden, and Pavel Bure, but no one could claim that those teams were built through the draft.

There is a much stronger case to be made for the Canucks team that went to the 2011 Stanley Cup Final.

The 2010–11 Canucks were one of the greatest teams of the modern era, dominating the rest of the NHL in every facet of the game en route to the first Presidents' Trophy in franchise history. They had the best offence, leading the league with 3.15 goals per game. They had the best defence and goaltending, leading the league with just 2.20 goals against per game. They had the best power play, scoring on 24.3 percent of their opportunities, and had the second-best penalty kill at 85.6 percent, just 0.5 percent behind the league-leading Pittsburgh Penguins.

The foundation of the team came mostly through the draft, starting with First-Team All-Stars Daniel and Henrik Sedin, drafted second and third in 1999. Daniel led the NHL in scoring with 104 points to win the Art Ross Trophy and was voted as the most outstanding player by his peers to win the Ted Lindsay Award. Henrik wasn't far behind at 98 points, with a league-leading 75 assists.

Ryan Kesler, drafted 23rd overall in 2003, exploded offensively in the 2010–11 season with 41 goals, destroying his previous career high of 26. Paradoxically, that offensive explosion helped him win the Frank J. Selke Award as the NHL's best defensive forward.

Alex Edler, drafted 91st overall in 2004, was the workhorse on defence, averaging 24:17 in ice time per game. He was a key component on both sides of special teams and put up 33 points in 55 games to lead the Canucks' defence in points per game.

Kevin Bieksa, drafted 151st overall in 2001, was one half of the Canucks' second pairing, which took on the toughest assignments. He tallied 10 points in 25 playoff games, including the goal that sent the Canucks to the Stanley Cup Final.

The one foundational piece of the Canucks' core that didn't come via the draft was goaltender Roberto Luongo, acquired via trade in 2006 from the Florida Panthers by then general manager Dave Nonis. Todd Bertuzzi, acquired in the Linden deal, was packaged up with Bryan Allen, who was the Canucks' fourth-overall pick in 1998, and goaltender Alex Auld for Luongo, defenceman Lukas Krajicek and a sixth-round pick in 2006.

Luongo brought an end to the "goalie graveyard" in Vancouver, and he was particularly good in the 2010–11 season, with a .928 save percentage and a career-low 2.11 goals against average, helping him to a share of the William M. Jennings Trophy for the league's lowest goals against tally.

THAT CORE, KEPT together with hometown discounts and some clever salary cap wizardry, was supplemented by trades and free agents.

Dan Hamhuis, Mikael Samuelsson, Manny Malhotra, and Raffi Torres were all added in free agency. Mike Gillis took advantage of the San Jose Sharks' need to clear cap space to trade a couple of prospect busts—2007 first-round pick Patrick White and 2006 third-round pick Daniel Rahimi—for Christian Ehrhoff. Creative work around the team's injured reserve list by assistant general manager Laurence Gilman gave the team room to add Chris Higgins and Maxim Lapierre at the trade deadline, bolstering the roster for the playoffs.

Not all of the trades were as successful. Gillis traded Steve Bernier, Michael Grabner, and the Canucks' first-round pick in 2010 to the Florida Panthers for defenceman Keith Ballard and depth forward Victor Oreskovich. Ballard struggled to put up points at the same rate as he did with the Panthers and was exposed defensively. In the playoffs, Ballard was a frequent healthy scratch despite the Canucks' injuries on defence, playing just 10 games and only one of them in the 2011 Stanley Cup Final.

"Keith suffered a fairly severe concussion very early in his tenure with us," says Gillis in defence of the deal. "You simply can't have enough puck-moving defencemen, particularly when you played the way we wanted the team to play, which was really high tempo, really quick transitional play, moving up the ice as quickly as possible, constant pressure on the opposition defence. You need puck-moving defencemen and Keith was one of those. Just, he got hurt.

"It's really too bad because he's a really good person, a great teammate."

In retrospect, Gillis wishes he had traded away more first-round draft picks, not fewer, while the Canucks were in their Cup window. The team was regularly picking in the twenties in the first round—picks that are less likely to produce NHL stars than the top half of the draft—so moving those picks for immediate help would be justified in pushing for a Cup. But it's easier said than done.

"Other teams are not stupid. They're not giving up value where they don't have to," said Gillis. "They're looking at their draft list and they're realizing that beyond this point, it's a total crapshoot. So, are they going to give up a player who isn't just a rental for a late first-round pick? Probably not."

While there was a limit on how much help Gillis could get the team in trades and free agency, the Canucks had several drafted players from the previous management regime to round out the roster.

SPEEDSTER MASON RAYMOND played a key role alongside Kesler on the Canucks' second line in 2010–11. Raymond and Kesler played a straight-ahead north-south game that complemented the Sedins' cycle game on the first line, varying the Canucks' attack.

Raymond was ranked 123rd among North American skaters by Central Scouting heading into the 2005 NHL Entry Draft. Taking him 51st overall in the second round seemed like a reach, but the Canucks ranked him a lot higher than Central Scouting and knew they weren't the only team interested in the fleet-footed forward.

"We had him rated at the bottom of the first round," said Nonis. "He's going to take time to develop but his offensive ability and his foot speed is real impressive."

Still, there was a risk to Raymond because he was already in his second year of draft eligibility and actually turned 20 in September, two days after the age cutoff for the draft. That gave him less time to develop compared to the youngest players in the draft, who were almost three years younger. Raymond didn't opt in to the 2004 draft in his first year of eligibility on the advice of his agent—a risky move as he might not have been drafted at all.

"I was a late bloomer," said Raymond on the *Sekeres & Price Show*. "My birthday is September 17th, and the 15th is the cutoff. I was drafted in the [Sidney] Crosby year with the '87s, which was the lockout year, but I'm actually an '85-born."

Raymond captured the attention of scouts with a massive season as the MVP of the AJHL, leading the league with 41 goals for the Camrose Kodiaks despite playing far fewer games than the league's other top scorers. Raymond was at his best at the RBC Cup, which was swarming with NHL scouts. He led the tournament in scoring with 10 points in five games and was named the top forward.

"I had some meetings with a whole bunch of teams, including Vancouver," said Raymond. "It was an odd year because there was no [in-person] draft because of the lockout year, so I got a phone call: lo and behold, there I was at 51st overall to the Canucks."

Raymond was vacationing at a cottage with his friend and fellow former Kodiak Dan Bertram, who was selected three picks later by the Chicago Blackhawks. The two of them toasted their good fortune with champagne.

With the rules changes that came after the 2004–05 lockout, Dave Nonis emphasized speed and skill over size and strength to his scouting staff, which led them toward Raymond, who could fly around the ice but was a very slight 165 pounds at the time of the draft.

"He's an extremely quick skater, a guy that can beat you wide and the puck doesn't slow him down. He's going to need time to develop and get a little stronger," said Nonis after the draft. "If you look at the rules package that was introduced last week, you have to start projecting some players like that into the game."

It was a prescient decision. In the clutch-and-grab era, Raymond might have struggled, but with the crackdown on hooking and holding, Raymond became a top-six forward on a Stanley Cup contender.

Raymond's best season came in 2009–10, when he scored 25 goals and had 53 points in 82 games. He was still effective at five-on-five in 2010–11 but the Canucks decided to load up the first power play unit, moving Kesler to the top unit with the Sedins. That left the second unit without their pivot and Raymond's scoring suffered.

Despite being limited to 15 goals and 39 points, Raymond's speed made him a puck-possession powerhouse and an effective complement to Kesler's transition game. He and Kesler were first and second on the Canucks in Corsi percentage—a statistic that measures shot attempts for and against when a player is on the ice at five-on-five. They were joined by Chris Higgins after the trade deadline and that line stayed together through most of the Canucks' 2011 playoff run.

Unfortunately, Raymond's playoffs abruptly ended in Game 6 of the Stanley Cup Final when he was jammed awkwardly into the boards by the Boston Bruins' Johnny Boychuk, fracturing two vertebrae and suffering nerve damage. After months of rehabilitation, much of it spent in a full back brace, Raymond was able to resume his career in the 2011–12 season, even if he was never quite the same.

Raymond frequently gets underrated by Canucks fans, but his speed was a crucial component of the best team in franchise history. His career ended on a high note: when the NHL barred its players from participating in the 2018 Winter Olympics, Raymond left the NHL to spend a season in Switzerland so he could play for Team Canada. Wearing an "A" as an alternate captain, Raymond won an Olympic bronze medal for his country before he retired.

THOMAS GRADIN DESERVES plenty of kudos for the Canucks drafting Swedes like the Sedins, Matthias Öhlund, and Edler, but his best late-round find was a Dane.

Jannik Hansen was just the second player born and raised in Denmark to play in the NHL, with Frans Nielsen preceding him by one season. Oddly enough, he wasn't the first Dane to ever be drafted by the Canucks; they selected Poul Popeil, who was born in Denmark but raised in Canada, in the 1970 expansion draft.

Hansen's father, Bent, was one of Denmark's top hockey players in the '70s and '80s, playing on the Danish national team with a couple of other fathers of future NHLers: Frits Nielsen and Olaf Eller, the fathers of Frans Nielsen and Lars Eller respectively. But Hansen wasn't necessarily eager to follow in his father's footsteps.

"As his parents, we always wanted Jannik to skate," said Bent to Peter Fredberg with the IIHF. "We took him to 'Kostalden' when he was two, three years old. But it wasn't on the cards at the time, as Jannik chose to play football instead, which he liked very much."

Kostalden, which literally translates to "cowshed," was Denmark's first covered ice rink and was actually called the Rødovre Skøjtehal (Ice Skating Hall). According to Hansen, it earned the cowshed nickname because it resembled a barn and the local team's hockey jerseys initially had a cow on them—the logo for the city of Rødovre—before later becoming the Rødovre Mighty Bulls and changing the logo to a bull.

Other sources say it was called the cowshed because of the odor from the ammonia used to keep the ice at the right temperature. The old barn was replaced by a new, ammonia-free facility, in 1995: the Rødovre Skøjte Arena

"In 1997, when he was 11 years old, he played his first match in Rødovre Skøjte Arena," said Bent. "He didn't know the rules, but he went at it nonetheless and was part of the club's first junior team that won the Danish championship.

Jannik has always had a go-do attitude, lots of willpower, and wouldn't let anything knock him out. I remember the football club tried to lure him back, but hockey won. We didn't pressure him. It was his choice."

Hansen's development was influenced by Danish hockey bringing in coaches from outside the country to jump-start their ailing program.

"My age group were the first players that they started a new development program," said Hansen to the *Globe and Mail* in 2011. "They brought in a couple Swedish coaches who brought the Swedish style to Denmark. You're seeing the fruit of that now."

In his draft year, Hansen was playing against men in Denmark's top league for the Mighty Bulls, tallying 12 goals and 19 points in 35 games, then had a strong performance at the 2004 World Under-18 Championships, finishing the tournament with seven points in six games. That was tied with Alexander Radulov and David Krejci, who were first- and second-round picks in 2004, and it was a sign that Hansen could compete with the best of his peers.

NHL scouts were more interested in his Danish teammate Peter Regin, who led Denmark in scoring at the World Under-18 with five goals and nine points and played the more valuable position at centre. Regin was picked in the third round by the Ottawa Senators, exactly 200 picks before Hansen.

Gradin and the Canucks, however, saw in Hansen a player whose style would adapt well to the NHL, with glimmers of a high-energy, two-way game and a tenacious will to improve. At one point, Gradin called Hansen the "most

North American-style player" on the Canucks, according to Iain MacIntyre of the *Vancouver Sun*.

As they did with Edler, the Canucks influenced Hansen's post-draft decision to play one more season in Europe then come over to North America to play a season in the WHL with the Portland Winter Hawks, making him the first Danish player to play in the WHL. He finished second on the Winter Hawks in scoring with 64 points in 64 games, then added seven goals and 13 points in 12 playoff games.

While Frans Nielsen beat Hansen to the NHL, Hansen was the first Danish citizen to play in the NHL playoffs. Hansen played the 2006–07 season with the Manitoba Moose in the AHL, but got called up for the NHL playoffs when Matt Cooke got injured. Apart from that and a couple of other NHL stints, however, Hansen spent two full seasons with the Moose while refining his two-way game and improving the elements he needed to make the NHL as a bottom-six, penalty-killing grinder.

"I was more of a go-to guy [with Portland], playing on the top line, the power play, being a guy they looked to score the goals we needed to win games," reflected Hansen in 2011 to Cam Cole of the *Sun*. "Coming into a league like this, but especially a team like this, there's only so many guys who can play on the power play and it's pretty talented players, so you've got to find other ways to contribute."

In the 2010–11 season, he contributed as a member of one of the best checking lines in the NHL alongside Manny Malhotra and Raffi Torres. That line absorbed tough matchups while starting the vast majority of their shifts in the defensive zone, freeing up the Sedin and Kesler lines to focus on offence. Hansen was also a key contributor to the penalty kill, playing the fourth-most shorthanded minutes behind Kesler, Hamhuis, and Malhotra.

He played the same role in the 2011 playoffs, though he was centred by Maxim Lapierre after Malhotra suffered a gruesome eye injury. Hansen, Lapierre, and Torres were a buzzsaw of an energy line throughout the playoffs and, led by Hansen, they also chipped in some scoring. Hansen managed nine points in 24 playoff games, good for eighth on the Canucks.

Hansen was also an important part of the Canucks' culture during that era. His teammates would joke that he was "the best practice player" on the team, but his all-out effort rubbed off on other players, as he challenged them to take practice as seriously as they did the games. It's something he learned from his captain on the Moose.

"Mike Keane gave me a rude awakening and made sure I was ready every day, not just in games but practices," said Hansen to Brad Ziemer of the *Sun*. "It just sort of carried over to here. He was extremely vocal and he wasn't afraid to let guys know if they were cutting corners."

The Sedins always considered him a big part of the team, with Henrik even mentioning him by name as one of the key culture carriers of the Canucks during his Hockey Hall of Fame induction speech.

"To Kevin Bieksa, Ryan Kesler, Alex Edler, and Jannik Hansen—you guys came up a couple of years after us," said Henrik. "Thanks for helping create a culture where results were just a by-product of our everyday process."

THE CANUCKS' BACKUP—AND occasional starter—in the playoffs was Cory Schneider, who was selected in the first round of the 2004 draft when the Canucks did what you're not supposed to do: draft for need.

At the time, the Canucks were known as a "goalie graveyard," with a series of goaltenders crashing and burning after Kirk McLean. Brian Burke gave Vancouver the label, insinuating that it was the fault of fans and media for putting too much pressure on the men between the pipes.

"I've never seen a city where people love goalies more than they do here," said Burke after he traded away Felix Potvin. "If you look at the goalies in the past, if they played well, they are gods. But this might be a goalie graveyard when you start struggling."

Goaltending ultimately led to the downfall of the West Coast Express–era Canucks, with Dan Cloutier collapsing in pivotal games in the 2002 and 2003 playoffs, then suffering an injury in the 2004 playoffs, but Burke wouldn't—or couldn't—upgrade the position. As a result, one of the most talented teams in Canucks history had plenty of regular-season success but never made it out of the second round.

At the 2003 draft, Burke tried to solve the team's goaltending woes by acquiring Miikka Kiprusoff, who was stuck battling for a backup job with the San Jose Sharks. According to Burke, he had a "handshake deal" with Sharks general manager Doug Wilson to trade a second-round pick for Kiprusoff, but the deal fell apart when Wilson asked for a conditional first-round pick if Kiprusoff became the team's starting goaltender, something that was a near-certainty.

That first-round pick would have been in 2004.

Instead of going to the Canucks, Kiprusoff was traded to the Calgary Flames for a conditional second-round pick, which was used on a pretty good defenceman for the Sharks: Marc-Edouard Vlasic. But Kiprusoff was even better for the Flames. In his first season with Calgary, he was the runner-up for the Vezina as the best goaltender in the NHL. In his second season, he won it.

The miss on Kiprusoff meant the Canucks still needed a goaltender in 2004, and new general manager Dave Nonis—Burke's former right-hand man—did what no Canucks general manager had done before: he drafted a goaltender in the first round, using the 26th overall pick that Burke refused to trade for Kiprusoff.

Coming out of high school hockey, Cory Schneider was tough to assess. His .960 save percentage for the Phillips Andover Academy led all goaltenders by a wide margin—the next best goaltender had a .931 save percentage—but the quality of competition varied widely at the high school level.

In international competition, however, Schneider proved he could thrive against the best of his peers. First, he helped Team USA win a gold medal at the 2003 Under-18 Junior World Cup—eventually known as the Hlinka Gretzky Cup—then he starred in the 2004 World Under-18 Championship just before the draft. He posted a .929 save percentage to carry Team USA to the final before falling just short of a gold medal against a high-powered Russian team led by Evgeni Malkin.

Schneider was already high on the Canucks' list after his season at Phillips Andover, where he was the rare goaltender to be named team captain. His star performances for Team

USA only moved him further up their list, particularly since they so badly needed a goaltender.

Central Scouting ranked Schneider seventh among just the North American goaltenders, but the Canucks had him in the top 10 overall on their draft board. They were afraid he wouldn't be available at 26th but couldn't arrange a deal to move up in the draft to take him earlier. Instead, they worked out a deal to trade down in the draft if Schneider wasn't available, planning to move the 26th pick for two second-round picks. That deal was scuttled when Schneider was still there.

"As the teams kept picking and I saw who was left, I saw Vancouver and I thought there was maybe a chance that they would pick me," said Schneider. "I never had any idea how interested they were. I am just glad that they selected me."

The argument could be made that even though he was drafted to fill a need, Schneider was also the best player available. Of the players taken immediately after Schneider, only Mike Green would arguably have been the better pick with the benefit of hindsight.

Schneider was the last of four goaltenders taken in the first round in 2004, behind Al Montoya, Devan Dubnyk, and Marek Schwarz. Montoya, taken sixth overall, became a journeyman who played more games in the AHL than in the NHL. Schwarz played just six NHL games. Dubnyk had a successful NHL career but, at his peak, Schneider was far better.

By the time Schneider signed his first NHL contract with the Canucks, however, the goalie graveyard was gone with the 2006 acquisition of Luongo. Suddenly, Schneider didn't fill a need anymore and it made it difficult for him to crack the Canucks' lineup.

It wasn't until 2010, six years after he was drafted, that Schneider made the NHL full-time as Luongo's backup. Soon, a goaltending controversy bloomed, as Schneider proved he was up to the task of being a number one goaltender.

In the 2010–11 season, Luongo was fantastic with a .928 save percentage. Schneider, in fewer starts, was ever-so-slightly better at .929. Schneider had a 16–4–2 record during the 2010–11 regular season and split the William M. Jennings Trophy with Luongo for the league's best goals against average.

In the playoffs, Schneider nearly stole the net from Luongo. The Canucks took a 3–0 series lead against the Chicago Blackhawks in the first round, but their rivals refused to go quietly. They scored six goals on Luongo in Game 4, prompting head coach Alain Vigneault to bring in Schneider in relief. Schneider came in again in Game 5 when Luongo allowed four goals on 12 shots.

That was enough to get Schneider his first-ever playoff start in Game 6 but he suffered cramps after failing to stop a penalty shot from Michael Frolik, the Blackhawks' third goal of the game. Luongo came back into the game and stopped every shot he faced in regulation to get the game to overtime. The Canucks still lost, but Luongo had earned back the crease and started every game the rest of the way in the 2011 playoffs.

THERE WAS ONE player drafted by Gillis who made an appearance in the 2011 playoffs: his first-ever draft pick in 2008, Cody Hodgson.

If everything had gone just right, however, the Canucks would have come out of the 2008 draft with not just Hodgson, but also one of the biggest thorns in their side over the next several seasons.

Hodgson was a very good prospect who had scored 40 goals and 85 points in 68 games for the Brampton Battalion in the OHL, but he wasn't originally in the Canucks' plans. That changed, thanks to a Canucks legend.

"Cody wasn't ranked in our top ten," said Gillis. "Kyle Beech was ranked ahead of him, if I remember. But Pat Quinn had him at the Under-18s and we talked to Pat about him. Pat and I had a good relationship and Pat obviously had a good relationship with a number of scouts that were still part of the Canucks. Pat spoke very highly of Cody, spoke very highly of his leadership, and that made him a target."

Quinn was the head coach of Team Canada at the 2008 World Under-18 Championship and Hodgson was not only the captain of the team but also led Canada in scoring with 12 points in seven games on a team with future stars like Matt Duchene, Jordan Eberle, and Taylor Hall. Quinn's seal of approval bumped Hodgson up the Canucks' list, but it wasn't a sure thing he'd be available where the Canucks were picking at 10th overall.

Hodgson slid down in the draft when the New York Islanders traded down twice from the fifth-overall pick and reached to take Josh Bailey ninth overall. That pick has looked better in retrospect—only Drew Doughty has played more games from the 2008 draft than Bailey—but the Canucks were happy to get Hodgson.

Before they picked Hodgson, the Canucks came close to pulling off a huge trade.

"There was an entire dynamic with Chicago at the time, who were picking 11th," said Gillis. "There was some back and forth with them about that pick and they wanted to pick Beech. We knew they wanted to pick Beech and they thought we were gonna pick Beech because he was a B.C. guy—that's how hockey guys think."

Gillis and the Canucks tried to make a deal with the Blackhawks where they agreed not to pick Beech in exchange for a player off the Blackhawks' roster, perhaps with some other pieces to the trade to make both sides happy.

The player the Canucks wanted was Dustin Byfuglien.

"They wanted to make sure we didn't pick Beech, so we asked them for Byfuglien in exchange," says Gillis. "He was on the fringes and he was constantly in trouble because of his weight and commitment levels and other things, so we thought it was a great opportunity to maybe get a player we thought had big potential in exchange for not selecting the player they wanted to select."

Unfortunately for the Canucks, the Blackhawks didn't bite on the deal. As much as Byfuglien rankled the hockey establishment at the time, he was also coming off his first full season with the Blackhawks, scoring 19 goals and 36 points in 67 games—solid production for the then-winger. The Blackhawks decided to hang onto Byfuglien and hope that the Canucks would let Beech slide to them anyway.

It was a good bet for the Blackhawks. The Canucks drafted Hodgson as they had always intended, leaving Beech for the Blackhawks. Byfuglien went on to terrorize the Canucks' crease for two more seasons with the Blackhawks, including two second-round exits for the Canucks in 2009 and 2010. If the Canucks had managed to pry Byfuglien out of Chicago, perhaps they would have slayed the dragon a bit sooner. By 2011, Byfuglien had been traded to the Atlanta Thrashers and the Canucks finally got past the Blackhawks.

Hodgson played a minor role in the 2011 playoffs, appearing in 12 games and recording one point, an assist. He didn't play a single game against the Bruins in the Stanley Cup Final but played a major part in what became colloquially known as "Game 8," when the Canucks enacted a small measure of revenge on the Bruins in their regular season rematch in the 2011–12 season.

Hodgson scored the game-winning goal in a 4–3 win over the Bruins and it was the best goal of his career: a blistering bardown slap shot off the rush that rocketed over the left shoulder of Tim Thomas, who had seemed so impossible to beat just seven months earlier. It was the highlight of "Game 8" and the highlight of Hodgson's career as a Canuck. He was traded to the Buffalo Sabres just over a month later.

LUC BOURDON

One significant draft pick was missing from the 2010–11 Canucks for tragic reasons. Apart from Cody Hodgson, the Canucks had just one other top-10 pick in the decade leading up to the 2010–11 season, when they drafted Luc Bourdon 10th overall in 2005.

Bourdon was intended to be a foundational piece of the Canucks' defence. At the 2005 World Under-18 Championship, Bourdon was named the top defenceman despite only recording one point, an assist, in six games. His physical, shutdown game was just that good and was matched with excellent mobility that had the Canucks believing he was the perfect defenceman for the new rules ushered in after the 2004–05 NHL lockout.

"If you look at the way the game is going to be played in the new NHL, guys who can get around the ice, who are agile, and obviously with size on top of that, it's a pretty enticing package," said Nonis. "He has very good foot speed, he's able to take away ice, and he makes a very good first pass."

The Canucks weren't alone in their high view of Bourdon, who was ranked sixth among North American skaters by Central Scouting.

"It was a consensus pick amongst our group," said chief scout Ron Delorme to Steve Ewen of *The Province*. "We all liked him. He's a good, two-way, reliable guy. The way to describe him is a guy that gets involved in both ends. He's not great in any one area but he'll show up in all of them."

Bourdon's development was derailed by a significant ankle injury in his first post-draft season, but by the time he was 20 he was back on track. He split time between the NHL and AHL in the 2007–08 season, playing 27 games with the Canucks. While he was in Vancouver, the undrafted Alex Burrows took the first-round pick under his wing.

"He didn't know a lot of people in Vancouver and I had been with Manitoba for a few years and I knew a little bit more of the guys and tried to help him out as much as I could," said Burrows. The two French-speaking Canucks became fast friends and looked forward to years of playing together in Vancouver in the future.

Instead, shortly after the 2007–08 season, Bourdon veered into an oncoming transport truck while riding his motorcycle, which he had purchased just three weeks earlier. Police said that a strong gust of wind likely pushed him into the path of the truck and that he died instantly.

It was a devastating loss for his family and the small town of Shippagan, New Brunswick, where Bourdon was a local hero. Bourdon had just turned 21 a few months earlier. It wasn't fair. It wasn't right.

Bourdon's Canucks teammates were shocked, most of all Burrows, who took the loss the hardest. The Canucks paid tribute to Bourdon ahead of the opening faceoff of the 2008–09 season and Burrows was overcome with emotion.

"It's going to be really tough for me," said Burrows to Jason Botchford of *The Province* ahead of the game. "Luc was one of my best friends on the team. Our friendship was only growing. He was a great friend and a great teammate. I will try to do my best to play my game and to play hard, even though it's going to be really, really tough.

"I'm sure Luc will be watching. I'm sure he's going to help me out."

Despite fighting back tears during the tribute video before the game, Burrows played inspired hockey, scoring not just one but two goals. After his first goal, Burrows borrowed a celebration from the late Bourdon, paying tribute to his friend by drawing an imaginary arrow and shooting it straight up to heaven.

"That was Luc's ceremony. He used to do that move after he scored goals in Junior—pulling the arrow and shooting it," said Burrows. "It was a little tribute to him. I thought about it right away when I scored."

It's a celebration that Burrows would bring back throughout his career, keeping Bourdon's memory alive.

Even in the 2010–11 playoffs, Bourdon was constantly on Burrows' mind. He said he would think about Bourdon during the national anthem before every game. When he scored the biggest goal of his career, "slaying the dragon" that was the Chicago Blackhawks in Game 7 of the first round, he tried to repeat Bourdon's favourite celebration.

"I wanted to get past the first guy and maybe shoot a couple into the upper deck, but I got clotheslined by the guys and couldn't," said Burrows.

Maybe Bourdon was with the Canucks in the 2011 playoffs after all.

13

BO HORVAT AND THE REBUILD THAT NEVER HAPPENED

"WE HAVE A TRADE TO ANNOUNCE," said NHL commissioner Gary Bettman, who then raised his eyebrows as the usual chorus of jeers and boos that typically greet his appearances rained down from the New Jersey crowd. "I think you're going to want to hear this."

The jeers turned first into stunned disbelief then into cheers as Bettman announced that the New Jersey Devils had just acquired Cory Schneider from the Vancouver Canucks for the ninth-overall pick in the 2013 draft.

"MY CONTRACT SUCKS."

That was Luongo on April 3, 2013, explaining why the Canucks hadn't moved him at that year's trade deadline. Trade rumours had been following the All-Star goaltender for nearly a year, with a potential trade back to his previous team, the Florida Panthers, falling through in the 2012 off-season.

The Canucks had two elite goaltenders, which is one more than can be on the ice at any given time. Cory Schneider put up better numbers than Luongo in two seasons as the team's backup and, in the 2012–13 season, took over as the number one. It seemed clear that Schneider was the goaltender of the future for Vancouver.

Luongo deserved to be the number one goaltender somewhere, so the Canucks tried to trade him, but there was a major stumbling block—Luongo's 12-year contract that he signed in 2009.

The long-term contract kept Luongo's cap hit to just $5.3 million by heavily front-loading the deal. The bulk of the money was to be paid in the first eight seasons, then fall to $1 million per season by the final two years. By the end of the contract, Luongo would be 43 years old.

The NHL head offices were not impressed, considering the contract a form of cap circumvention. Assuming Luongo retired before the end of his contract, those added years artificially extended the length of the deal just to get his cap hit down. That lower cap hit was essential for the Canucks to not only keep their core group together but also add to it. The Canucks took full advantage of this in the 2010–11 season, putting together a roster that would have been far more difficult to assemble if Luongo had the higher cap hit that a shorter-term deal would have entailed.

So, after they approved the deal in 2009, the NHL did more than just patch the loophole the Canucks exploited— they retroactively penalized the Canucks and the few other teams that had signed similar deals. The new rule stated that if a player retired before the end of a back-diving contract, the team would receive a salary cap penalty equivalent to the amount they previously benefited from the lower cap hit.

The new rule was so obviously targeted at Luongo and the Canucks that it was dubbed "the Luongo Rule." Making matters worse, the rule applied not only to the team that signed the player but also to any other teams he played for if they also got a cap benefit from the back-diving deal.

That made Luongo even harder to trade, as any team taking on the goaltender and his contract had to be wary of salary cap complications in the future from the Luongo Rule.

In other words, his contract sucked.

Still, it was thought that Luongo would be easier to trade at the 2013 NHL Entry Draft, as it would be less complicated to sort out the details of a deal after the season was over. A year-long debacle would surely come to a close and allow the Canucks to move forward with Schneider as the team's number-one goaltender for years to come.

AT THE TIME of the 2013 draft, the Canucks were at a crossroads. While they won the Northwest Division for the fifth-straight season, they were swept in the first round by the San Jose Sharks, their second-straight first-round exit. General manager Mike Gillis decided it was time for a bold move: a rebuild.

Canucks ownership, headed up by Francesco Aquilini, wasn't keen on the idea. After all, the team was just two years removed from a trip to the Stanley Cup Final and one year removed from winning the Presidents' Trophy and a rebuild would mean missing the playoffs for an unknown number of years, with no guarantees of future success.

A compromise was reached: the team fired Alain Vigneault as head coach and brought in firebrand John Tortorella, in hopes of whipping the team back into shape with his blunt and abrasive approach. Meanwhile, Gillis and his management team would quietly start putting pieces in place for a rebuild in case their pitch fell on more receptive ears in the future.

"Our plan was to move six or seven players," said Gillis. "We were planning on basically rebuilding the entire team. We had really desirable players like Ryan Kesler, Kevin Bieksa, Jannik Hansen, Chris Higgins, and Alex Burrows—guys that had Stanley Cup Finals experience and were still very productive players."

With ownership not convinced of the need for a rebuild after the 2012–13 season, management set their sights two years in the future.

"We thought we'd be in a position to have another really high draft pick through trading those other players and have multiple picks moving forward," said Gillis. "The '15 draft was an extraordinarily strong draft—that's what we were aiming for."

The first step was more immediate: finding a way to take the team's biggest boondoggle—the goaltending situation—and turn it into the first piece of this prospective rebuild.

The scouting staff, headed up by the newly promoted Eric Crawford, had a target in mind at the 2013 draft: a prospect who would not be available to them with their own first-round pick at 24th overall; a prospect that would only be available if they made a major trade.

"Mike's plan along with the other members of senior management was that we had to start building from underneath through the draft," said Crawford to The Athletic's Pierre LeBrun. "That was really our first draft where we were looking to rebuild this group."

The prospect they wanted as the first piece of that rebuild was Bo Horvat.

BO HORVAT GOT his start battling his younger brother, Cal Horvat, in floor hockey in the basement of their home in London, Ontario. Their father, Tim Horvat, played the part of referee, dropping the puck and keeping things honest.

Tim had been a dominant scorer for the St. Thomas Stars in the Western Ontario Hockey League in the '80s, leading the Junior B league in scoring in the 1986–87 season with 42 goals and 103 points in 41 games. The season prior, he finished second behind his older brother, Ron Horvat. Tim's performance for the Stars even earned him a cup of coffee with the London Knights in the OHL—Bo's eventual team— but that's as far as his hockey dream would go.

With multiple family members in hockey, it was inevitable that Bo would end up on the ice, though it happened remarkably quickly.

"Bo started walking at eight months and he was on skates by nine months," said Tim on the *Behind the Gear* podcast. "I had the single-blade Lange skates and he would walk around the house in them all day. He wouldn't take them off."

Bo took to the ice like he was born on it and established himself as a top-flight hockey player at a young age. Even when he was just starting out in hockey, he was far more mature than his tender years would suggest.

"What really stood out to me with Bo is how hard he worked," said Tim. "He wouldn't be the flash-and-dash guy, really.... He hated to get scored on. He would work just as hard coming back because he did not like getting scored on. It still bugs him the most today."

That's not to say Bo didn't love to score goals. When the Horvat family moved into a new house with a basement, Tim painted the concrete floor into a hockey rink with a net on one wall. Bo would spend hours in the basement firing pucks at the wall.

"That's just something he wanted to do," said Tim. "I didn't force him to go down and shoot pucks."

The two-way habits that Horvat developed at a young age stuck with him and got him to the OHL, playing for the London Knights team that Tim couldn't quite stick with. In his draft year, Horvat was placed on the second line behind Max Domi on the first line and he finished the season under a point per game with 61 points in 67 games.

While he attracted the attention of scouts with his complete game, scouts questioned Horvat's upside, with scouting reports projecting him as a third-line centre rather than a top-six forward. Accordingly, Horvat was generally ranked outside the top 10 in public draft rankings. Inside the Canucks' room, however, they had Horvat much higher.

"We didn't have him at the top, there was [Aleksander] Barkov and a couple high-end players ahead of him," said Laurence Gilman in a TSN 1040 interview. "We had him very high.

"Our position on Bo was that we felt he was going to be a player cut in the same mold as a Patrice Bergeron or Jonathan Toews without the prolific offensive upside. We saw him as second-line centre who was going to be an exceptional two-way centre—a matchup player who would shut down the opposing team's top offensive players, a guy on your power play, a guy who could kill penalties, and a guy who'd be a leader on your team."

One scout, in particular, led the charge.

"It wasn't a consensus. Dan Palango was the one guy who argued the most for Horvat, who was really confident in his ability," said Gillis. "Dan was a relatively new scout, so there was that whole dynamic, but Dan was extremely confident and we trusted his judgment."

Beyond what he did on the ice, Horvat's maturity stood out to Palango.

"Interviewing Bo at 18 was similar to the person you see now: focussed, businesslike, mature," said Palango. "I remember meeting Mike at a game in Windsor and he was there with Laurence Gilman, Eric Crawford, and Lorne Henning to see Plymouth play Windsor—Ryan Hartman versus Kirby Rychel, who guys on our staff liked. I told Mike he should have driven an hour down the road to see London because the player there, Bo, was better than both these guys."

Horvat was initially a tough sell to the rest of the scouting staff. His numbers didn't jump off the page and there were question marks about his skating. Since acquiring a first-round pick high enough to take Horvat wouldn't be cheap, some were skeptical that he was worth the cost.

"His skating was a bit of an issue, but we thought he would work as hard as he possibly could to overcome any deficiencies in his game," said Gillis, who saw him as a potential replacement for when the team traded Ryan Kesler. "Where we were trying to go in moving Kesler, he would have eventually fit into that role really well, we thought. It was identifying Horvat as a prospect but it was also part of our plan moving forward."

Most importantly, Gillis saw Horvat as the closest the Canucks could get to a sure thing outside of a top-three pick in order to kick-start their under-the-table rebuild.

Bo Horvat dons a Canucks jersey for the first time at the 2013 NHL Entry Draft with Laurence Gilman, Ron Delorme, and Stan Smyl.

"No matter what was going to happen, he was going to play 400 games in the NHL," said Gillis. "There's no denying that he had the strength, he had the size, he had the work ethic, the attitude—barring some catastrophic injury of some sort or something completely unpredictable happening, he was going to be a second- or third-line centre in the National Hockey League, no matter what.

"It's pretty rare that you can pick someone from six to ten who you're that confident in. The drop-off in some years is right after the first-overall pick, and sometimes that's not even a great pick. It's profound how the NHL draft works. The drop off in reliability is incredible and where you put that line is almost always in the top ten."

It helped that Horvat made a strong argument in his own favour with a dominant playoff performance, scoring 16 goals in 21 games to lead the OHL playoffs in goal scoring. By the time of the draft, everyone was on board.

"There were sexier players at that time that were in the wheelhouse but we kept coming back to Bo," said Crawford.

"Eventually everyone agreed on Bo, but it took time," Palango agreed.

In order to get Horvat, however, the Canucks needed another first-round pick and not just any first-round pick: they had to get into the top 10.

GILLIS HAD TO reckon with two elements as he aimed for Horvat: an untenable goaltending situation and an owner who didn't want a rebuild. That meant the valuable veterans who might have netted a strong trade return were off limits, as they were key parts of the Canucks' roster.

One of their two goaltenders could be traded, however, but only one of them might deliver a top-10 pick: the one whose contract didn't suck. Cory Schneider was younger, cheaper, and arguably better than Roberto Luongo during the 2012–13 season.

"Cory was technically a more valuable player when it came to what other teams were looking for," said Gillis. "For our purposes, Roberto was under a long-term contract, he was a perennial All-Star, we knew exactly what we had in him. We had to do something, so we made the best move that we thought we could make."

The trouble was finding a very specific trade partner: one that needed a number-one goaltender, was picking in the top 10 of the draft, and was willing to trade a high draft pick.

"Trading goaltenders is really difficult," said Gillis. "Teams already have two or three in their pipeline that they're confident in, or even a starter for that matter. It's extremely difficult to get value in return."

First, the Canucks targeted the Edmonton Oilers, who held the seventh-overall pick. The Oilers had three recent first-overall picks—Taylor Hall, Ryan Nugent-Hopkins, and Nail Yakupov—but goaltending had frequently let them down and they had just missed the playoffs for a seventh-straight season. The day before the draft, the Canucks held a meeting with the Oilers—Gillis, Laurence Gilman, Lorne Henning, and Stan Smyl for the Canucks and Kevin Lowe, Craig MacTavish, and Scott Howson for the Oilers—looking to nail down a deal, but it never came together.

From the Oilers' side, they believed they had made a better offer than what the Canucks got back from the Devils, and the Canucks didn't take the deal. Some hockey insiders speculated that the Canucks decided they didn't want to deal Schneider within the division and have to face him repeatedly in the coming years.

According to Gillis, that's not what happened. He claims there was a deal on the table with the Oilers that involved not just the seventh-overall pick, but also the Oilers' second-round pick and an unnamed prospect defenceman. As Gillis remembers it, the Oilers said no.

"We gave them the opportunity to get Cory and we were absolutely dumbfounded they didn't do that," said Gillis. "But they chose not to."

Fortunately, the Canucks had a backup plan. Gillis had a deal already in place with Lou Lamoriello and the Devils, who held the ninth overall pick and needed an heir apparent for the 41-year-old Martin Brodeur. The Devils were hosting the 2013 draft, presenting the perfect opportunity to make a big splash in front of the home crowd.

If the Canucks were unable to find another trade and Horvat was still available at ninth overall, then the Canucks would trade Schneider to the Devils. Perhaps that's why Gillis felt so comfortable asking for more than just the seventh-overall pick from the Oilers. He had a deal with the Devils in his back pocket.

THE TRADE SENT a shock wave through the NHL and, in particular, through the Canucks fan base.

"At the time, we were vilified for that trade," recalled Gillis, as fans saw scouting reports describing Horvat as a third-line centre and were outraged that the team's young goaltender of the future got such a paltry return.

Even Tim Horvat, elated as he was to see his son drafted into the NHL, couldn't help but be stunned and worried for what Bo was about to go through in the hockey-mad market of Vancouver.

"I was so happy, but I sat back down and I thought to myself, 'Why couldn't this kid just get drafted normally?'" said Tim. "Because now he's always going to be compared to Cory Schneider, who is a great goaltender, a great guy for the organization.... The hardest part for me was how much the press and the fans were ripping Bo that didn't even know about him.

"All they looked at was his points in the OHL and they weren't off the charts. They thought they could have got more for [Schneider]...I just knew deep down, they didn't know Bo. They didn't know the kid, how hard he's worked, and what kind of kid he is. That hurt as a dad."

"Just wait," he added, "Just let him show you."

The trade was also a shock to Roberto Luongo, who at least got a little advanced warning when Aquilini made the surprising move of flying to Florida and visiting Luongo at his off-season home. Aquilini informed Luongo of the trade just moments before it was announced at the draft.

While everyone else was stunned, however, the Canucks draft table was thrilled. Palango in particular told everyone who would listen, "We may be drafting our next captain."

He was exactly right.

THE ONLY TROUBLE with Horvat as the first piece of a rebuild is that the rebuild never happened. After the Tortorella-coached Canucks crashed out of playoff contention, Gillis was fired and a new general manager, Jim Benning, was brought in who shared ownership's view that the team didn't need rebuilding at all.

"This is a team we can turn around in a hurry," said Benning when he was hired, and that was the approach he took year after year.

The Canucks did make the playoffs in Benning's first season, but then missed the playoffs in six of his next seven seasons as general manager. The team refused to even utter the word "rebuild" until 2017, four years after Horvat was drafted.

When Horvat was traded ahead of the 2023 trade deadline, he was the captain of a sinking ship, making the playoffs just twice in his 10 seasons with the Canucks.

THATCHER DEMKO

The 2014 NHL Entry Draft was rich with goaltenders, including the Vezina-winning Igor Shesterkin, the Vezina-deserving Ilya Sorokin, and several other NHL goaltenders such as Ville Husso, Elvis Merzlikins, Kaapo Kahkonen, and Alex Nedeljkovic.

And yet, somehow, not a single goaltender was taken in the first round of the 2014 draft. That included the top-ranked goaltender, Thatcher Demko, who was snapped up by the Canucks in the second round, 36th overall.

Thatcher Demko stops a shot from Calgary Flames winger Tyler Toffoli.

Demko was projected to be a first-round pick after a stellar season at Boston College, where he earned the starting job as a 17-year-old freshman—the youngest player in college hockey that season. Born and raised in California, Demko didn't have the typical background of an elite hockey prospect—but, then again, he wasn't a typical Californian.

"I'm an abnormal California kid," said Demko to Iain MacIntyre of the *Vancouver Sun*. "I don't have the tan going like all my friends do. I'm not at the beach. I'm always stuck in the rink—no sun there."

It's not just that Demko was from California that made him unique. He had taken an unusual development path as well. Growing up in San Diego, Demko had to travel to find ice time, elite competition, and high-level coaching, but the hard work paid off. He earned his way to the US National Team Development Program and fast-tracked his schooling to get to

Boston College a year early. When he was starting in the NCAA as a freshman, he was supposed to still be a senior in high school.

Demko had already faced college competition as a 16-year-old with the USNTDP and had excelled, with an 8–2–3 record, including wins against top schools including Michigan and Merrimack. In one game against the University of Minnesota, Demko made 39 saves on 41 shots for a 2–2 tie, including two saves with his shoulder popped out of its socket after a Minnesota forward fell on him.

That competitiveness, combined with his 6'4" stature and elite athleticism, made him highly sought-after by college programs, and Boston College pushed hard to recruit him. Their diligence paid off, as Demko became a star between the pipes as a freshman, outperforming one of his Boston College predecessors: Cory Schneider.

Schneider managed a .916 save percentage in his freshman year at Boston College and that was after he had already been drafted by the Canucks. Demko's .919 save percentage was one of the best ever by an under-19 goaltender in the NCAA. It's no wonder he was the top-ranked goaltender in the 2014 draft.

"He was so far ahead of the under-aged players last year that if he was draft-eligible in 2013 he would probably have been drafted high; that's how far he was ahead then and is now," said NHL Central Scouting's Al Jensen.

So, how did such a highly acclaimed goaltender fall out of the first round? One reason is that teams were starting to get gun-shy about drafting goaltenders with first-round picks in general. It's tough to project how an 18-year-old goaltending prospect will develop, and a few too many first-round busts led to a trend in top goaltenders slipping out of the first round.

Another concern was Demko's health. Demko had labrum tears in his hips that he—and every NHL team—knew would eventually require surgery. He had felt this pain and stiffness in his hips since he was 15 but had been able to play through it and still perform at an elite level. In order to keep playing at that level, however, arthroscopic surgery to repair the tears would soon be necessary.

It's a common surgery for top goaltenders, akin to Tommy John surgery for pitchers in baseball, but all surgery comes with risks, and it likely played a part in every NHL team passing on Demko in the first round of the 2014 draft.

The Canucks, however, were happy to take the risk and surprised that he had made it that far in the draft.

"Thatcher was a great interview in Toronto," said Trevor Linden, who had become the Canucks' president of hockey operations. "He's really a smart kid and a hardworking kid. He's dedicated, super-focussed. I really didn't think we'd get a shot at him at 36."

The Canucks needed a goaltender of the future. Both Cory Schneider and Roberto Luongo were gone—Schneider traded at the 2013 draft and Luongo traded a few months before the 2014 draft. Luongo demanded a trade after Canucks head coach John Tortorella snubbed the legend by starting backup Eddie Lack for the team's marquee outdoor game. Even with top goaltending prospect Jacob Markstrom, who the Canucks had received in return for Luongo from the Florida Panthers, the Canucks' future between the pipes was uncertain. General manager Jim Benning and the team's scouting staff felt that Demko was the answer.

"We believe he's going to be a number-one goalie," said Benning at the draft. "He's 6′4″, he's calm, he's got quick feet, he's hard to beat down low. I was able, because I lived in Boston, to see him play, like, ten times last year. For a freshman playing at the college level, he had an excellent season."

Demko played another year with torn labrums, posting a .925 save percentage at Boston College and a .934 save percentage with Team USA at the 2015 World Junior Championship, before finally undergoing surgery.

"You don't want to ever have surgery until it's absolutely necessary," said Boston College head coach Jerry York, "and it was absolutely necessary."

Demko's surgery was performed by Dr. Bryan Kelly, a specialist in sports medicine and hip preservation, who had performed the same surgery for the Canucks' nemesis: Tim Thomas. If not for Dr. Kelly, the Canucks may very well have won the 2011 Stanley Cup, as Thomas gave credit to the surgeon when he accepted the 2011 Vezina Trophy as the NHL's top goaltender.

"A little bit over a year ago I had a hip surgery and I didn't know if I'd be able to play at the level that I had become accustomed to playing with ever again," said Thomas. "I'd like to thank Dr. Bryan Kelly for doing the hip surgery and doing such a fantastic job."

Of course, without Dr. Kelly, the Canucks might not have Thatcher Demko playing at an elite level either. After the surgery, which involves stitching up the tears in the labrum and smoothing off the top of the femur to prevent future tears, Demko felt better than ever.

"Way better than new," said Demko to the NHL's Kevin Woodley after the surgery. "It should be fixed forever now.

I had zero degrees of internal rotation last season and two weeks after the operation I was already at 20 degrees, so it was almost immediate."

"I have just been looking forward to the day I can play pain-free for about four years," he added.

The increased mobility made him a monster in his junior year with Boston College, when he posted a .935 save percentage and 1.88 goals against average. He won the 2016 Mike Richter Award—named after another Canucks nemesis—as the NCAA's most outstanding goaltender before signing his entry-level contract with the Canucks.

It took another four years before Demko was an NHL regular—another reason why goaltenders are seldom first-round picks—but he became the number-one goaltender the Canucks believed he could be. He proved it in the 2020 playoffs when he came in to replace Jacob Markstrom in the Canucks' series against the Vegas Golden Knights.

Demko faced 125 shots across three starts. He stopped 123 of them, allowing just two goals against for a .985 save percentage. While the Canucks came up short in Game 7, losing 1–0, the Golden Knights were so shaken by Demko's dominance that they bowed out to the Dallas Stars in five games in the following round.

"There's no doubt that the last couple games of the Vancouver series against Demko rattled our confidence," said Golden Knights head coach Pete DeBoer.

Thanks to his surgically repaired hips, Demko should be rattling the confidence of the Canucks' opponents for years to come.

14

ELIAS PETTERSSON, OR HOW TO FIND A FRANCHISE PLAYER WITHOUT A FIRST-OVERALL PICK

THE VANCOUVER CANUCKS are not the only NHL team that has never picked first overall in their history, but they've gone longer than any other team. For instance, the Calgary Flames have similarly never picked first, but they came into the league two years after the Canucks, in 1972, as the Atlanta Flames, so they haven't suffered quite as long.

Over time, Canucks fans have learned that their team can't depend on lottery luck to get superstars. It's still possible to get the best player in the draft—or close to it—without the first-overall pick. Through a mix of hard work, boldness, and luck, the Canucks managed that feat with Pavel Bure, who was one of the best players in the 1989 NHL Entry Draft with Mats Sundin, Sergei Fedorov, and Nicklas Lidstrom.

The Canucks did it again in 1999, getting not just the best player in the draft but the *two* best players when they selected Daniel and Henrik Sedin.

In 2017, the Canucks once again got the best player in the draft without picking first overall. It took a dreadful season, some terrible luck in the draft lottery, and a contentious debate for the Canucks to draft Elias Pettersson.

THE 2016-17 CANUCKS season wasn't supposed to be one of the worst in franchise history. General manager Jim Benning had made two major acquisitions to quickly get the Canucks back to the playoffs. Benning felt there were two major weaknesses on the Canucks' roster—size on defence and the declining play of the Sedins—and paid handsomely to address them.

First, he sent 2014 first-round pick Jared McCann and 2016 second- and fourth-round picks for defenceman Erik Gudbranson and a fifth-round pick. Second, he signed Loui Eriksson in free agency to a six-year deal worth $6 million per season. The 31-year-old winger was coming off a 30-goal season for the Boston Bruins and had experience playing with the Sedins in international competition with Team Sweden, winning gold at the 2013 World Championship, followed by a silver medal at the 2014 Olympics.

Trevor Linden and Elias Pettersson in conversation at the 2017
NHL Entry Draft.

Things started going wrong right from the first game
of the season, when Eriksson scored an own goal into the
Canucks' net on a delayed penalty. Eriksson managed just
24 points in 65 games—his lowest point total since his rookie
year—and it was a sign of things to come.

"When we signed him, we expected him to be a consistent
20-goal scorer," said Benning a few years later. "He hasn't
done that. That part, that's been disappointing."

Meanwhile, Gudbranson crashed and burned in his first
season in Vancouver. He struggled early, with the Canucks getting outscored 27-to-15 when he was on the ice at five-on-five,
then had season-ending wrist surgery after 30 games.

The Canucks' two major additions, designed to propel
the team back to the playoffs, were instead a major reason
why they were one of the worst teams in the NHL. Their
30 wins were the fewest for the Canucks in the salary cap era

and their 182 goals set a new franchise record for the fewest goals in a full season.

The one upside is their terrible season ensured the Canucks would have excellent odds at getting a high pick in the 2017 NHL Entry Draft. The Canucks finished second-last with 69 points, one point below both the Arizona Coyotes and New Jersey Devils. The only team worse than the Canucks was the Colorado Avalanche, who had just 48 points, giving the Canucks the second-best odds in the draft lottery.

The draft lottery was introduced in 1995 to dissuade teams from tanking—intentionally losing as many games as possible to ensure they get the first-overall pick in the next draft. The entire point of the lottery was to make it so finishing at the bottom of the standings didn't guarantee you a top pick in the draft.

In 2016, the Canucks dropped two spots in the draft order, from third to fifth overall. It happened again in 2017—for the second year in a row, the Canucks dropped in the draft lottery to the fifth-overall pick, this time with three teams passing them in the draft order. This was the draft lottery working exactly as intended: the worst teams didn't automatically get the top picks.

The Canucks made the mistake of drafting for need in 2016. They prioritized defence, picking Olli Juolevi ahead of his London Knights teammate Matthew Tkachuk. Juolevi played just 24 games for the Canucks, while Tkachuk went on to post back-to-back 40-plus goal, 100-plus point seasons for the Calgary Flames and Florida Panthers.

The Canucks couldn't afford to make a similar mistake in 2017. As frustrating as it was to fall to fifth again, the

Canucks needed to find a way to draft a star to turn the team's fortunes around.

They weren't alone in their frustration. The last-place Avalanche, with the best odds of winning the lottery and landing in the top-three picks, instead slid down to fourth, just ahead of the Canucks. In a piece of karmic justice, however, the Avalanche and the Canucks ended up with the two best players in the draft.

THE CONSENSUS TOP-TWO players in the 2017 draft were a pair of centres out of major junior: Nolan Patrick with the Brandon Wheat Kings in the WHL and Nico Hischier with the Halifax Mooseheads in the QMJHL. As much as drafting for need backfired in 2016, the Canucks couldn't deny that they needed a centre. With Henrik Sedin heading into his final season, the Canucks were hoping they could find a future first-line centre to replace him.

By losing the draft lottery, however, the Canucks likely weren't going to get a shot at either Patrick or Hischier. Fortunately, the 2017 draft was full of centres.

International Scouting Services (ISS) ranked 6′3″ Windsor Spitfires centre Gabriel Vilardi third overall, right behind Patrick and Hischier. Another 6′3″ centre, Cody Glass, who dominated the WHL with the Portland Winterhawks, was ranked sixth. Right after at seventh was talented high school centre Casey Mittelstadt, who had impressed scouts with outstanding international performances at the Ivan Hlinka Cup and the Under-18 World Championship.

Then there was a centre out of Sweden with a slight build but sublime skill: Elias Pettersson. But not everyone in the scouting business was high on the slim Swede. ISS had Pettersson ranked all the way down at 20th overall, and they weren't alone in slotting him in the bottom half of the first round. Corey Pronman at ESPN had Pettersson 17th overall, while Sportsnet's rankings compiled by Jeff Marek had him 15th.

While there were a few prospect pundits who were high on Pettersson, the general consensus was that Vilardi, Glass, and Mittelstadt were ahead of him. They were bigger, stronger, and more NHL-ready.

Quietly, however, the Canucks were extremely high on Pettersson. They didn't just have Pettersson ranked ahead of Vilardi, Glass, and Mittelstadt; they had him ranked higher than Patrick and Hischier.

BY THE TIME of the 2017 NHL Draft, Pettersson had grown weary of being questioned about his size. He felt he had answered those questions by putting up 41 points in 43 games against men in the HockeyAllsvenskan. Besides, he had plenty of experience playing against those bigger than him. Growing up in the tiny town of Ånge, he spent long hours playing against his older brother Emil, who was picked in the sixth round of the 2013 draft by the Nashville Predators.

"He always had to play on our level to be able to play with us, to not play with his friends or kids his age," said Emil to the NHL's Nick Cotsonika.

Ånge only had a few thousand people, but it had an ice rink, where Elias and Emil's father, Torbjörn Pettersson, drove the Zamboni. That meant he had keys to the building and the Pettersson brothers spent hours at the rink, with Elias skating every day after school in addition to hockey practice in the evening.

"Just using your imagination," said Pettersson. "I don't remember doing certain drills. I was just skating, having fun. Growing up, that was the [most fun] thing I could do...I was able to be on the ice more than maybe guys who played in a bigger city."

While the unstructured ice time helped Pettersson's creativity, he also took a methodical approach to improving his game, right from a young age. When his dad suggested that riding a unicycle would improve his balance on the ice, Pettersson diligently spent hours every day learning to ride. Next, he taught himself to juggle with the same deliberate approach, then combined the two, improving his balance, hand-eye coordination, and ability to multitask even in the face of his older brother poking fun at him for being a circus performer.

Pettersson took that same methodical approach to improving his game on the ice. Dissatisfied with his shot, Pettersson spent the off-season after he was drafted dissecting every aspect of it, breaking down his shot into a dozen distinct components and working on each of them individually. As a result, his shot became one of the biggest strengths of his game, with flawless technique. At the 2023 NHL All-Star Skills Competition, that technique led to a 103.2 mph slap shot to win the Hardest Shot contest.

At 15, Pettersson left home to play in the youth program in nearby Timrå. Not long after, he caught the attention of the Canucks.

"We'd had him under close observation since he was 16," said then Canucks director of amateur scouting Judd Brackett to Gunnar Nordström of *Expressen*. "Early on, we gave Elias Pettersson the 'priority watch' stamp, which means that he's a talent we have to keep an extra eye on."

As a 16-year-old during the 2014–15 season, Pettersson lit up the J18 Allsvenskan league, racking up 20 goals and 38 points in 18 games. He played a handful of games in the J20 SuperElit league and dominated against the older players in that league as well, putting up 13 points in six games. He also made his first international appearance, playing with Sweden's Under-17 team.

Inge Hammarström, the Canucks' European scout, lived near Timrå and gave the earliest scouting reports on the rising star, long before any other Canucks scouts saw him play.

"I tried early on to say that Elias was the most talented player in the entire draft that year because he was in my eyes," said Hammarström to Nordström. "But you have to be incredibly lucky to land a draft pick like this if you don't pick first overall."

More Canucks scouts than just Hammarström grew enamoured with Pettersson's elite skill. The Canucks sent crossover scouts to Sweden and they came back raving about the slight kid with the superb hockey sense and deft touch with the puck. The team sent at least six scouts to each of his international tournaments—Four Nations, Five Nations, Under-18 Championship, Ivan Hlinka—all of which added to the growing sense within the scouting staff that Pettersson was a future star who deserved to be near the top of their draft list.

Elias Pettersson after getting selected fifth overall by the Canucks at the 2017 NHL *Entry Draft.*

According to Brackett, no one person deserves the credit for the Canucks getting Pettersson. It was a collaborative effort.

"It starts with an identification process early on, and then people come in from all over and put him against players from their region and vice versa. There's a real process to it," said Brackett. "We have Inge Hammarström over there and Thomas [Gradin] traveled there, but Elias played in the U20 tournament in November...and we had plenty of guys that cross over to Sweden. So, there's no one person that drafts. If there's a player we like, we have long discussions about that player. It's definitely a group effort when we find someone special like Pettersson."

Those long discussions centred around just how high the Canucks should rank Pettersson, specifically among the other top centres in the draft. Those discussions were fierce, as Hammarström and some other scouts firmly believed that

Pettersson was the best centre available in the draft—not just the best centre after Patrick and Hischier, but the best centre, period.

Trevor Linden, now the Canucks' president of hockey operations, gave a subtle hint to Ben Kuzma of *The Province* that they might not be as high on Patrick and Hischier as the rest of the hockey world.

"There's no win or lose; we're going to get a good player and keep building," said Linden ahead of the draft lottery. "A plug-and-play player is good, but maybe the player we pick at four or five becomes a better pro. And I do believe that."

Patrick and Hischier were undoubtedly "plug-and-play" prospects. Both made the jump to the NHL the season after they were drafted, while everyone else taken in the first round spent at least one more season outside of the NHL. But, despite Patrick and Hischier making the NHL sooner, the players taken at four and five became better players when they made the NHL, just as Linden suggested they would.

Others in the Canucks' room disagreed that Pettersson was the best centre but not because they were high on Patrick or Hischier. Instead, general manager Jim Benning made an argument that Cody Glass, the talented two-way centre out of the WHL, deserved to be a lot higher on the Canucks' draft board, perhaps even ahead of Pettersson.

Benning liked everything about Glass' game and felt that he fit the Canucks' biggest needs.

"Cody's a guy that has real good intangibles," said Benning ahead of the draft. "He's a playmaking centreman, but when we talk about the hard work and intensity and willingness to compete, he does all those things too. He's a well-rounded two-way player."

With his background as an amateur scout, Benning continued to scout as general manager of the Canucks. But there's a limit to how much scouting a general manager can do with all of their other responsibilities. With Glass playing on the West Coast, Benning had more opportunities to see him play compared to Pettersson in Sweden. With that in mind, it shouldn't be a surprise that Benning needed a little bit of convincing that Pettersson deserved to be so high on the Canucks' list.

Typically, a general manager will only see a top prospect like Pettersson at big international tournaments, and Pettersson had an underwhelming performance at the 2017 World Junior Championships, managing just a single assist in six games. He left a lot of NHL scouts wanting more. Prospect expert Corey Pronman, in his mea culpa for having Pettersson ranked so low ahead of the draft, said that he knew multiple teams had Pettersson ranked first overall on their draft boards, while others had him much lower, and there was a clear split between the two.

"What's more interesting is the divide that emerged, from talking to numerous teams, between the scouts who saw Pettersson mostly in international play, like me, or those who saw him with his club team," said Pronman. "The former group didn't like him that much, the latter were salivating at the thought of picking him. It's why some teams had him rated very high [one to three] and others had him outside their top ten."

The divide wasn't just between teams but within the Canucks as well. The scouts who had seen Pettersson regularly with Timrå argued that his performance in the Allsvenskan should trump how he played against his peers in international play.

"I really think it's important that you take the whole body of work into it by the time you get to June," said Brackett.

"Can you help yourself at World Juniors? Yes. But it is a U20 tournament—it's generally difficult for draft-eligible players, so I try not to be overly critical of someone that maybe we've seen earlier and have really strong reports on, but maybe he struggled a bit or didn't have the same impact.

"Obviously, there are some that can compete there and do well and help themselves, but we need to stay focused on the whole year. We really can't knock someone down or prop them up based on one tournament."

The side arguing for Pettersson had a conviction borne out of years of hard work.

"We watched him for two years. We interviewed him. We talked to his coaches. We talked to players who played with him and against him. Everything came back positive," said Brackett. "Then we had guys in the office who gave us support from the analytical side."

The analytics on Pettersson were overwhelming. No prospect in his draft year had ever scored like Pettersson in the Allsvenskan. The closest comparisons were NHL stars like William Nylander and David Pastrnak, but Pettersson significantly outscored even them in their draft years. The Canucks' internal data argued heavily that Pettersson had the potential to be not just a top-six centre, but a franchise forward.

ONE OF THE people most responsible for the Canucks drafting Pettersson was Trevor Linden. It's not that Linden scouted Pettersson or even argued for him; what Linden did was argue for the process.

Linden wasn't happy with the process that led to drafting Juolevi in 2016. It was scattered, with multiple competing draft lists and a mandate that the Canucks had to pick a defenceman. While Brackett was ostensibly in charge as director of amateur scouting, some prospects that he was high on didn't even end up on the Canucks' final draft list.

As president of hockey operations, Linden felt he need to get more involved during the 2017 draft meetings, insisting on more thorough discussion and debate to make sure that every opinion was heard. Linden would later describe the importance of the scouting staff having "autonomy" to make the right pick.

"There were some heated debates in our meetings after we knew we were going to be at five," said Linden to Jason Botchford of *The Province.* "The conviction those guys showed, they fought hard. It was a good, healthy debate."

"At the end of the day," he added, "our guys led by Judd, and the guys who had seen [Pettersson] the most, were adamant that he be our guy."

Former Canucks executive Chris Gear wrote an article for Daily Faceoff about how fighting over prospects is a key part of the process, pointing to Pettersson as a prototypical example.

"The best scouts," Gear said, "are the ones willing to stick their necks out and fight the fight. As an example, those around the Canucks' war room who vigorously insisted that the wafer-thin Elias Pettersson would be a better player than the brick-walled Cody Glass weren't putting forward the easy take, but it was the right one, and their belief and willingness to stand behind it ensured that the Canucks indeed got the right man."

With the conviction of the scouts who had seen Pettersson the most and the weight of analytical evidence on their side, the debate between Pettersson and Glass was won by the Pettersson apologists. By the time of the draft, the question was settled: Pettersson was ranked firmly ahead of Glass and Benning was fully and enthusiastically on board.

In fact, Benning was so completely sold on Pettersson over Glass that he attempted to trade down from fifth overall to sixth with George McPhee, general manager of the Vegas Golden Knights, who he knew was high on Glass. A mic'd up Benning laid out the logic in a behind-the-scenes video posted by the Canucks.

"If the top four guys go, right, then if they want to take Glass, then we go down one spot, we get Pe— our guy," said Benning, hoping to add an additional pick—reportedly a second-round pick—while still getting Pettersson.

Ultimately, McPhee declined the trade. Perhaps he caught wind of the Canucks' enthusiasm for Pettersson and realized he could get Glass without losing another pick. The Canucks might have had an easier time trading down if they had won the draft lottery, giving them a top-three pick.

Hischier went first overall to the New Jersey Devils, while Patrick went second to the Philadelphia Flyers. If the Canucks had won the draft lottery, they wouldn't have picked either player, but they didn't have Pettersson ranked first either. Instead, they had defenceman Cale Makar at the top of their draft board, then Pettersson, a ranking that looks prescient now.

Just as Linden said, the players that went fourth and fifth ended up being the best players in the draft. Makar, picked fourth by the Colorado Avalanche, already has a Norris

Trophy as the top defenceman in the NHL. If the Avalanche had instead picked a centre like Glass or Vilardi, the Canucks would have had a conundrum at fifth overall: the elite defenceman in Makar or the franchise forward in Pettersson?

Ultimately, it's a moot point. The Canucks were thrilled to pick Pettersson, though some were simply relieved—Hammarström described it as a weight of bricks being lifted from his shoulders—and the Canucks ultimately got their own elite defenceman in the 2018 draft.

PETTERSSON WASTED LITTLE time getting to work on proving he was the right pick for the Canucks.

"I'll never forget it. We drafted him on Friday and on the Saturday he came back down to our table," said Linden to Botchford. "That is rare in itself. He then asked us about every single player we drafted, wanting to know all about them.

"Then Sunday he flies out to Vancouver. I was in the office early Monday morning. He shows up there in his gym clothes already and says, 'Hey, I need to work out.' He's a driven and committed kid and that is going to serve him well."

Pettersson followed up his unprecedented draft year in the Allsvenskan with an equally unprecedented post-draft year in the SHL with the Växjö Lakers, leading the SHL in scoring in both the regular season and playoffs. His 56 points in 44 games broke a 42-year-old record held by Kent "Magic Man" Nilsson for the most points ever by a junior-aged player in the SHL, passing Canucks greats Thomas Gradin, Markus Näslund, and the Sedins along the way.

"We have not taught Elias anything about the game of hockey," said Växjö head coach Sam Hallam after Pettersson broke Nilsson's record. "He is teaching us."

Pettersson continued to teach lessons in his rookie year in the NHL, as he electrified Canucks fans with his dazzling dekes and astonishing shot. He broke the Canucks' franchise record for most points by a rookie, passing Pavel Bure and Ivan Hlinka with 66 points in 71 games and won the Calder Trophy as the NHL's rookie of the year.

Six years after he was drafted, Pettersson now leads the entire 2017 draft in points, putting up 102 points in 80 games after 2022–23.

The Pettersson pick is a lesson in listening to scouts, paying attention to analytics, and not being afraid to take a big swing on a player with superstar potential, even if it goes against industry consensus. If the Canucks had played it safe with the bigger, stronger, and seemingly more NHL-ready Cody Glass, they would have missed out on an elite centre with the potential to be the best player in Canucks history.

BROCK BOESER

Before Elias Pettersson, another blue-chip prospect gave the Canucks hope for a post-Sedin future.

Brock Boeser took the NHL by storm in his rookie year. He scored 29 goals in 62 games and was the clear frontrunner for the Calder Trophy before a fluke back injury ended his season. He represented the Canucks at the All-Star Game and not only won the Accuracy Shooting contest at the Skills

Competition but also was named the All-Star Game MVP the next day as he paced the Pacific Division to the win.

Before all that, Boeser was a high school hockey star in Minnesota, where he first caught the eye of the Canucks.

Ted Hampson was the Canucks scout in charge of the Midwest, so he was the first to scout Boeser in Minnesota, then with the Waterloo Black Hawks in the USHL. Hampson had been embedded in hockey his entire life—as a star player for the Flin Flon Bombers in the '50s, then one season with the Vancouver Canucks when they were still in the WHL, and then 980 games in the NHL and WHA, where he won both leagues' awards for gentlemanly play, the Lady Byng Trophy and the Paul Daneau Trophy.

The gentleman continued his hockey career after he retired from playing, stepping into the stands as a scout. He started out with NHL Central Scouting, then spent 21 years as the St. Louis Blues' director of amateur scouting. Two of the players he pushed for the Blues to draft were future Canucks Cliff Ronning and Bret Hedican.

Hampson then worked for two years as chief scout of the Colorado Avalanche before joining the Canucks as an amateur scout in 2006. His long history in the game gave him confidence in his instincts when he watched young prospects.

"It's just going to games and being there and getting enough looks at a guy," said Hampson to the *Flin Flon Reminder*. "You have your gut feeling about players, and everybody has that. Sometimes a player strikes you in a certain way. It might be your type of player, it might be a player like somebody you admired and so you kind of lock in on that guy. But the big, strong, talented guys are easy to spot."

Hampson was 79 when he watched Boeser in his draft year but he still had a keen eye that could see that Boeser was big, strong, and talented. Boeser racked up 35 goals and 68 points in 57 games in the USHL in his draft year and he had size, strength on the puck, and—most eye-catching of all—a laser beam of a wrist shot.

Hampson wasn't the only Canucks scout pushing for Boeser. Wyatt Smith, a relatively new scout with Vancouver, also spent considerable time scouting Boeser alongside Hampson, while Judd Brackett also scouted the USHL prior to his promotion to director of amateur scouting. When Boeser captained Team USA to a bronze medal at the Ivan Hlinka tournament and was one of the top players at the World Junior-A Challenge, the Canucks had plenty of scouts on hand.

As the Canucks got to know Boeser as a person, they were even more convinced that he deserved to be high on their draft board. Boeser's character was impeccable and he had faced more than his share of tragedy and adversity already in his life. He had lost a close friend in a car accident, which also critically injured another friend. His father was diagnosed with Parkinson's disease, then suffered a traumatic brain injury in his own car accident.

Through it all, hockey was Boeser's escape and his way to pay tribute to those he cared about. Working through that adversity refined his character and gave him a different perspective. As a result, Boeser's kindness and generosity with others impressed the Canucks nearly as much as his NHL-caliber shot.

"He's a really good person who has persevered through personal circumstances that could have really affected him," said his mom, Laurie Boeser. "He learned from those things in a positive way. It helped him mature and made him realize that hard things happen in life and you have to work through them."

The Canucks were far from the only team scouting Boeser. So, why did Boeser, who led the USHL in goalscoring and was dominant in international competition, last until 23rd overall in the 2015 draft?

One reason is that the USHL was still underrated as a league for top prospects. A year earlier, Dylan Larkin didn't get picked until 15th overall—now he's top-five in scoring from the 2014 draft. Kyle Connor led the USHL in points in the 2014–15 season with 12 more than Boeser and even he didn't get drafted until 17th overall. Now Connor has more career goals than second-overall pick Jack Eichel.

In the following years, the USHL got much more respect, particularly among players in the US National Team Development Program. Five of the six drafts following 2015 saw at least one top-10 pick out of the USHL. In fact, in 2019, three of the top-10 picks in the draft came out of the USHL, including first-overall pick Jack Hughes. If the USHL had earned that respect even a year earlier, Boeser might not have slid to the Canucks at 23rd overall.

The Canucks were shocked he was still available.

"There's no way Boeser is getting to us," said general manager Jim Benning early in the first round. "We're still 13 more picks [away]."

Thanks to the work of Hampson and the Canucks' other scouts, the Canucks were so high on Boeser that they were already lamenting he wouldn't be available as the 10th-overall pick was being made. Fortunately for the Canucks, other teams weren't as high on Boeser as they were.

15

QUINN HUGHES, THE NO. 1 DEFENCEMAN

THE CANUCKS TRIED to draft a superstar defenceman with their first-ever draft pick in 1970. Nearly 50 years later, they finally managed to do it.

It wasn't a spin of a carnival wheel that delivered Quinn Hughes to the Canucks, but it felt just about as lucky. The stars aligned just right and one of those stars landed right in the Canucks' lap.

HUGHES GREW UP embedded in hockey. His father, Jim Hughes, was a onetime college hockey star as a defenceman for Providence College and played a season in Sweden before embarking on a career as a coach. That job saw him bounce around North America, including a stint in Florida as assistant coach of the IHL's Orlando Solar Bears.

That's where Quinn and his brother, Jack, were born, making them two of just 18 players in NHL history born in Florida. They didn't stay there long, moving with Jim as he joined the Boston Bruins and then Manchester Monarchs. Finally, Toronto became home when Jim spent a long stint in the Maple Leafs' organization, first as an assistant coach with the Toronto Marlies in the AHL, then director of player development with the Leafs.

The Hughes brothers—Quinn, Jack, and youngest brother Luke—grew up at the rink surrounded by professional hockey players. They would sit in the stands at practices, keenly watching the drills and scrimmages, and spent long hours skating at the outdoor rink at Toronto's Wedgewood Park, developing their skating, skills, and creativity.

"They grew their passion for the game outdoors," said Jim to ESPN's Chris Peters. "There was no structure. They just had fun, but everything was a competition."

Their dad may have been a professional hockey coach, but their mom was their first coach. Ellen Weinberg-Hughes was an elite athlete who played soccer, lacrosse, and hockey at the University of New Hampshire. Ellen went to UNH on a soccer scholarship but walked onto the hockey team as a defenceman. By her senior year, she was the captain of both teams.

Ellen was renowned for her smooth skating and ability to break the puck out of the defensive zone with her crisp passing—a familiar description for Canucks fans who have watched Quinn in Vancouver. She represented Team USA at the 1992 World Championship, where she won a silver medal and was named to the All-Tournament All-Star Team as one of the top two defencemen in the tournament. Unfortunately, a knee injury ended her hockey career before she could fulfill her dream of playing in the Olympics when women's hockey was introduced in 2002.

Ellen was the one who taught her boys to skate, and her influence can be seen in Quinn's seemingly effortless mobility.

"She could wheel a bit," said Quinn to ESPN in a typically Hughesian understatement. "She was an awesome player."

Quinn was described as the best skater in the 2018 draft and Ellen was a major influence on that. Some didn't stop short at just the best skater in the draft either.

"He's the best skater I've ever seen," said Canucks director of amateur scouting Judd Brackett.

Jim didn't neglect his sons' hockey education by any means. The same high-level instruction that he was giving the Leafs' top prospects was getting passed onto Quinn and his brothers when they were preteens. Any time the family took in a game on TV together, Jim would break down plays in real time, supercharging the brothers' hockey IQs.

The Hughes brothers even got to see an elite prospect on an everyday basis when William Nylander billeted with the Hughes family. It was a crash course in the type of day-to-day dedication it would take for the brothers to one day make the NHL.

Hughes wasn't a diamond in the rough or a late bloomer. Every NHL team knew who he was from a young age as he starred for the US National Team Development Program (USNTDP). He was a standout in international tournaments with Team USA and even earned a call to play in the 2018

World Championship, where he looked comfortable playing with and against some of the best players in the world.

With his elite combination of skill, skating, and hockey sense, Hughes was a lock to be a top-10 pick in the 2018 NHL Entry Draft—not a single public draft ranking had Hughes lower than tenth overall. The only thing that kept Hughes from competing for first overall was his size. At 5'10", Hughes had some scouts worried that he wouldn't be able to win puck battles against the bigger, stronger players in the NHL.

That wasn't a concern for the Canucks, who believed Hughes' skating and intelligence would outweigh his size.

"Quinn's ability to defend is still going to be predicated on his mobility and reads and angles. He's not going to be a guy that's going to push guys off of pucks very often, but that's not going to limit his ability to defend," said Brackett. "He's going to do the majority of his defence with possession time, honestly. He's a smart player, a competitive player—he wants to win. So he's going to put himself in places to separate pucks and intercept passes."

Besides, Hughes' elite offensive talent and ability to quarter-back the power play fit everything the Canucks were looking for in the 2018 draft. The trouble was that they didn't think it was possible that Hughes would be available by the time they picked.

THE 2018 DRAFT lottery brought some familiar disappointment to the Canucks. In the Sedins' final season, the Canucks slid into the NHL's basement again, giving them the sixth-best odds in the lottery, but they were once again passed by a team with lower odds, moving them to seventh overall.

Quinn Hughes (left) defends against his younger brother, Jack Hughes, who was the first-overall pick in 2019.

While there was a fierce debate the year before about drafting Elias Pettersson, there was barely any debate about Hughes. Everyone in the Canucks' scouting meetings was on the same page: if Rasmus Dahlin was obviously the best defenceman available in the draft and the consensus first-overall pick in 2018, the Canucks believed that Hughes was just as obviously the next best defenceman.

"The other defencemen at the top of the draft are real quality defencemen; they bring different traits," said Brackett to Jason Botchford of *The Province*. "But for us with Quinn, it was the skating, the possession, and the puck recovery. We talked about wanting to play faster and improving the power play, and these are all things he hit on. It was a real fit for us."

In fact, the Canucks had Hughes ranked third overall on their draft board, much higher than the public consensus. It was a given that the Buffalo Sabres would take Dahlin first overall, then Andrei Svechnikov would go second overall to the Carolina Hurricanes, but the Canucks felt Hughes was right there with them in that top tier.

With that in mind, the Canucks knew the chances of Hughes being available to them at seventh overall were slim, as they were far from the only team high on Hughes. While general manager Jim Benning looked to trade up, the Canucks scouting staff, led by Brackett, had to prepare for the draft with the understanding that Hughes would likely be gone by the time they picked.

Picking third to sixth were the Montreal Canadiens, Ottawa Senators, Arizona Coyotes, and Detroit Red Wings. The Canadiens were expected to pass up the consensus third-ranked Filip Zadina to instead draft for their biggest need at centre by taking Jesperi Kotkaniemi. The Finnish forward, originally expected to go in the middle of the first round, rocketed up draft boards after a strong performance at the World Under-18 Championship.

The Coyotes were unlikely to pick a defenceman given their desperate need for scoring and with a 20-year-old Jakob Chychrun already heading into his third NHL season.

But either the Senators or the Red Wings could easily take Hughes. For the Senators, Erik Karlsson had just finished his final season in Ottawa and was traded to the San Jose Sharks later that summer. Drafting Hughes as an heir for Karlsson made sense.

Meanwhile, the Red Wings were known to be targeting defencemen at sixth overall and Hughes had played both his junior and college hockey in Michigan, right in the Red Wings' backyard. At the 2018 World Championship with Team USA,

Hughes roomed with Red Wings forward Dylan Larkin and was coached by Red Wings head coach Jeff Blashill, who came away impressed with the young defenceman.

"When I watched him I thought to myself, 'That's a skill set that's transferable,'" said Blashill. "Some guys are really good players in college or junior, but maybe they're not explosive enough or maybe they're not big enough or maybe they're not fast enough.

"His skill set, for me, was transferable because he is super explosive. I mean, super explosive. It wasn't explosive for college hockey, it wasn't explosive for the World Championships. It's explosive with the best players in the world."

It seemed like it would take a miracle for Hughes to get past the Red Wings to the Canucks at seventh overall. Instead, it just took a couple of general managers falling into the trap of drafting for need.

THE FIRST AND second picks went as expected, with Dahlin and Svechnikov going to the Sabres and Hurricanes. Then the Canadiens followed through on the rumours they were reaching for Kotkaniemi. Then the Senators passed on Hughes and picked one of his closest friends instead—power forward Brady Tkachuk, who had been Hughes' roommate with the USNTDP.

That left Zadina available for the Coyotes at fifth. It seemed obvious how the picks would go. The Coyotes would take Zadina fifth overall, then, at sixth, the Red Wings would happily snap up Hughes. That would leave the Canucks with the best of the rest and they couldn't really complain. There were plenty of good prospects still available.

Quinn Hughes at the 2018 NHL Entry Draft with then head of analytics Jonathan Wall (left) and president of hockey operations Trevor Linden (right).

But then the Coyotes decided they needed a centre. Barrett Hayton was projected to be a first-round pick, but few had him ranked in the top 10 and no one had him in their top five. No one, that is, except the Coyotes and, possibly, the Canucks themselves, as Benning admitted after the draft.

"We had Hayton really high too," said Benning to The Athletic. "And Arizona's built a real good defence, so there was a possibility that they could draft a forward."

Coyotes general manager John Chayka liked Tkachuk, Hayton, and Hughes, in that order, all ahead of Zadina. When the Senators took Tkachuk, Chayka simply went to the next name on the Coyotes' list. The question was whether the Coyotes overrated Hayton because of their desire for a centre.

Zadina's slide down the draft created a buzz. Even at the Canucks' table, Zadina slipping past the Senators and Coyotes had assistant general manager John Weisbrod second-guessing their draft board. Even though the Canucks had Hughes ranked above Zadina, Weisbrod couldn't help but ask Brackett what they would do if the Red Wings passed up both players.

"Zadina or Hughes?" asked Weisbrod. Brackett was emphatic in his reply: "Hughes."

With Zadina suddenly available, the Red Wings' intentions to pick a defenceman fell by the wayside. Red Wings general manager Ken Holland had to admit that picking Zadina wasn't the plan.

"We did our ranking, our final list and my expectations coming in were that we were going to take a defenceman," said Holland to The Athletic. "We didn't expect Zadina to be on the board when we picked."

But even if Zadina didn't fall, Hughes likely would have slipped to the Canucks anyway. According to Hughes himself, the Red Wings had no intention of drafting him.

"I was kind of told a couple of days earlier that I wasn't going to the Red Wings," said Hughes to Ben Kuzma of *The Province*. "I just wrapped my head around that."

The Red Wings did want a defenceman at the draft, but there were four defencemen in the tier after Dahlin—Hughes, Evan Bouchard, Noah Dobson, and Adam Boqvist—and little consensus in the public square over who was best. In hindsight, Hughes towers over the others but, at the time, it seemed perfectly reasonable to prefer one of the bigger defencemen.

If Zadina hadn't fallen, the Red Wings would reportedly have taken Evan Bouchard, not Hughes. In fact, one source suggested the Red Wings had both Bouchard and Dobson ranked ahead of Hughes.

As much as it seemed like Zadina sliding out of the top-five to the Red Wings delivered Hughes to the Canucks, it was the Coyotes who were actually the bigger threat to take Hughes. If they hadn't overrated Hayton, Hughes would be in Arizona instead of Vancouver.

AS THE RED WINGS announced the selection of Zadina, the staff at the Canucks' draft table were outwardly calm, but inwardly jubilant. Jonathan Wall, the Canucks' director of hockey operations, later called it "a hard poker face moment" as they tried to hide their excitement. Wall said they took just five seconds of their allotted time to get their selection of Hughes into the system.

Weisbrod, however, couldn't help but breathe a visible sigh of relief and give a small fist pump. He had been keeping an eye on Hughes longer than anyone else at the Canucks' draft table, longer than Brackett or any of the scouts. He was literally in the hospital when Hughes was born.

Weisbrod was a longtime friend of Jim Hughes, as they grew up together on Long Island and played against each other in the NCAA. When Weisbrod's playing career was cut short by a shoulder injury, he went into management, first with the Albany River Rats in the AHL, then with the IHL's Orlando Solar Bears in 1997.

Former Canuck Curt Fraser was the head coach of the Solar Bears until he left to take a job as the first head coach of the Atlanta Thrashers in the NHL. Fraser's departure left a hole in the coaching staff and, needing someone to improve the team's defence, Weisbrod thought of his old friend Jim Hughes and brought him on as an assistant coach—his first job coaching in professional hockey after three years in the NCAA.

Two weeks into Jim's first season with the Solar Bears, along came Quinn.

Weisbrod tried not to let his friendship with the Hughes family influence the Canucks' scouting discussions but he couldn't help but be thrilled when Quinn fell into their laps at seventh overall. Eighteen years after he was at the hospital to welcome Quinn into the world as a newborn, he welcomed him to the Canucks on the stage at the 2018 NHL Entry Draft.

"I was at the hospital when Quinn was born but that's really a coincidental side piece," said Weisbrod. "Obviously, this is a business, we're trying to draft the best players we can and, without question, we felt that this was the best player there at that spot."

Meanwhile, Benning could barely contain himself in an interview with Elliotte Friedman on the draft floor.

"I'm so excited for our fans right now. I didn't think he was going to be there, but I'm so happy that he was," said Benning with a wide smile on his face. "I'm over the moon."

THE CANUCKS GOT Hughes because the Canadiens and Coyotes drafted for need instead of taking the best player available. For the Canucks, Hughes represented the best of both worlds.

"We focus mostly on best available and at times maybe that intersects," said Brackett. "For us, Quinn was best available and also biggest need."

"We didn't think he was going to be there for us at seven," said Benning, "and the fact that he made it to seven and he's a defenceman and he's a power play guy: he fit all of our needs."

In the years since the draft, Hughes has proven that he was definitively the best player available. He's already set a new franchise record for points by a Canucks defenceman, finally passing the record set by Doug Lidster 35 years earlier. He did it twice, in fact, putting up 68 points in the 2021–22 season, then breaking his own record with 76 points in 2022–23.

After four seasons with the Canucks, Hughes has 241 points in 283 games—more points than first-overall pick Rasmus Dahlin, who has played one more season than Hughes. Only forwards Brady Tkachuk and Andrei Svechnikov have more points than Hughes from the 2018 draft and they've each played an extra season too.

It turns out, the Canucks were wrong to rank Hughes third overall on their draft board in 2018; they should have ranked him first.

HOW TO GET A TOP-10 PICK WRONG

The Canucks nailed two top-10 picks when they selected Elias Pettersson and Quinn Hughes, but they haven't done quite so well in their history with other top-10 picks. There are numerous examples of them getting a top-10 pick wrong, such as Dennis Ververgaert over Lanny McDonald in 1973, Jere Gillis over Doug Wilson in 1977, or Dan Woodley over Brian Leetch in 1986.

You don't have to go that far into the past, however. The Canucks blew top-10 picks in 2014 and 2016 when they drafted Jake Virtanen sixth overall and Olli Juolevi fifth

overall, just ahead of players who went on to far more successful careers.

When William Nylander and Nikolaj Ehlers, taken eighth
and ninth in the 2014 draft, quickly proved to be better players than Virtanen, Canucks fans wondered who deserved to
shoulder the blame. Fingers were pointed at Benning, who
made Virtanen his first-ever draft pick; Trevor Linden, the
president of hockey operations; and even Francesco Aquilini,
the team's owner.

The truth is, all three wanted Virtanen, whether because
of his size, speed, and shot, or because he was born and raised
in B.C. and represented a great marketing opportunity. There
were voices within the scouting department who argued for
Nylander, notably Thomas Gradin, but when the leadership
is in lockstep, there's no dissuading them.

The Canucks' high view of Virtanen wasn't far from the
consensus. While some public draft rankings had him further
down in the first round—TSN's Craig Button boldly bumped
him out of the first round altogether at 48th overall—most
rankings saw him as a top-10 pick.

Intelligent voices within the Canucks community, however, such as CanucksArmy's coterie of analytics experts,
argued persuasively for Nylander and Ehlers over Virtanen.
Several of the experts involved in those 2014 rankings—Josh
Weissbock, Cam Lawrence, Rhys Jessop, and Cam Charron—
were hired by NHL teams partly because of this type of work
in draft analytics.

The Canucks ignored a number of red flags with Virtanen.
He was the third-highest scorer on his own line with the
Calgary Hitmen. He had just 26 assists with his 45 goals, an

indication of his one-dimensional game. While he had blazing speed, he lacked east-west mobility and any sense of deception that would help that speed translate to the NHL. But the biggest red flag was the lack of all the intangibles that would drive him to become a better player. Frankly, the less said about his character at this point, the better.

Brackett talked about that element being the most difficult aspect of scouting. The key is not just figuring out who is the best player at the time of the draft but who will become the best player in two, four, or six years.

"They're 17, 18 years old, and it's not just drive," said Brackett. "It's the willingness to accept coaching or to make changes with your body and what you fuel it with. Maybe some feel like they don't need to do this or there's a corner to cut, and it hurts them down the line. It's not just the will and the drive—that's part of it—but it's also being receptive, being coachable."

The Canucks missed these red flags because they were fixated on physicality above all else. Benning said that the Canucks really only considered two players at sixth overall: Virtanen and the 6'3" Michael Dal Colle.

"We zoned in on those guys," said Benning to Jason Botchford of *The Province*. "It was either Dal Colle or Jake... if you watch the NHL players, you need guys with size and strength. Guys who can get to the net and deflect pucks to get rebounds. We were looking for that style of player. We were happy that's where we ended up."

Dal Colle was notably the only player picked in the top 10 who had a worse NHL career than Virtanen. He played just 112 games with the New York Islanders, scoring a paltry 21 points before he was cut loose and signed in Finland.

Ehlers and Nylander were never on Benning's radar at sixth overall. He didn't want a smaller, skilled player with his first pick as an NHL general manager; he wanted a power forward.

"We're going to get back to a meat-and-potatoes type style of in the trenches, play hard," said Benning. "So, we never gave it much consideration."

Ironically, Virtanen appeared to be more interested in eating meat and potatoes than playing hard, with his conditioning repeatedly called into question. He never became the power forward that Benning hoped he could be.

IT WASN'T ENTIRELY Olli Juolevi's fault that he became a bust, as injuries played a major role in derailing his development. Even with that in mind, he was clearly the wrong pick for the Canucks in 2016, with his London Knights teammate, Matthew Tkachuk, becoming one of the best players in the NHL.

There's no hindsight involved in the Juolevi pick being a mistake: not a single significant public draft ranking heading into the 2016 NHL Entry Draft had Juolevi ahead of Tkachuk. While Juolevi was consistently ranked in the top ten by draft experts, Tkachuk was consistently ranked in the top five.

Tkachuk racked up 107 points in 57 regular season games in the OHL, then elevated his game in the playoffs, scoring 20 goals and adding 20 assists in 18 games. He combined his elite skill with an agitating edge, making him a favourite of both old-school hockey men and modern draft analysts.

The one question mark with Tkachuk was how much of his production was a result of playing on a line with top prospect Mitch Marner and another quality junior player in Christian Dvorak. But if that was a question for Tkachuk, it was doubly so for Juolevi, who had the benefit of feeding the puck to all three players.

Unfortunately, the Canucks were fixated on picking a defenceman despite the overwhelming consensus that Tkachuk was the better prospect.

The Canucks had not drafted a defenceman in the first round since Luc Bourdon in 2005. With several top defencemen available—not just Juolevi but also Jakob Chychrun, Mikhail Sergachev, and Charlie McAvoy—Benning was convinced that 2016 was the right time to draft the team's next great defenceman.

"All things being equal, we'll take a defenceman," said Benning ahead of the draft. "The three players at the top of the draft have a chance to be special but after that, if the defenceman and forward are equal, we'll take the defenceman."

All things weren't equal between Juolevi and Tkachuk, however, and yet they took Juolevi anyway. Behind the scenes, the mandate was clear: unless centre Pierre Luc Dubois fell to them, the Canucks were taking a defenceman at fifth overall, whether the scouting staff liked it or not. Benning publicly admitted years later that was their mindset.

"We didn't have any defencemen coming through the system at the time, so we made the pick based on positional need or fit with our group versus taking the best player," said Benning on Sportsnet 650 after trading the struggling Juolevi to the Florida Panthers.

That focus on drafting for need cost the Canucks dearly, as Tkachuk became a 40-goal, 100-point player, while Juolevi has yet to establish himself as an NHL defenceman.

16

THE FUTURE

UNLIKE IN 1970, the modern NHL doesn't use a carnival wheel to decide who gets the first-overall pick in the draft. Instead, the league uses a lottery machine manufactured by the same company that designs machines for state and provincial lotteries across North America.

The machine is loaded up with 14 balls numbered 1 to 14, which bounce randomly in the machine until a designated person, who literally faces the wall so he can't see the machine, calls out to take a ball from the machine every 20 seconds. Four balls are drawn, creating a sequence of four numbers.

As long as you don't care about the order of the numbers, there are exactly 1,001 combinations you can make with 14 numbered balls. One combination is designated "pick again," leaving 1,000 combinations that the NHL can dole out to give every team a specific percentage of winning the draft lottery.

The end result for the Canucks has been exactly the same as the wheel in 1970: disappointment.

The 2023 draft lottery had a particularly special prize: lifelong Canucks fan and potential generational talent Connor Bedard. The Canucks had just a 3 percent chance of winning the first-overall pick to draft Bedard—30 combinations of four numbers. The odds were much worse than the 50 percent chance they had to pick Gilbert Perreault, but the Canucks still came agonizingly close.

The winning combination was 4-5-9-13. One of the Canucks' 30 combinations was 4-5-9-12.

Missed it by *thaaaaat* much.

Just like that, instead of picking first overall, the Canucks picked 11th overall. There's that number 11 again, just like the result of the wheel spun way back in 1970 that cost them Gilbert Perreault.

But the Canucks have shown that it's possible to draft a star player without needing to use the first-overall pick. They've done it before with the likes of Trevor Linden, Pavel Bure, Daniel and Henrik Sedin, Elias Pettersson, and Quinn Hughes.

Perhaps Vasily Podkolzin, drafted 10th overall in 2019, can be the next great Russian Canuck. Maybe Jonathan Lekkerimäki, selected 15th overall in 2022, can follow in the footsteps of the great Swedish forwards throughout Canucks history. And it's possible that Tom Willander, taken 11th overall in the 2023 draft, can take the Canucks back to the Stanley Cup Final. Maybe this time they can actually win it.

It'll take a lot of hard work, a lot of talent, and a lot of luck.

Just like the draft.

APPENDIX

VANCOUVER CANUCKS DRAFT HISTORY

(Games current through 2022-23 season)

1970

Round	Num.	Player	Pos	GP	G	A	Pts	PIM
1	2	Dale Tallon	D	642	98	238	336	568
2	16	Jim Hargreaves	D	66	1	7	8	105
3	30	Ed Dyck	G	49	0	0	0	0
4	44	Brent Taylor	RW					
5	58	Bill McFadden	C					
6	72	Dave Gilmour	LW					

1971

Round	Num.	Player	Pos	GP	G	A	Pts	PIM
1	3	Jocelyn Guevremont	D	571	84	223	307	319
2	17	Bobby Lalonde	C	641	124	210	334	298
3	39	Richard Lemieux	C	274	39	82	121	132
5	59	Mike McNiven	RW					

6	73	Tim Steeves	D	
7	87	Bill Green	D	
8	101	Norm Cherrey	RW	
8	102	Bob Murphy	LW	

1972

Round	Num.	Player	Pos	GP	G	A	Pts	PIM
1	3	Don Lever	LW	1,020	313	367	680	593
2	19	Bryan McSheffrey	RW	90	13	7	20	44
3	35	Paul Raymer	LW					
4	51	Ron Homenuke	RW	1	0	0	0	0
5	67	Larry Bolonchuk	D	74	3	9	12	97
6	83	Dave McLelland	G	2	0	0	0	0
7	99	Danny Gloor	C	2	0	0	0	0
8	115	Dennis McCord	D	3	0	0	0	6
9	131	Steve Stone	RW	2	0	0	0	0

1973

Round	Num.	Player	Pos	GP	G	A	Pts	PIM
1	3	Dennis Ververgaert	RW	583	176	216	392	247
1	9	Bob Dailey	D	561	94	231	325	814
2	19	Paulin Bordeleau	C	183	33	56	89	47
3	35	Paul Sheard	LW					
4	51	Keith Mackie	D					
5	67	Paul O'Neil	C	6	0	0	0	0
6	83	Jim Cowell	C					
7	99	Clay Hebenton	G					
8	115	John Senkpiel	RW					
9	131	Peter Folco	D	2	0	0	0	0
10	146	Terry McDougall	C					

1974

Round	Num.	Player	Pos	GP	G	A	Pts	PIM
2	23	Ron Sedlbauer	LW	430	143	86	229	210
3	41	John Hughes	D	70	2	14	16	211
4	59	Harold Snepsts	D	1,033	38	195	233	2,009
5	77	Mike Rogers	C	484	202	317	519	184
6	95	Andy Spruce	LW	172	31	42	73	111
7	113	Jim Clarke	D					
8	130	Robbie Watt	LW					
9	147	Marc Gaudreault	D					

1975

Round	Num.	Player	Pos	GP	G	A	Pts	PIM
1	10	Rick Blight	RW	326	96	125	221	170
2	28	Brad Gassoff	LW	122	19	17	36	163
3	46	Normand LaPointe	G					
4	64	Glen Richardson	LW	24	3	6	9	19
5	82	Doug Murray	LW					
6	100	Bob Watson	RW					
7	118	Brian Shmyr	C					
8	136	Allan Fleck	LW					
9	152	Bob McNeice	LW					
11	182	Sid Veysey	C	1	0	0	0	0

1976

Round	Num.	Player	Pos	GP	G	A	Pts	PIM
2	26	Bob Manno	C/D	371	41	131	172	274
3	44	Rob Flockhart	LW	55	2	5	7	14
4	62	Elmer Ray	LW					
5	80	Rick Durston	LW					
6	98	Rob Tudor	C	28	4	4	8	19
7	114	Brad Rhiness	C					
8	122	Stu Ostlund	C					

1977

Round	Num.	Player	Pos	GP	G	A	Pts	PIM
1	4	Jere Gillis	LW	386	78	95	173	230
2	22	Jeff Bandura	D	2	0	1	1	0
3	40	Glen Hanlon	G	477	0	11	11	237
4	56	Dave Morrow	D					
4	58	Murray Bannerman	G	289	0	10	10	37
5	76	Steve Hazlett	LW	1	0	0	0	0
6	94	Brian Drumm	LW					
7	112	Ray Creasy	C					

1978

Round	Num.	Player	Pos	GP	G	A	Pts	PIM
1	4	Bill Derlago	C	555	189	227	416	247
2	22	Curt Fraser	LW	704	193	240	433	1,306
3	40	Stan Smyl	RW	896	262	411	673	1,556
4	56	Harald Luckner	LW					
4	57	Brad Smith	RW	222	28	34	62	591
6	90	Gerry Minor	C	140	11	21	32	173
7	107	Dave Ross	RW					
8	124	Steve O'Neill	LW					
9	141	Charlie Antetomaso	D					
10	158	Rick Martens	G					

1979

Round	Num.	Player	Pos	GP	G	A	Pts	PIM
1	5	Rick Vaive	RW	876	441	347	788	1,445
2	26	Brent Ashton	C	998	284	345	629	635
3	47	Ken Ellacott	G	12	0	0	0	0
4	68	Art Rutland	C					
5	89	Dirk Graham	RW	772	219	270	489	917
6	110	Shane Swan	D					

1980

Round	Num.	Player	Pos	GP	G	A	Pts	PIM
1	7	Rick Lanz	D	569	65	221	286	448
3	49	Andy Schliebener	D	84	2	11	13	74
4	70	Marc Crawford	LW	176	19	31	50	229
5	91	Darrell May	G	6	0	1	1	2
6	112	Ken Berry	RW	55	8	10	18	30
7	133	Doug Lidster	D	897	75	268	343	679
8	154	John O'Connor	D					
9	175	Patrik Sundstrom	RW	679	219	369	588	349
10	196	Grant Martin	C	44	0	4	4	55

1981

Round	Num.	Player	Pos	GP	G	A	Pts	PIM
1	10	Garth Butcher	D	897	48	158	206	2,302
3	52	Jean-Marc Lanthier	RW	105	16	16	32	29
4	73	Wendell Young	G	187	0	10	10	20
5	105	Moe Lemay	LW	317	72	94	166	442
6	115	Stu Kulak	RW	90	8	4	12	130
7	136	Bruce Holloway	D	2	0	0	0	0
8	157	Petri Skriko	LW	541	183	222	405	246
9	178	Frank Caprice	G	102	0	3	3	17
10	199	Rejean Vignola	C					

1982

Round	Num.	Player	Pos	GP	G	A	Pts	PIM
1	11	Michel Petit	D	827	90	238	328	1,839
3	53	Yves Lapointe	LW					
4	71	Shawn Kilroy	G					
6	116	Taylor Hall	RW	41	7	9	16	29
7	137	Parie Proft	D					
8	158	Newell Brown	C					
9	179	Don McLaren	RW					
10	200	Al Raymond	LW					

11	221	Steve Driscoll	LW						
12	242	Shawn Green	RW						

1983

Round	Num.	Player	Pos	GP	G	A	Pts	PIM
1	9	Cam Neely	RW	726	395	299	694	1,241
2	30	David Bruce	LW	234	48	39	87	338
3	50	Scott Tottle	RW					
4	70	Tim Lorenz	LW					
5	90	Doug Quinn	D					
6	110	Dave Lowry	LW	1,084	164	187	351	1,191
7	130	Terry Maki	LW					
8	150	John Labatt	C					
9	170	Allan Measures	D					
10	190	Roger Grillo	D					
11	210	Steve Kayser	D					
12	230	Jay Mazur	RW	47	11	7	18	20

1984

Round	Num.	Player	Pos	GP	G	A	Pts	PIM
1	10	J.J. Daigneault	D	899	53	197	250	687
2	31	Jeff Rohlicek	C	9	0	0	0	8
3	52	David Saunders	LW	56	7	13	20	10
3	55	Landis Chaulk	LW					
3	58	Mike Stevens	LW	23	1	4	5	29
4	73	Brian Bertuzzi	D					
5	94	Brett MacDonald	D	1	0	0	0	0
6	115	Jeff Korchinski	D					
7	136	Blaine Chrest	C					
8	157	Jim Agnew	D	81	0	1	1	257
9	178	Rex Grant	G					
10	198	Ed Lowney	RW					
11	219	Doug Clarke	D					
12	239	Ed Kister	D					

1985

Round	Num.	Player	Pos	GP	G	A	Pts	PIM
1	4	Jim Sandlak	RW	549	110	119	229	821
2	25	Troy Gamble	G	72	0	1	1	22
3	46	Shane Doyle	D					
4	67	Randy Siska	C					
5	88	Robert Kron	C	771	144	194	338	119
6	109	Martin Hrstka	LW					
7	130	Brian McFarlane	RW					
8	151	Hakan Ahlund	RW					
9	172	Curtis Hunt	D					
10	193	Carl Valimont	D					
11	214	Igor Larionov	C	921	169	475	644	474
12	235	Darren Taylor	LW					

1986

Round	Num.	Player	Pos	GP	G	A	Pts	PIM
1	7	Dan Woodley	C	5	2	0	2	17
3	49	Don Gibson	D	14	0	3	3	20
4	70	Ronnie Stern	RW	638	75	86	161	2,077
5	91	Eric Murano	C					
6	112	Steve Herniman	D					
7	133	Jon Helgeson	LW					
8	154	Jeff Noble	C					
9	175	Matt Merten	G					
10	196	Marc Lyons	D					
11	217	Todd Hawkins	LW	10	0	0	0	15
12	238	Vladimir Krutov	LW	61	11	23	34	20

1987

Round	Num.	Player	Pos	GP	G	A	Pts	PIM
2	24	Rob Murphy	C	125	9	12	21	152
3	45	Steve Veilleux	D					
4	66	Doug Torrel	RW					

5	87	Sean Fabian	D					
6	108	Garry Valk	LW	777	100	156	256	747
7	129	Todd Fanning	G					
8	150	Viktor Tumeneu	C					
9	171	Craig Daly	D					
10	192	John Fletcher	G					
11	213	Roger Hansson	RW					
12	233	Neil Eisenhut	C	16	1	3	4	21
12	234	Matt Evo	LW					

1988

Round	Num.	Player	Pos	GP	G	A	Pts	PIM
1	2	Trevor Linden	C	1,382	375	492	867	895
2	33	Leif Rohlin	D	96	8	24	32	40
3	44	Dane Jackson	RW	45	12	6	18	58
6	107	Corrie D'Alessio	G	1	0	0	0	0
6	122	Phil Von Stefenelli	D	33	0	5	5	23
7	128	Dixon Ward	RW	537	95	129	224	431
8	149	Greg Geldart	C					
9	170	Roger Akerstrom	D					
10	191	Paul Constantin	LW					
11	212	Chris Wolanin	D					
12	233	Stefan Nilsson	RW					

1989

Round	Num.	Player	Pos	GP	G	A	Pts	PIM
1	8	Jason Herter	D	1	0	1	1	0
2	29	Rob Woodward	LW					
4	71	Brett Hauer	D	37	4	4	8	38
6	113	Pavel Bure	RW	702	437	342	779	484
7	134	Jim Revenberg	RW					
8	155	Rob Sangster	LW					
9	176	Sandy Moger	RW	236	41	38	79	212

10	197	Gus Morschauser	G
11	218	Hayden O'Rear	D
12	239	Darcy Cahill	C
12	248	Jan Bergman	D

1990

Round	Num.	Player	Pos	GP	G	A	Pts	PIM
1	2	Petr Nedved	LW	982	310	407	717	708
1	18	Shawn Antoski	LW	183	3	5	8	599
2	23	Jiri Slegr	D	622	56	193	249	838
4	65	Darin Bader	LW					
5	86	Gino Odjick	LW	605	64	73	137	2567
7	128	Daryl Filipek	D					
8	149	Paul O'Hagan	D					
9	170	Mark Cipriano	D					
10	191	Troy Neumeier	D					
11	212	Tyler Ertel	C					
12	233	Karri Kivi	D					

1991

Round	Num.	Player	Pos	GP	G	A	Pts	PIM
1	7	Alek Stojanov	RW	107	2	5	7	222
2	29	Jassen Cullimore	D	812	26	85	111	704
3	51	Sean Pronger	C	260	23	36	59	159
5	95	Dan Kesa	RW	139	8	22	30	66
6	117	Evgeny Namestnikov	D	43	0	9	9	24
7	139	Brent Thurston	LW					
8	161	Eric Johnson	RW					
9	183	David Neilson	LW					
10	205	Brad Barton	D					
11	227	Jason Fitzsimmons	G					
12	249	Xavier Majic	C					

1992

Round	Num.	Player	Pos	GP	G	A	Pts	PIM
1	21	Libor Polasek	C					
2	40	Mike Peca	C	864	176	289	465	798
2	45	Mike Fountain	G	11	0	0	0	2
3	69	Jeff Connolly	RW					
4	93	Brent Tully	D					
5	110	Brian Loney	RW	12	2	3	5	6
5	117	Adrian Aucoin	D	1,108	121	278	399	793
6	141	Jason Clark	LW					
7	165	Scott Hollis	RW					
9	213	Sonny Mignacca	G					
10	237	Mark Wotton	D	43	3	6	9	25
11	261	Aaron Boh	D					

1993

Round	Num.	Player	Pos	GP	G	A	Pts	PIM
1	20	Mike Wilson	D	336	16	41	57	264
2	46	Rick Girard	C					
4	98	Dieter Kochan	G	21	0	0	0	0
5	124	Scott Walker	RW	829	151	246	397	1,162
6	150	Troy Creuer	D					
7	176	Evgeny Babariko	C					
8	202	Sean Tallaire	RW					
10	254	Bert Robertsson	D	123	4	10	14	75
11	280	Sergei Tkachenko	G					

1994

Round	Num.	Player	Pos	GP	G	A	Pts	PIM
1	13	Mattias Ohlund	D	909	93	250	343	885
2	39	Rob Gordon	C	4	0	0	0	2
2	42	Dave Scatchard	C	659	128	141	269	1,040
3	65	Chad Allan	D					
4	92	Mike Dubinsky	RW					

5	117	Yanick Dube	C					
7	169	Yuri Kuznetsov	C					
8	195	Rob Trumbley	RW					
9	221	Bill Muckalt	RW	256	40	57	97	204
10	247	Tyson Nash	LW	374	27	37	64	673
11	273	Robert Longpre	C					

1995

Round	Num.	Player	Pos	GP	G	A	Pts	PIM
2	40	Chris McAllister	D	301	4	17	21	634
3	61	Larry Courville	LW	33	1	2	3	16
3	66	Peter Schaefer	LW	572	99	162	261	200
4	92	Lloyd Shaw	D					
5	120	Todd Norman	LW					
6	144	Brent Sopel	D	659	44	174	218	309
7	170	Stu Bodtker	C					
8	196	Tyler Willis	RW					
9	222	Jason Cugnet	G					

1996

Round	Num.	Player	Pos	GP	G	A	Pts	PIM
1	12	Josh Holden	C	60	5	9	14	16
3	75	Zenith Komarniski	D	21	1	1	2	10
4	93	Jonas Soling	RW					
5	121	Tyler Prosofsky	RW					
6	147	Nolan McDonald	G					
7	175	Clint Cabana	D					
8	201	Jeff Scissons	C					
9	227	Lubomir Vaic	LW	9	1	1	2	2

1997

Round	Num.	Player	Pos	GP	G	A	Pts	PIM
1	10	Brad Ference	D	250	4	30	34	565
2	34	Ryan Bonni	D	3	0	0	0	0
2	36	Harold Druken	C	146	27	36	63	36
3	64	Kyle Freadrich	LW	23	0	1	1	75
4	90	Chris Stanley	C					
5	114	David Darguzas	LW					
5	117	Matt Cockell	G					
6	144	Matt Cooke	LW	1,046	167	231	398	1,135
6	148	Larry Shapley	RW					
7	171	Rod Leroux	D					
8	201	Denis Martynyuk	LW					
9	227	Peter Brady	G					

1998

Round	Num.	Player	Pos	GP	G	A	Pts	PIM
1	4	Bryan Allen	D	721	29	107	136	839
2	31	Artem Chubarov	C	228	25	33	58	40
3	68	Jarkko Ruutu	LW	652	58	84	142	1,078
3	81	Justin Morrison	RW					
4	90	Regan Darby	D					
5	136	David Jonsson	RW					
5	140	Rick Bertran	D					
6	149	Paul Cabana	RW					
7	177	Vince Malts	RW					
8	204	Graig Mischler	C					
8	219	Curtis Valentine	LW					
9	232	Jason Metcalfe	D					

1999

Round	Num.	Player	Pos	GP	G	A	Pts	PIM
1	2	Daniel Sedin	LW	1,306	393	648	1,041	546
1	3	Henrik Sedin	C	1,330	240	830	1,070	680

3	69	Rene Vydareny	D
5	129	Ryan Thorpe	LW
6	172	Josh Reed	D
7	189	Kevin Swanson	G
8	218	Markus Kankaanpera	D
9	271	Darrell Hay	D

2000

Round	Num.	Player	Pos	GP	G	A	Pts	PIM
1	23	Nathan Smith	C	26	0	0	0	14
3	71	Thatcher Bell	C					
3	93	Tim Branham	D					
5	144	Pavel Duma	C					
7	208	Brandon Reid	C	13	2	4	6	0
8	241	Nathan Barrett	C					
9	272	Tim Smith	C					

2001

Round	Num.	Player	Pos	GP	G	A	Pts	PIM
1	16	R.J. Umberger	C	779	180	212	392	312
3	66	Fedor Fedorov	C	18	0	2	2	14
4	114	Evgeny Gladskikh	RW					
5	151	Kevin Bieksa	D	808	63	215	278	1,124
7	212	Jason King	RW	59	12	11	23	8
8	245	Konstantin Mikhailov	C					

2002

Round	Num.	Player	Pos	GP	G	A	Pts	PIM
2	49	Kirill Koltsov	D					
2	55	Denis Grot	D					
3	68	Brett Skinner	D	11	0	0	0	4

Round	Num.	Player	Pos	GP	G	A	Pts	PIM
3	83	Lukas Mensator	G					
4	114	John Laliberte	LW					
5	151	Rob McVicar	G	1	0	0	0	0
7	214	Marc-Andre Roy	LW					
7	223	Ilya Krikunov	LW					
8	247	Matt Violin	G					
9	277	Thomas Nussli	LW					
9	278	Matt Gens	RW					

2003

Round	Num.	Player	Pos	GP	G	A	Pts	PIM
1	23	Ryan Kesler	C	1,001	258	315	573	920
2	60	Marc-Andre Bernier	RW					
4	111	Brandon Nolan	C	6	0	1	1	0
4	128	Ty Morris	RW					
5	160	Nicklas Danielsson	LW					
6	190	Chad Brownlee	D					
7	222	Francois-Pierre Guenette	C					
8	252	Sergei Topol	LW					
8	254	Nathan McIver	D	36	0	1	1	95
9	285	Matthew Hansen	D					

2004

Round	Num.	Player	Pos	GP	G	A	Pts	PIM
1	26	Cory Schneider	G	410	0	9	9	4
3	91	Alexander Edler	D	1,030	104	335	439	733
4	125	Andrew Sarauer	LW					
5	159	Mike Brown	RW	407	19	17	36	778
6	189	Julien Ellis	G					
8	254	David Schulz	D					
9	287	Jannik Hansen	RW	626	109	147	256	282

2005

Round	Num.	Player	Pos	GP	G	A	Pts	PIM
1	10	Luc Bourdon	D	36	2	0	2	24
2	51	Mason Raymond	LW	546	115	136	251	156
4	114	Alexandre Vincent	G					
5	138	Matt Butcher	C					
6	185	Kris Fredheim	D	3	0	0	0	2
7	205	Mario Bliznak	C	6	1	0	1	0

2006

Round	Num.	Player	Pos	GP	G	A	Pts	PIM
1	14	Michael Grabner	RW	640	175	101	276	110
3	82	Daniel Rahimi	D					
6	163	Sergei Shirokov	RW	8	1	0	1	2
6	167	Juraj Simek	LW					
7	197	Evan Fuller	C					

2007

Round	Num.	Player	Pos	GP	G	A	Pts	PIM
1	25	Patrick White	C					
2	33	Taylor Ellington	D					
5	145	Charles-Antoine Messier	C					
5	146	Ilya Kablukov	C					
6	176	Taylor Matson	C					
7	206	Dan Gendur	C					

2008

Round	Num.	Player	Pos	GP	G	A	Pts	PIM
1	10	Cody Hodgson	C	328	64	78	142	68
2	41	Yann Sauve	D	8	0	0	0	0
5	131	Prabh Rai	C					
6	161	Mats Josten-Froshaug	C					
7	191	Morgan Clark	G					

2009

Round	Num.	Player	Pos	GP	G	A	Pts	PIM
1	22	Jordan Schroeder	LW	165	18	24	42	14
2	53	Anton Rodin	RW	3	0	1	1	0
3	83	Kevin Connauton	D	360	28	52	80	188
4	113	Jeremy Price	D					
5	143	Peter Andersson	D					
6	173	Joe Cannata	G					
7	187	Steven Anthony	LW					

2010

Round	Num.	Player	Pos	GP	G	A	Pts	PIM
4	115	Patrick McNally	D					
5	145	Adam Polasek	D					
6	172	Alex Friesen	C	1	0	0	0	0
6	175	Jonathan Iilahti	G					
7	205	Sawyer Hannay	D					

2011

Round	Num.	Player	Pos	GP	G	A	Pts	PIM
1	29	Nicklas Jensen	RW	31	3	3	6	10
3	71	David Honzik	G					
3	90	Alexandre Grenier	RW	9	0	0	0	2
4	101	Joseph LaBate	LW	13	0	0	0	21
4	120	Ludwig Blomstrand	LW					
5	150	Frankie Corrado	D	76	3	5	8	40
6	180	Pathrik Westerholm	LW					
7	210	Henrik Tommernes	D					

2012

Round	Num.	Player	Pos	GP	G	A	Pts	PIM
1	26	Brendan Gaunce	C	153	11	13	24	61
2	57	Alexandre Mallet	C					

5	147	Ben Hutton	D	468	22	90	112	174
6	177	Wesley Myron	C					
7	207	Matthew Beattie	RW					

2013

Round	Num.	Player	Pos	GP	G	A	Pts	PIM
1	9	Bo Horvat	C	651	208	228	436	206
1	24	Hunter Shinkaruk	LW	15	2	2	4	4
3	85	Cole Cassels	C					
4	115	Jordan Subban	D					
5	145	Anton Cederholm	D					
6	175	Mike Williamson	D					
7	205	Miles Liberati	D					

2014

Round	Num.	Player	Pos	GP	G	A	Pts	PIM
1	6	Jake Virtanen	RW	317	55	45	100	219
1	24	Jared McCann	LW	506	133	142	275	169
2	36	Thatcher Demko	G	168	0	4	4	6
3	66	Nikita Tryamkin	D	79	3	8	11	74
5	126	Gustav Forsling	D	318	36	86	122	108
6	156	Kyle Pettit	C					
7	186	Mackenze Stewart	D					

2015

Round	Num.	Player	Pos	GP	G	A	Pts	PIM
1	23	Brock Boeser	RW	398	139	172	311	112
3	66	Guillaume Brisebois	D	27	1	2	3	6
4	114	Dmitry Zhukenov	C					
5	144	Carl Neill	D					
5	149	Adam Gaudette	C	218	27	43	70	84
6	174	Lukas Jasek	RW					
7	210	Tate Olson	D					

2016

Round	Num.	Player	Pos	GP	G	A	Pts	PIM
1	5	Olli Juolevi	D	41	2	1	3	6
3	64	William Lockwood	RW	28	0	1	1	11
5	140	Cole Candella	D					
6	154	Jakob Stukel	LW					
7	184	Rodrigo Abols	C					
7	194	Brett McKenzie	LW					

2017

Round	Num.	Player	Pos	GP	G	A	Pts	PIM
1	5	Elias Pettersson	C	325	136	187	323	62
2	33	Kole Lind	RW	30	2	6	8	12
2	55	Jonah Gadjovich	LW	79	4	6	10	148
3	64	Michael DiPietro	G	3	0	0	0	0
4	95	Jack Rathbone	D	28	2	3	5	4
5	135	Kristoffer Gunnarsson	D					
6	181	Petrus Palmu	RW					
7	188	Matt Brassard	D					

2018

Round	Num.	Player	Pos	GP	G	A	Pts	PIM
1	7	Quinn Hughes	D	283	26	215	241	108
2	37	Jett Woo	D					
3	68	Tyler Madden	C					
5	130	Toni Utunen	D					
6	186	Artem Manukyan	RW					
7	192	Matthew Thiessen	G					

2019

Round	Num.	Player	Pos	GP	G	A	Pts	PIM
1	10	Vasili Podkolzin	RW	118	18	15	33	35
2	40	Nils Hoglander	LW	141	26	28	54	46
4	122	Ethan Keppen	LW					

5	133	Carson Focht	C					
6	156	Arturs Silovs	G	5	0	0	0	0
6	175	Karel Plasek	RW					
6	180	Jack Malone	RW					
7	195	Aidan Mcdonough	LW	6	1	0	1	2
7	215	Arvid Costmar	C					

2020

Round	Num.	Player	Pos	GP	G	A	Pts	PIM
3	82	Joni Jurmo	D					
4	113	Jackson Kunz	LW					
5	144	Jacob Truscott	D					
6	175	Dmitry Zlodeyev	C					
7	191	Viktor Persson	D					

2021

Round	Num.	Player	Pos	GP	G	A	Pts	PIM
2	41	Danila Klimovich	RW					
5	137	Aku Koskenvuo	G					
5	140	Jonathan Myrenberg	D					
6	169	Hugo Gabrielson	D					
6	178	Connor Lockhart	C					
7	201	Lucas Forsell	LW					

2022

Round	Num.	Player	Pos	GP	G	A	Pts	PIM
1	15	Jonathan Lekkerimaki	RW					
3	80	Elias Pettersson	D					
4	112	Daimon Gardner	C					
5	144	Ty Young	G					
6	176	Jackson Dorrington	D					
7	208	Kirill Kudryavtsev	D					

2023

Round	Num.	Player	Pos	GP	G	A	Pts	PIM
1	11	Tom Willander	D					
3	75	Hunter Brzustewicz	D					
3	89	Sawyer Mynio	D					
4	105	Ty Mueller	C					
4	107	Vilmer Alriksson	LW					
6	171	Aiden Celebrini	D					

SOURCES

Books

Burke, Brian and Stephen Brunt. *Burke's Law: A Life in Hockey* (Toronto, Ontario: Viking Canada, 2020).

Dowbiggin, Bruce. *Ice Storm: the Rise and Fall of the Greatest Vancouver Canucks Team Ever* (Vancouver, BC: Greystone Books, 2014).

Drance, Thomas and Mike Halford. *100 Things Canucks Fans Should Know & Do Before They Die* (Chicago, Illinois: Triumph Books, 2017).

Dwyer, Eric. *Hockey's Young Superstars* (Vancouver, BC: Polestar Press Ltd, 1992).

Imlach, Punch with Scott Young. *Heaven and Hell in the NHL* (Toronto, Ontario: Goodread Biography, 1986).

Jenish, D'Arcy. *The NHL: 100 Years of On-Ice Action and Boardroom Battles* (Toronto, Ontario: Doubleday Canada, 2013).

Jewison, Norm. *The Vancouver Canucks: The First Twenty Years* (Vancouver, BC: Raincoast Books, 1990).

Robson, Dan. *Quinn: The Life of a Hockey Legend* (Toronto, Ontario: Viking, 2015).

St. James, Helene. *On the Clock: Detroit Red Wings: Behind the Scenes with the Detroit Red Wings at the NHL Draft* (Chicago, Illinois: Triumph Books, 2022).

Wire Services, Newspapers, and Magazines

Associated Press

Canadian Press

Chicago Tribune

Edmonton Journal

Expressen

Flin Flon Reminder

Globe & Mail

Hartford Courant

The Hockey News

The Ledger

Los Angeles Times

Montreal Gazette

Montreal Star

New York Daily News

Ogonyok

Orlando Sentinel

Philadelphia Daily News

Philadelphia Inquirer

Pittsburgh Press

The Province

Sentinel-Tribune

Sports Illustrated

Star Tribune

Tampa Tribune

Toronto Star

Vancouver Sun

Washington Post

Windsor Star

Websites

bcsportshall.com

canucks.com

canucksarmy.com

cbc.ca

dailyfaceoff.com

dropyourgloves.com

eliteprospects.com

eprinkside.com

espn.com

expressen.se

greatesthockeylegends.com

griffinshockey.com

hockeydb.com

hockey-reference.com

iihf.com

newspapers.com

nhl.com

passittobulis.com

sportsnet.ca

theathletic.com

tsn.ca

twitter.com

usahockey.com

web.archive.com

wheatkings.com

youtube.com

ACKNOWLEDGMENTS

THIS BOOK WOULDN'T HAVE ever been finished without my wife, Rachael, and her invisible labour to keep our family healthy, happy, and sane. I'm particularly grateful for her endless patience when I found something interesting in my research and felt the need to tell her immediately. Thank you.

Thank you to my parents, who got me into both sports and writing at a young age. Your love, support, and encouragement mean the world to me.

I wouldn't be writing about hockey for a living without Harrison Mooney, with whom I started the hockey blog Pass it to Bulis back in 2010. Thank you for immediately agreeing when I suggested "Pass it to Bulis" as the name for our blog, a decision that sounds ludicrous in retrospect.

Thanks to my fellow Canucks scribe Patrick Johnston, who provided a sounding board and crucial feedback throughout the writing of this book. Someday, we'll write something together.

I am very grateful to the current and former scouts, executives, and players who took the time to speak to me, whether it was on the record, on background, or off the record, to help point me in the right direction. I'm particularly thankful to Mike Penny, who was incredibly generous with his time and knowledge, and I'm sincerely apologetic for having to poke holes in the legend of how he helped the Canucks draft Pavel Bure.

Many thanks to my boss at Vancouver Is Awesome, Bob Kronbauer, for lending me his newspapers.com account, which was an essential resource.

I owe a great debt to the many fantastic sports reporters that came before me in Vancouver. This book would not have been possible without their work on the Canucks beat, capturing quotes and telling the stories of the Canucks over the last 50-plus years. There are almost too many writers to name, so I sincerely apologize if I forget anyone: Hal Sigurdson, Tom Watt, Jim Kearney, Eric Whitehead, Jim Taylor, Clancy Loranger, Lyndon Little, Arv Olson, Archie McDonald, Mike Beamish, Jack Keating, Tony Gallagher, Lee Bacchus, Gary Kingston, David Banks, Elliott Pap, Ben Kuzma, Iain MacIntyre, Ed Willes, Cam Cole, Brad Ziemer, Steve Ewen, Jason Botchford, Patrick Johnston, Kevin Woodley, Thomas Drance, and Harman Dayal.

Thank you to the team at Triumph Books, particularly my editors Darcy Waskiewicz and Michelle Bruton and director of author engagement Bill Ames, who were so easy to work with and eased so much of the stress of writing my first book.

A massive chunk of this book was written at one of the branches of the Surrey Library, which provided a quiet place to work away from the noises that three boisterous boys inevitably make. Support your local library, folks.

Finally, a shout out to the Black Aces. I would've gone crazy over the last decade without you guys.